WITHDRAWN

𝔖tandard 𝔏ibrary 𝔈dition

THE WRITINGS OF
BRET HARTE

WITH INTRODUCTIONS, GLOSSARY, AND
INDEXES

ILLUSTRATED BY PHOTOGRAVURES

VOLUME XVII

Its jaws met in his throat

The Writings of Bret Harte

STANDARD LIBRARY EDITION

A
NIECE OF SNAPSHOT HARRY'S

AND OTHER TALES

BY

BRET HARTE

AMS Press, Inc.

New York

AMS Press, Inc.

New York, N. Y. 10003

1966

Manufactured in the United States of America

CONTENTS

	PAGE
A Niece of Snapshot Harry's	1
What happened at the Fonda	50
Mr. Bilson's Housekeeper	75
Jimmy's Big Brother from California	104
The Youngest Miss Piper	126
A Widow of the Santa Ana Valley	145
The Mermaid of Lighthouse Point	164
Three Vagabonds of Trinidad	186
A Mercury of the Foot-Hills	202
Colonel Starbottle for the Plaintiff	230
The Landlord of the Big Flume Hotel	263
The Reincarnation of Smith	282
Lanty Foster's Mistake	310
An Ali Baba of the Sierras	329
The Four Guardians of Lagrange	340

LIST OF ILLUSTRATIONS

PAGE

ITS JAWS MET IN HIS THROAT (see page
201) . . . . *Frontispiece* *Arthur I. Keller*
VIGNETTE ON ENGRAVED TITLE-PAGE (see
page 72) . . . . *R. Farrington Elwell*
"PLEASE DON'T ASK ME WHY" . . . . *H. E. Townsend* . . 92
A SERAPE-DRAPED HORSEMAN . . . . . *R. Farrington Elwell* 150
GAZING FIXEDLY AT THE GROWING LIGHT *Alice Barber Stephens* 176
"I THOUGHT YOU WERE THAT HORSE-
THIEF" . . . . *Denman Fink* . . . 326

A NIECE OF SNAPSHOT HARRY'S, AND OTHER TALES

A NIECE OF SNAPSHOT HARRY'S

I

THERE was a slight jarring through the whole frame of the coach, a grinding and hissing from the brakes, and then a sudden jolt as the vehicle ran upon and recoiled from the taut pole-straps of the now arrested horses. The murmur of a voice in the road was heard, followed by the impatient accents of Yuba Bill, the driver.

"Wha-a-t? Speak up, can't ye?"

Here the voice uttered something in a louder key, but equally unintelligible to the now interested and fully awakened passengers.

One of them dropped the window nearest him and looked out. He could see the faint glistening of a rain-washed lantern near the wheelers' heads, mingling with the stronger coach lights, and the glow of a distant open cabin door through the leaves and branches of the roadside. The sound of falling rain on the roof, a soft swaying of wind-tossed trees, and an impatient movement on the box-seat were all they heard. Then Yuba Bill's voice rose again, apparently in answer to the other.

"Why, that's half a mile away!"

"Yes, but ye might have dropped onto it in the dark, and it's all on the down grade," responded the strange voice more audibly.

The passengers were now thoroughly aroused.

"What's up, Ned?" asked the one at the window of the nearest of two figures that had descended from the box.

"Tree fallen across the road," said Ned, the expressman, briefly.

"I don't see no tree," responded the passenger, leaning out of the window towards the obscurity ahead.

"Now, that's onfortnit!" said Yuba Bill grimly; "but ef any gentleman will only lend him an opery glass, mebbe he can see round the curve and over the other side o' the hill where it is. Now, then," addressing the stranger with the lantern, "bring along your axes, can't ye?"

"Here's one, Bill," said an officious outside passenger, producing the instrument he had taken from its strap in the boot. It was the "regulation" axe, beautifully shaped, highly polished, and utterly ineffective, as Bill well knew.

"We ain't cuttin' no kindlin's," he said scornfully; then he added brusquely to the stranger: "Fetch out your biggest wood axe — you've got one, ye know — and look sharp."

"I don't think Bill need be so d—d rough with the stranger, considering he's saved the coach a very bad smash," suggested a reflective young journalist in the next seat. "He talks as if the man was responsible."

"He ain't quite sure if that isn't the fact," said the express messenger, in a lowered voice.

"Why? What do you mean?" clamored the others excitedly.

"Well — *this* is about the spot where the up coach was robbed six months ago," returned the messenger.

"Dear me!" said the lady in the back seat, rising with a half hysterical laugh, "hadn't we better get out before they come?"

"There is not the slightest danger, madam," said a quiet, observant man, who had scarcely spoken before, "or the expressman would not have told us; nor would he, I fancy, have left his post beside the treasure on the box."

The slight sarcasm implied in this was enough to redden the expressman's cheek in the light of the coach lamp which Yuba Bill had just unshipped and brought to the window. He would have made some tart rejoinder, but was prevented by Yuba Bill addressing the passengers: "Ye 'll have to put up with *one* light, I reckon, until we 've got this job finished."

"How long will it last, Bill?" asked the man nearest the window.

"Well," said Bill, with a contemptuous glance at the elegant coach axe he was carrying in his hand, "considerin' these purty first-class highly expensive hash choppers that the kempany furnishes us, I reckon it may take an hour."

"But is there no place where we can wait?" asked the lady anxiously. "I see a light in that house yonder."

"Ye might try it, though the kempany, as a rule, ain't in the habit o' makin' social calls there," returned Bill, with a certain grim significance. Then, turning to some outside passengers, he added, "Now, then! them ez is goin' to help me tackle that tree, trot down! I reckon that blitherin' idiot" (the stranger with the lantern, who had disappeared) "will have sense enough to fetch us some ropes with his darned axe."

The passengers thus addressed, apparently miners and workingmen, good-humoredly descended, all except one, who seemed disinclined to leave the much coveted seat on the box beside the driver.

"I 'll look after your places and keep my own," he said, with a laugh, as the others followed Bill through the dripping rain. When they had disappeared, the young journalist turned to the lady.

"If you would really like to go to that house, I will gladly accompany you." It was possible that in addition to his youthful chivalry there was a little youthful resentment of Yuba Bill's domineering prejudices in his attitude. However, the quiet, observant passenger lifted a look of approval to him, and added, in his previous level, half contemptuous tone: —

"You'll be quite as well there as here, madam, and there is certainly no reason for your stopping in the coach when the driver chooses to leave it."

The passengers looked at each other. The stranger spoke with authority, and Bill had certainly been a little arbitrary!

"I'll go too," said the passenger by the window. "And you'll come, won't you, Ned?" he added to the express messenger. The young man hesitated; he was recently appointed, and as yet fresh to the business — but he was not to be taught his duty by an officious stranger! He resented the interference youthfully by doing the very thing he would have preferred *not* to do, and with assumed carelessness — yet feeling in his pocket to assure himself that the key of the treasure compartment was safe — turned to follow them.

"Won't *you* come too?" said the journalist, politely addressing the cynical passenger.

"No, I thank you! I'll take charge of the coach," was the smiling rejoinder, as he settled himself more comfortably in his seat.

The little procession moved away in silence. Oddly enough, no one, except the lady, really cared to go, and two — the expressman and journalist — would have preferred to remain on the coach. But the national instinct of questioning any purely arbitrary authority probably was a sufficient impulse. As they neared the opened door of what appeared to be a four-roomed, unpainted, redwood boarded cabin, the passenger who had occupied the seat near the window said, —

"I 'll go first and sample the shanty."

He was not, however, so far in advance of them but that the others could hear quite distinctly his offhand introduction of their party on the threshold, and the somewhat lukewarm response of the inmates. "We thought we 'd just drop in and be sociable until the coach was ready to start again," he continued, as the other passengers entered. "This yer gentleman is Ned Brice, Adams & Co.'s expressman; this yer is Frank Frenshaw, editor of the 'Mountain Banner;' this yer 's a lady, so it ain't necessary to give *her* name, I reckon, — even if we knowed it! Mine 's Sam Heckshill of Heckshill & Dobbs's Flour Mills of Stockton, whar, ef you ever come that way, I 'll be happy to return the compliment and hospitality."

The room they had entered had little of comfort and brightness in it except the fire of pine logs which roared and crackled in the adobe chimney. The air would have been too warm but for the strong west wind and rain which entered the open door freely. There was no other light than the fire, and its tremulous and ever-changing brilliancy gave a spasmodic mobility to the faces of those turned towards it, or threw into stronger shadow the features that were turned away. Yet by this uncertain light they could see the figures of a man and two women. The man rose and, with a certain apathetic gesture that seemed to partake more of weariness and long suffering than positive discourtesy, tendered seats on chairs, boxes, and even logs to the self-invited guests. The stage party were surprised to see that this man was the stranger who had held the lantern in the road.

"Ah! then you did n't go with Bill to help clear the road?" said the expressman surprisedly.

The man slowly drew up his tall, shambling figure before the fire and then facing them, with his hands behind him, as slowly lowered himself again as if to bring his speech to the level of his hearers and give a lazier and more deliberate effect to his long-drawn utterance.

"Well — no!" he said slowly. "I — did n't — go — with — no — Bill — to — help — clear — the road! I — don't — reckon — *to* go — with — no — Bill — to — clear — *any* road! I 've just whittled this thing down to a pint, and it 's this — I ain't no stage kempany's nigger! So far as turnin' out and warnin' 'em agin goin' to smash over a fallen tree, and slap down into the cañon with a passel of innercent passengers, I 'm that much a white man, but I ain't no *nigger* to work clearing things away for 'em, nor I ain't no scrub to work beside 'em." He slowly straightened himself up again, and, with his former apathetic air, looking down upon one of the women who was setting a coffee-pot on the coals, added, "But I reckon my old woman here kin give you some coffee and whiskey — ef you keer for it."

Unfortunately the young expressman was more loyal to Bill than diplomatic. "If Bill 's a little rough," he said, with a heightened color, "perhaps he has some excuse for it. You forget it 's only six months ago that this coach was 'held up' not a hundred yards from this spot."

The woman with the coffee-pot here faced about, stood up, and, either from design or some odd coincidence, fell into the same dogged attitude that her husband had previously taken, except that she rested her hands on her hips. She was prematurely aged, like many of her class, and her black, snake-like locks, twisting loose from her comb as she lifted her head, showed threads of white against the firelight. Then with slow and implacable deliberation she said: —

"We 'forget!' Well! not much, sonny! We ain't forgot it, and we ain't goin' to forget it, neither! We ain't bin likely to forget it for any time the last six months. What with visitations from the county constables, snoopin's round from 'Frisco detectives, droppin's-in from newspaper

men, and yawpin's and starin's from tramps and strangers
on the road — we have n't had a chance to disremember
much! And when at last Hiram tackled the head stage
agent at Marysville, and allowed that this yer pesterin' and
persecutin' had got ter stop — what did that yer head agent
tell him? Told him to 'shet his head,' and be thankful
that his 'thievin' old shanty was n't burnt down around
his ears!' Forget that six months ago the coach was held
up near here? Not much, sonny — not much!"

The situation was embarrassing to the guests, as ordinary politeness called for some expression of sympathy with
their gloomy hostess, and yet a selfish instinct of humanity
warned them that there must be some foundation for this
general distrust of the public. The journalist was troubled
in his conscience; the expressman took refuge in an official
reticence; the lady coughed slightly, and drew nearer to
the fire with a vague but safe compliment to its brightness
and comfort. It devolved upon Mr. Heckshill, who felt
the responsibility of his late airy introduction of the party,
to boldly keep up his rôle, with an equally non-committal,
light-hearted philosophy.

"Well, ma'am," he said, addressing his hostess, "it's a
queer world, and no man's got *sabe* enough to say what's
the rights and wrongs o' anything. Some folks believe one
thing and act upon it, and other folks think differently and
act upon *that!* The only thing ye kin safely say is that
things is ez they be! My rule here and at the mill is jest
to take things ez I find 'em!"

It occurred to the journalist that Mr. Heckshill had the
reputation, in his earlier career, of "taking" such things
as unoccupied lands and timber "as he found them," without much reference to their actual owners. Apparently he
was acting upon the same principle now, as he reached for
the demijohn of whiskey with the ingenuous pleasantry,
"Did somebody say whiskey, or did I dream it?"

But this did not satisfy Frenshaw. "I suppose," he said, ignoring Heckshill's diplomatic philosophy, "that you may have been the victim of some misunderstanding or some unfortunate coincidence. Perhaps the company may have confounded you with your neighbors, who are believed to be friendly to the gang; or you may have made some injudicious acquaintances. Perhaps " —

He was stopped by a suppressed but not unmusical giggle, which appeared to come from the woman in the corner who had not yet spoken, and whose face and figure in the shadow he had previously overlooked. But he could now see that her outline was slim and graceful, and the contour of her head charming, — facts that had evidently not escaped the observation of the expressman and Mr. Heckshill, and that might have accounted for the cautious reticence of the one and the comfortable moralizing of the other.

The old woman cast an uneasy glance on the fair giggler, but replied to Frenshaw : —

"That's it! 'injerdishus acquaintances!' But just because we might happen to have friends, or even be sorter related to folks in another line o' business that ain't none o' ours, the kempany hain't no call to persecute *us* for it! S'pose we do happen to know some one like " —

"Spit it out, aunty, now you've started in! *I* don't mind," said the fair giggler, now apparently casting off all restraint in an outburst of laughter.

"Well," said the old woman, with dogged desperation, "suppose, then, that that young girl thar is the niece of Snapshot Harry, who stopped the coach the last time " —

"And ain't ashamed of it, either!" interrupted the young girl, rising and disclosing in the firelight an audacious but wonderfully pretty face; "and supposing he *is* my uncle, that ain't any cause for their bedevilin' my poor old cousins Hiram and Sophy thar!" For all the indignation of her words, her little white teeth flashed mischievously in the dancing light, as if she rather enjoyed the embarrassment of her audience, not excluding her own relatives. Evidently cousin Sophy thought so too.

"It's all very well for you to laugh, Flo, you limb!" she retorted querulously, yet with an admiring glance at the girl, "for ye know thar ain't a man dare touch ye even with a word; but it's mighty hard on me and Hiram, all the same."

"Never you mind, Sophy dear," said the girl, placing her hand half affectionately, half humorously on the old woman's shoulder; "mebbe I won't always be a discredit and a bother to you. Jest you hold your hosses, and wait until uncle Harry 'holds up' the next Pioneer Coach," — the dancing devil in her eyes glanced as if accidentally on the young expressman, — "and he'll make a big enough pile to send me to Europe, and you'll be quit o' me."

The embarrassment, suspiciousness, and uneasiness of the coach party here found relief in a half hysteric explosion of laughter, in which even the dogged Hiram and Sophy joined. It seemed as impossible to withstand the girl's invincible audacity as her beauty. She was quick to perceive her advantage, and, with a responsive laugh and a picturesque gesture of invitation, said: —

"Now that's all settled, ye'd better waltz in and have your whiskey and coffee afore the stage starts. Ye kin comfort yourselves that it ain't stolen or pizoned, even if it is served up to ye by Snapshot Harry's niece!" With another easy gesture she swung the demijohn over her arm, and, offering a tin cup to each of the men, filled them in turn.

The ice thus broken, or perhaps thus perilously skated over, the passengers were as profuse in their thanks and apologies as they had been constrained and artificial before. Heckshill and Frenshaw vied with each other for a glance from the audacious Flo. If their compliments partook of an extravagance that was at times ironical, the girl was evidently not deceived by it, but replied in kind. Only the expressman, who seemed to have fallen under the spell of her audacious glances, was uneasy at the license of the others, yet himself dumb towards her. The lady discreetly drew nearer to the fire, the old woman, and her coffee; Hiram subsided into his apathetic attitude by the fire.

A shout from the road at last proclaimed the return of Yuba Bill and his helpers. It had the singular effect of startling the party into a vague and uneasy consciousness of indiscretion, as if it had been the voice of the outer world of law and order, and their manner again became constrained. The leavetaking was hurried and perfunctory; the diplomatic Heckshill again lapsed into glittering generalities about "the best of friends parting." Only the expressman lingered for a moment on the doorstep in the light of the fire and the girl's dancing eyes.

"I hope," he stammered, with a very youthful blush, "to come the next time — with — with — a better introduction."

"Uncle Harry's," she said, with a quick laugh and a mock courtesy, as she turned away.

Once out of hearing, the party broke into hurried comment and criticism of the scene they had just witnessed, and particularly of the fair actress who had played so important a part, averring their emphatic intention of wresting the facts from Yuba Bill at once, and cross-examining him closely; but oddly enough, reaching the coach and that redoubted individual, no one seemed to care to take the initiative, and they all scrambled hurriedly to their seats without a word. How far Yuba Bill's irritability and imperious haste contributed to this, or whether a fear that he might in turn catechise them kept them silent, no one knew. The cynically observant passenger was not there; he and the sole occupant of the box-seat, they were told, had joined the clearing party some moments before, and would be picked up by Yuba Bill later on.

Five minutes after Bill had gathered up the reins, they reached the scene of obstruction. The great pine-tree which had fallen from the steep bank above and stretched across the road had been partly lopped of its branches, divided in two lengths, which were now rolled to either side of the track, leaving barely space for the coach to pass. The huge vehicle "slowed up" as Yuba Bill skillfully guided his six horses through this narrow alley, whose tassels of pine, glistening with wet, brushed the panels and sides of the coach, and effectually excluded any view from its windows. Seen from the coach top, the horses appeared to be cleaving their way through a dark, shining olive sea, that parted before and closed behind them, as they slowly passed. The leaders were just emerging from it, and Bill was gathering up his slackened reins, when a peremptory voice called, "Halt!" At the same moment the coach lights flashed upon a masked and motionless horseman in the road. Bill made an impulsive reach for his whip, but in the same instant checked himself, reined in his horses with a suppressed oath, and sat perfectly rigid. Not so the expressman, who caught up his rifle, but it was arrested by Bill's arm, and his voice in his ear!

"Too late! — we 're covered! — don't be a d—d fool!"

The inside passengers, still encompassed by obscurity, knew only that the stage had stopped. The "outsiders" knew, by experience, that they were covered by unseen guns in the wayside branches, and scarcely moved.

"I did n't think it was the square thing to stop you, Bill, till you 'd got through your work," said a masterful but not unpleasant voice, "and if you 'll just hand down the express box, I 'll pass you and the rest of your load through free. But as we 're both in a hurry, you 'd better look lively about it."

"Hand it down," said Bill gruffly to the expressman.

The expressman turned with a white cheek but blazing eyes to the compartment below his seat. He lingered, apparently in some difficulty with the lock of the compartment, but finally brought out the box and handed it to another armed and masked figure that appeared mysteriously from the branches beside the wheels.

"Thank you!" said the voice; "you can slide on now."

"And thank you for nothing," said Bill, gathering up his reins. "It's the first time any of your kind had to throw down a tree to hold me up!"

"You're lying, Bill! — though you don't know it," said the voice cheerfully. "Far from throwing down a tree to stop you, it was *I* sent word along the road to warn you from crashing down upon it, and sending you and your load to h—ll before your time! Drive on!"

The angry Bill waited for no second comment, but laying his whip over the backs of his team, drove furiously forward. So rapidly had the whole scene passed that the inside passengers knew nothing of it, and even those on the top of the coach roused from their stupor and inglorious inaction only to cling desperately to the terribly swaying coach as it thundered down the grade and try to keep their equilibrium. Yet, furious as was their speed, Yuba Bill could not help noticing that the expressman from time to time cast a hurried glance behind him. Bill knew that the young man had shown readiness and nerve in the attack, although both were hopeless; yet he was so much concerned at his set white face and compressed lips that when, at the end of three miles' unabated speed, they galloped up to the first station, he seized the young man by the arm, and, as the clamor of the news they had brought rose around them, dragged him past the wondering crowd, caught a decanter from the bar, and, opening the door of a side room, pushed him into it and closed the door behind them.

"Look yar, Brice! Stop it! Quit it right thar!" he said emphatically, laying his large hand on the young fellow's shoulder. "Be a man! You 've shown you are one, green ez you are, for you had the sand in ye — the clear grit to-night, yet you 'd have been a dead man now, if I had n't stopped ye! Man! you had no show from the beginning! You 've done your level best to save your treasure, and I 'm your witness to the kempany, and proud of it, too! So shet your head and — and," pouring out a glass of whiskey, "swaller that!"

But Brice waved him aside with burning eyes and dry lips.

"You don't know it all, Bill!" he said, with a half choked voice.

"All what?"

"Swear that you 'll keep it a secret," he said feverishly, gripping Bill's arm in turn, "and I 'll tell you."

"Go on!"

"*The coach was robbed before that!*"

"Wot yer say?" ejaculated Bill.

"The treasure — a packet of greenbacks — had been taken from the box before the gang stopped us!"

"The h—ll, you say!"

"Listen! When you told me to hand down the box, I had an idea — a d—d fool one, perhaps — of taking that package out and jumping from the coach with it. I knew they would fire at me only; I might get away, but if they killed me, I 'd have done only my duty, and nobody else would have got hurt. But when I got to the box I found that the lock had been forced and the money was gone. I managed to snap the lock again before I handed it down. I thought they might discover it at once and chase us, but they did n't."

"And then thar war no greenbacks in the box that they took?" gasped Bill, with staring eyes.

"No!"

Bill raised his hand in the air as if in solemn adjuration, and then brought it down on his knee, doubling up in a fit of uncontrollable but perfectly noiseless laughter. "Oh, Lord!" he gasped, "hol' me afore I bust right open! Hush," he went on, with a jerk of his fingers towards the next room, "not a word o' this to any one! It's too much to keep, I know; it's nearly killing me! but we must swaller it ourselves! Oh, Jerusalem the Golden! Oh, Brice! Think o' that face o' Snapshot Harry's ez he opened that treasure box afore his gang in the brush! And he allers *so* keen and *so* easy and *so* cock sure! Created snakes! I'd go through this every trip for one sight of him as he just riz up from that box and cussed!" He again shook with inward convulsions till his face grew purple, and even the red came back to the younger man's cheek.

"But this don't bring the money back, Bill," said Brice gloomily.

Yuba Bill swallowed the glass of whiskey at a gulp, wiped his mouth and eyes, smothered a second explosion, and then gravely confronted Brice.

"When do you think it was taken, and how?"

"It must have been taken when I left the coach on the road and went over to that settler's cabin," said Brice bitterly. "Yet I believed everything was safe, and I left two men — both passengers — one inside and one on the box, that man who sat the other side of you."

"Jee whillikins!" ejaculated Bill, with his hand to his forehead, "the men I clean forgot to pick up in the road, and now I reckon they never intended to be picked up, either."

"No doubt a part of the gang," said Brice, with increased bitterness; "I see it all now."

"No!" said Bill decisively, "that ain't Snapshot Harry's style; he's a clean fighter, with no underhand tricks. And I don't believe he threw down that tree, either. Look yer, sonny!" he added, suddenly laying his hand on Brice's shoulder, "a hundred to one that that was the work of a couple o' d—d sneaks or traitors in that gang who kem along as passengers. I never took any stock in that coyote who paid extra for his box-seat."

Brice knew that Bill never looked kindly on any passenger who, by bribing the ticket agent, secured this favorite seat, which Bill felt was due to his personal friends and was in his own selection. He only returned gloomily: —

"I don't see what difference it makes to us which robber got the money."

"Ye don't," said Bill, raising his head, with a sudden twinkle in his eyes. "Then ye don't know Snapshot Harry. Do ye suppose he's goin' to sit down and twiddle his thumbs with that skin game played on him? No, sir," he continued, with a thoughtful deliberation, drawing his fingers slowly through his long beard, "he spotted it — and smelt out the whole trick ez soon ez he opened that box, and that's why he didn't foller us! He'll hunt those sneak thieves into h—ll but what he'll get 'em, and," he went on still more slowly, "by the livin' hokey! I reckon, sonny, that's jest how ye'll get your chance to chip in!"

"I don't understand," said Brice impatiently.

"Well," said Bill, with more provoking slowness, as if he were communing with himself rather than Brice, "Harry's mighty proud and high toned, and to be given away like this has cut down into his heart, you bet. It ain't the money he's thinkin' of; it's this split in the gang — the loss of his power ez boss, ye see — and ef he could get hold o' them chaps he'd let the money slide ez long ez they didn't get it. So you've got a detective on your side that's worth the whole police force of Californy! Ye never heard anything about Snapshot Harry, did ye?" asked Bill carelessly, raising his eyes to Brice's eager face.

The young man flushed slightly. "Very little," he said.

At the same time a vision of the pretty girl in the settler's cabin flashed upon him with a new significance.

"He's more than half white, in some ways," said Bill thoughtfully, "and they say he lives somewhere about here in a cabin in the bush, with a crippled sister and her darter, who both swear by him. It might n't be hard to find him — ef a man was dead set on it."

Brice faced about with determined eyes. "I'll do it," he said quietly.

"Ye might," said Bill, still more deliberately stroking his beard, "mention my name, ef ye ever get to see him."

"Your name," ejaculated the astonished Brice.

"My name," repeated Bill calmly. "He knows it's my bounden duty to kill him ef I get the chance, and I know that he'd plug me full o' holes in a minit ef thar war a necessity for it. But in these yer affairs, sonny, it seems to be the understood thing by the kempany that I'm to keep fiery young squirts like you, and chuckle-headed passengers like them" — jerking his thumb towards the other room — "from gettin' themselves killed by their rashness. So ontil the kempany fill the top o' that coach with men who ain't got any business to do *but* fightin' other men who ain't got any other business to do *but* to fight them — the odds are agin us! Harry has always acted square to me — that's how I know he ain't in this sneak-thief business, and why he did n't foller us, suspectin' suthin', and I've always acted square to him. All the same, I'd like ter hev seen his face when that box was opened! Lordy!" Here Bill again collapsed in his silent paroxysm of mirth. "Ye might tell him how I laughed!"

"I would hardly do that, Bill," said the young man, smiling in spite of himself. "But you've given me an idea, and I'll work it out."

Bill glanced at the young fellow's kindling eyes and flushing cheek, and nodded. "Well, rastle with that idea later on, sonny. I'll fix you all right in my report to the kempany, but the rest you must work alone. I've started out the usual posse, circus-ridin' down the road after Harry. He'd be a rough customer to meet just now," continued Bill, with a chuckle, "ef thar was the ghost of a chance o' them comin' up with him, for him and his gang is scattered miles away by this." He paused, tossed off another glass of whiskey, wiped his mouth, and saying to Brice, with a wink, "It's about time to go and comfort them thar passengers," led the way through the crowded barroom into the stage office.

The spectacle of Bill's humorously satisfied face and Brice's bright eyes and heightened color was singularly effective. The "inside" passengers, who had experienced neither the excitement nor the danger of the robbery, yet had been obliged to listen to the hairbreadth escapes of the others, pooh-poohed the whole affair, and even the "outsides" themselves were at last convinced that the robbery was a slight one, with little or no loss to the company. The clamor subsided almost as suddenly as it had arisen; the wiser passengers fashioned their attitude on the sangfroid of Yuba Bill, and the whole coach load presently rolled away as complacently as if nothing had happened.

II

The robbery furnished the usual amount of copy for the local press. There was the inevitable compliment to Yuba Bill for his well-known coolness; the conduct of the young expressman, "who, though new to the service, displayed an intrepidity that only succumbed to numbers," was highly commended, and even the passengers received their meed of praise, not forgetting the lady, "who accepted the incident with the light-hearted pleasantry characteristic of the Californian woman." There was the usual allusion to the necessity of a Vigilance Committee to cope with this "organized lawlessness," but it is to be feared that the readers of "The Red Dog Clarion," however ready to lynch a horse thief, were of the opinion that rich stage express companies were quite able to take care of their own property.

It was with full cognizance of these facts and their uselessness to him that the next morning Mr. Ned Brice turned from the road where the coach had halted on the previous night and approached the settler's cabin. If a little less sanguine than he was in Yuba Bill's presence, he was still doggedly inflexible in his design, whatever it might have been, for he had not revealed it even to Yuba Bill. It was his own; it was probably crude and youthful in its directness, but for that reason it was probably more convincing than the vacillations of older counsel.

He paused a moment at the closed door, conscious, however, of some hurried movement within which signified that his approach had been observed. The door was opened, and disclosed only the old woman. The same dogged expression was on her face as when he had last seen it, with the addition of querulous expectancy. In reply to his polite "Good-morning," she abruptly faced him with her hands still on the door.

"Ye kin stop right there! Ef yer want ter make any talk about this yar robbery, ye might ez well skedaddle to oncet, for we ain't ' takin' any ' to-day!"

"I have no wish to talk about the robbery," said Brice quietly, "and as far as I can prevent it, you will not be troubled by any questions. If you doubt my word or the intentions of the company, perhaps you will kindly read that."

He drew from his pocket a still damp copy of "The Red Dog Clarion" and pointed to a paragraph.

"Wot's that?" she said querulously, feeling for her spectacles.

"Shall I read it?"

"Go on."

He read it slowly aloud. I grieve to say it had been jointly concocted the night before at the office of the "Clarion" by himself and the young journalist — the latter's assistance being his own personal tribute to the graces of Miss Flo. It read as follows: —

"The greatest assistance was rendered by Hiram Tarbox, Esq., a resident of the vicinity, in removing the obstruction, which was, no doubt, the preliminary work of some of the robber gang, and in providing hospitality for the delayed passengers. In fact, but for the timely warning of Yuba Bill by Mr. Tarbox, the coach might have crashed into the tree at that dangerous point, and an accident ensued more disastrous to life and limb than the robbery itself."

The sudden and unmistakable delight that expanded the old woman's mouth was so convincing that it might have given Brice a tinge of remorse over the success of his stratagem, had he not been utterly absorbed in his purpose. "Hiram!" she shouted suddenly.

The old man appeared from some back door with a promptness that proved his near proximity, and glanced angrily at Brice until he caught sight of his wife's face. Then his anger changed to wonder.

"Read that again, young feller," she said exultingly.

Brice reread the paragraph aloud for Mr. Tarbox's benefit.

"That 'ar 'Hiram Tarbox, Esquire,' means *you*, Hiram," she gasped, in delighted explanation.

Hiram seized the paper, read the paragraph himself, spread out the whole page, examined it carefully, and then a fatuous grin began slowly to extend itself over his whole face, invading his eyes and ears, until the heavy, harsh, dogged lines of his nostrils and jaws had utterly disappeared.

"B' gosh!" he said, "that's square! Kin I keep it?"

"Certainly," said Brice.   "I brought it for you."

"Is that all ye came for?" said Hiram with sudden suspicion.

"No," said the young man frankly.   Yet he hesitated a moment as he added, "I would like to see Miss Flora."

His hesitation and heightened color were more disarming to suspicion than the most elaborate and carefully prepared indifference.   With their knowledge of and pride in their relative's fascinations they felt it could have but one meaning!   Hiram wiped his mouth with his hand, assumed a demure expression, glanced at his wife, and answered: —

"She ain't here now."

Mr. Brice's face displayed his disappointment.   But the true lover holds a talisman potent with old and young. Mrs. Tarbox felt a sneaking maternal pity for this suddenly stricken Strephon.

"She's gone home," she added more gently — "went at sun-up this mornin'."

"Home," repeated Brice.   "Where's that?"

Mrs. Tarbox looked at her husband and hesitated.   Then she said — a little in her old manner — "Her uncle's."

"Can you direct me the way there?" asked Brice simply.

The astonishment in their faces presently darkened into suspicion again.   "Ef that's your little game," began Hiram, with a lowering brow —

"I have no little game but to see her and speak with her," said Brice boldly.   "I am alone and unarmed, as you see," he continued, pointing to his empty belt and small dispatch bag slung on his shoulder, "and certainly unable to do any one any harm.   I am willing to take what risks there are.   And as no one knows of my intention, nor of my coming here, whatever might happen to me, no one need know it.   You would be safe from questioning."

There was that hopeful determination in his manner that

overrode their resigned doggedness. "Ef we knew how to direct you thar," said the old woman cautiously, "ye'd be killed outer hand afore ye even set eyes on the girl. The house is in a holler with hills kept by spies; ye'd be a dead man as soon as ye crossed its boundary."

"Wot do *you* know about it?" interrupted her husband quickly, in querulous warning. "Wot are ye talkin' about?"

"You leave me alone, Hiram! I ain't goin' to let that young feller get popped off without a show, or without knowin' jest wot he's got to tackle, nohow ye kin fix it! And can't ye see he's bound to go, whatever ye says?"

Mr. Tarbox saw this fact plainly in Brice's eyes, and hesitated.

"The most that I kin tell ye," he said gloomily, "is the way the gal takes when she goes from here, but how far it is, or if it ain't a blind, I can't swar, for I hev n't bin thar myself, and Harry never comes here but on an off night, when the coach ain't runnin' and thar's no travel." He stopped suddenly and uneasily, as if he had said too much.

"Thar ye go, Hiram, and ye talk of others gabblin'! So ye might as well tell the young feller how that thar ain't but one way, and that's the way Harry takes, too, when he comes yer oncet in an age to talk to his own flesh and blood, and see a Christian face that ain't agin him!"

Mr. Tarbox was silent. "Ye know whar the tree was thrown down on the road," he said at last.

"Yes."

"The mountain rises straight up on the right side of the road, all hazel brush and thorn — whar a goat could n't climb."

"Yes."

"But that's a lie! for thar's a little trail, not a foot wide, runs up from the road for a mile, keepin' it in view all the while, but bein' hidden by the brush. Ye kin see everything from thar, and hear a teamster spit on the road."

"Go on," said Brice impatiently.

"Then it goes up and over the ridge, and down the other side into a little gulch until it comes to the cañon of the North Fork, where the stage road crosses over the bridge high up. The trail winds round the bank of the Fork and comes out on the *left* side of the stage road about a thousand feet below it. That's the valley and hollow whar Harry lives, and that's the only way it can be found. For all along the *left* of the stage road is a sheer pitch down that thousand feet, whar no one kin git up or down."

"I understand," said Brice, with sparkling eyes. "I'll find my way all right."

"And when ye git thar, look out for yourself!" put in the woman earnestly. "Ye may have regular greenhorn's luck and pick up Flo afore ye cross the boundary, for she's that bold that when she gets lonesome o' stayin' thar she goes wanderin' out o' bounds."

"Hev ye any weppin, — any shootin'-iron about ye?" asked Tarbox, with a latent suspicion.

The young man smiled, and again showed his empty belt. "None!" he said truthfully.

"I ain't sure ef that ain't the safest thing arter all with a shot like Harry," remarked the old man grimly. "Well, so long!" he added, and turned away.

It was clearly a leavetaking, and Brice, warmly thanking them both, returned to the road.

It was not far to the scene of the obstruction, yet but for Tarbox's timely hint, the little trail up the mountain side would have escaped his observation. Ascending, he soon found himself creeping along a narrow ledge of rock, hidden from the road that ran fifty yards below by a thick network growth of thorn and bramble, which still enabled him to see its whole parallel length. Perilous in the extreme to any hesitating foot, at one point, directly above the obstruction, the ledge itself was missing — broken away by the fall of the tree from the forest crest higher up. For an instant Brice stood dizzy and irresolute before the gap. Looking down for a foothold, his eye caught the faint imprint of a woman's shoe on a clayey rock projecting midway of the chasm. It must have been the young girl's footprint made that morning, for the narrow toe was pointed in the direction she would go! Where *she* could pass should he shrink from going? Without further hesitation he twined his fingers around the roots above him, and half swung, half pulled himself along until he once more felt the ledge below him.

From time to time, as he went on along the difficult track, the narrow little toe-print pointed the way to him, like an arrow through the wilds. It was a pleasant thought, and yet a perplexing one. Would he have undertaken this quest just to see her? Would he be content with that if his other motive failed? For as he made his way up to the ridge he was more than once assailed by doubts of the practical success of his enterprise. In the excitement of last night, and even the hopefulness of the early morning, it seemed an easy thing to persuade the vain and eccentric highwayman that their interests might be identical, and to convince him that his, Brice's, assistance to recover the stolen greenbacks and insure the punishment of the robber, with the possible addition of a reward from the express company, would be an inducement for them to work together. The risks that he was running seemed to his youthful fancy to atone for any defects in his logic or his plans. Yet as he crossed the ridge, leaving the civilized highway behind him, and descended the narrow trail, which grew wilder at each step, his arguments seemed no longer so convincing. He now hurried forward, however, with a feverish haste to anticipate the worst that might befall him.

The trail grew more intricate in the deep ferns; the friendly little footprint had vanished in this primeval wilderness. As he pushed through the gorge, he could hear at last the roar of the North Fork forcing its way through the cañon that crossed the gorge at right angles. At last he reached its current, shut in by two narrow precipitous walls that were spanned five hundred feet above by the stage road over a perilous bridge. As he approached the gloomy cañon, he remembered that the river, seen from above, seemed to have no banks, but to have cut its way through the solid rock. He found, however, a faint ledge made by caught driftwood from the current and the débris of the overhanging cliffs. Again the narrow footprint on the ooze was his guide. At last, emerging from the cañon, a strange view burst upon his sight. The river turned abruptly to the right, and, following the mountain side, left a small hollow completely walled in by the surrounding heights. To his left was the ridge he had descended from on the other side, and he now understood the singular detour he had made. He was on the other side of the stage road also, which ran along the mountain shelf a thousand feet above him. The wall, a sheer cliff, made the hollow inaccessible from that side. Little hills covered with buckeye encompassed it. It looked like a sylvan retreat, and yet was as secure in its isolation and approaches as the outlaw's den that it was.

He was gazing at the singular prospect when a shot rang in the air. It seemed to come from a distance, and he interpreted it as a signal. But it was followed presently by another; and putting his hand to his hat to keep it from falling, he found that the upturned brim had been pierced by a bullet. He stopped at this evident hint, and, taking his dispatch bag from his shoulder, placed it significantly upon a boulder, and looked around as if to await the appearance of the unseen marksman. The rifle shot rang out

again, the bag quivered, and turned over with a bullet hole
through it!

He took out his white handkerchief and waved it. Another shot followed, and the handkerchief was snapped from
his fingers, torn from corner to corner. A feeling of desperation and fury seized him; he was being played with by
a masked and skillful assassin, who only waited until it
pleased him to fire the deadly shot! But this time he could
see the rifle smoke drifting from under a sycamore not a
hundred yards away. He set his white lips together, but
with a determined face and unfaltering step walked directly
towards it. In another moment he believed and almost
hoped that all would be over. With such a marksman he
would not be maimed, but killed outright.

He had not covered half the distance before a man lounged
out from behind the tree carelessly shouldering his rifle.
He was tall but slightly built, with an amused, critical manner, and nothing about him to suggest the bloodthirsty assassin. He met Brice halfway, dropping his rifle slantingly
across his breast with his hands lightly grasping the lock,
and gazed at the young man curiously.

"You look as if you'd had a big scare, old man, but
you've clear grit for all that!" he said, with a critical and
reassuring smile. "Now, what are you doing here? Stay,"
he continued as Brice's parched lips prevented him from replying immediately. "I ought to know your face. Hello!
you're the expressman!" His glance suddenly shifted,
and swept past Brice over the ground beyond him to the
entrance of the hollow, but his smile returned as he apparently satisfied himself that the young man was alone.
"Well, what do you want?"

"I want to see Snapshot Harry," said Brice, with an effort. His voice came back more slowly than his color,
but that was perhaps hurried by a sense of shame at his
physical weakness.

"What you want is a drop o' whiskey," said the stranger good humoredly, taking his arm, "and we'll find it in that shanty just behind the tree." To Brice's surprise, a few steps in that direction revealed a fair-sized cabin, with a slight pretentiousness about it of neatness, comfort, and picturesque effect, far superior to the Tarbox shanty. A few flowers were in boxes on the window — signs, as Brice fancied, of feminine taste. When they reached the threshold, somewhat of this quality was also visible in the interior. When Brice had partaken of the whiskey, the stranger, who had kept silence, pointed to a chair, and said smilingly: —

"I am Henry Dimwood, alias Snapshot Harry, and this is my house."

"I came to speak with you about the robbery of greenbacks from the coach last night," began Brice hurriedly, with a sudden access of hope at his reception. "I mean, of course," — he stopped and hesitated, — "the actual robbery before *you* stopped us."

"What!" said Harry, springing to his feet, "do you mean to say *you* knew it?"

Brice's heart sank, but he remained steadfast and truthful. "Yes," he said, "I knew it when I handed down the box. I saw that the lock had been forced, but I snapped it together again. It was my fault. Perhaps I should have warned you, but I am solely to blame."

"Did Yuba Bill know of it?" asked the highwayman, with singular excitement.

"Not at the time, I give you my word!" replied Brice quickly, thinking only of loyalty to his old comrade. "I never told him till we reached the station."

"And he knew it then?" repeated Harry eagerly.

"Yes."

"Did he say anything? Did he do anything? Did he look astonished?"

Brice remembered Bill's uncontrollable merriment, but replied vaguely and diplomatically, "He was certainly astonished."

A laugh gathered in Snapshot Harry's eyes which at last overspread his whole face, and finally shook his frame as he sat helplessly down again. Then, wiping his eyes, he said in a shaky voice: —

"It would have been sure death to have trusted myself near that station, but I think I'd have risked it just to have seen Bill's face when you told him! Just think of it! Bill, who was a match for anybody! Bill, who was never caught napping! Bill, who only wanted supreme control of things to wipe me off the face of the earth! Bill, who knew how everything was done, and could stop it if he chose, and then to have been *robbed twice in one evening by my gang!* Yes, sir! Yuba Bill and his rotten old coach were *gone through twice inside half an hour* by the gang!"

"Then you knew of it too?" said Brice, in uneasy astonishment.

"Afterwards, my young friend — like Yuba Bill — afterwards." He stopped; his whole expression changed. "It was done by two sneaking hounds," he said sharply; "one whom I suspected before, and one, a new hand, a pal of his. They were detached to watch the coach and be satisfied that the greenbacks were aboard, for it isn't my style to 'hold up' except for something special. They were to take seats on the coach as far as Ringwood Station, three miles below where we held you up, and to get out there and pass the word to us that it was all right. They didn't; that made us a little extra careful, seeing something was wrong, but never suspecting *them*. We found out afterwards that they got one of my scouts to cut down that tree, saying it was my orders and a part of our game, calculating in the stoppage and confusion to collar the swag and get off with it. Without knowing it, *you* played into their hands by going into Tarbox's cabin."

"But how did you know this?" interrupted Brice, in wonder.

"They forgot one thing," continued Snapshot Harry grimly. "They forgot that half an hour before and half an hour after a stage is stopped we have that road patrolled, every foot of it. While I was opening the box in the brush, the two fools, sneaking along the road, came slap upon one of my patrols, and then tried to run for it. One was dropped, but before he was plugged full of holes and hung up on a tree, he confessed, and said the other man who escaped had the greenbacks."

Brice's face fell. "Then they are lost," he said bitterly.

"Not unless he eats them — as he may want to do before I'm done on him, for he must either starve or come out. That road is still watched by my men from Tarbox's cabin to the bridge. He's there somewhere, and can't get forward or backward. Look!" he said, rising and going to the door. "That road," he pointed to the stage road, — a narrow ledge flanked on one side by a precipitous mountain wall, and on the other by an equally precipitate descent, — "is his limit and tether, and he can't escape on either side."

"But the trail?"

"There is but one entrance to it, — the way you came, and that is guarded too. From the time you entered it until you reached the bottom, you were signaled here from point to point! *He* would have been dropped! I merely gave *you* a hint of what might have happened to you, if you were up to any little game! You took it like a white man. Come, now! What is your business?"

Thus challenged, Brice plunged with youthful hopefulness into his plan; if, as he voiced it, it seemed to him a little extravagant, he was buoyed up by the frankness of the highwayman, who also had treated the double robbery with a levity that seemed almost as extravagant. He suggested that they should work together to recover the money; that the express company should know that the unprecedented stealthy introduction of robbers in the guise of passengers was not Snapshot Harry's method, and he repudiated it as unmanly and unsportsmanlike; and that, by using his superior skill and knowledge of the locality to recover the money and deliver the culprit into the company's hands, he would not only earn the reward that they should offer, but that he would evoke a sentiment that all Californians would understand and respect. The highwayman listened with a tolerant smile, but, to Brice's surprise, this appeal to his vanity touched him less than the prospective punishment of the thief.

"It would serve the d—d hound right," he muttered, "if, instead of being shot like a man, he was made to 'do time' in prison, like the ordinary sneak thief that he is." When Brice had concluded, he said briefly, "The only trouble with your plans, my young friend, is that about twenty-five men have got to consider them, and have *their* say about it. Every man in my gang is a shareholder in these greenbacks, for I work on the square; and it's for him to say whether he'll give them up for a reward and the good opinion of the express company. Perhaps," he went on, with a peculiar smile, "it's just as well that you tried it on me first! However, I'll sound the boys, and see what comes of it, but not until you're safe off the premises."

"And you'll let me assist you?" said Brice eagerly.

Snapshot Harry smiled again. "Well, if you come across the d—d thief, and you recognize him and can get the greenbacks from him, I'll pass over the game to you." He rose and added, apparently by way of farewell, "Perhaps it's just as well that I should give you a guide part

of the way to prevent accidents." He went to a door leading to an adjoining room, and called "Flo!"

Brice's heart leaped! If he had forgotten her in the excitement of his interview, he atoned for it by a vivid blush.
Her own color was a little heightened as she slipped into
the room, but the two managed to look demurely at each
other, without a word of recognition.

"This is my niece, Flora," said Snapshot Harry, with
a slight wave of the hand that was by no means uncourtly,
"and her company will keep you from any impertinent
questioning as well as if I were with you. This is Mr.
Brice, Flo, who came to see me on business, and has quite
forgotten my practical joking."

The girl acknowledged Brice's bow with a shyness very
different from her manner of the evening before. Brice
felt embarrassed and evidently showed it, for his host, with
a smile, put an end to the constraint by shaking the young
man's hand heartily, bidding him good-by, and accompany-
ing him to the door.

Once on their way, Mr. Brice's spirits returned. "I
told you last night," he said, "that I hoped to meet you
the next time with a better introduction. You suggested
your uncle's. Well, are you satisfied?"

"But you didn't come to see *me*," said the girl mischievously.

"How do you know what my intentions were?" returned
the young man gayly, gazing at the girl's charming face
with a serious doubt as to the singleness of his own intentions.

"Oh, because I know," she answered, with a toss of her
brown head. "I heard what you said to uncle Harry."

Mr. Brice's brow contracted. "Perhaps you saw me
too, when I came," he said, with a slight touch of bitterness as he thought of his reception.

Miss Flo laughed. Brice walked on silently; the girl

was heartless and worthy of her education. After a pause she said demurely, "*I* knew he would n't hurt you — but *you* did n't. That 's where you showed your grit in walking straight on."

"And I suppose you were greatly amused," he replied scornfully.

The girl lifted her arms a little wearily, as with a half sigh she readjusted her brown braids under her uncle's gray slouch hat, which she had caught up as she passed out. "Thar ain't much to laugh at here!" she said. "But it was mighty funny when you tried to put your hat straight, and then found thar was that bullet hole right through the brim! And the way you stared at it — Lordy!"

Her musical laugh was infectious, and swept away his outraged dignity. He laughed too. At last she said, gazing at his hat, "It won't do for you to go back to your folks wearin' that sort o' thing. Here! Take mine!" With a saucy movement she audaciously lifted his hat from his head, and placed her own upon it.

"But this is your uncle's hat," he remonstrated.

"All the same; he spoiled yours," she laughed, adjusting his hat upon her own head. "But I 'll keep yours to remember you by. I 'll loop it up by this hole, and it 'll look mighty purty. Jes' see!" She plucked a wild rose from a bush by the wayside, and, passing the stalk through the bullet hole, pinned the brim against the crown by a thorn. "There," she said, putting on the hat again with a little affectation of coquetry, "how 's that?"

Mr. Brice thought it very picturesque and becoming to the graceful head and laughing eyes beneath it, and said so. Then, becoming in his turn audacious, he drew nearer to her side.

"I suppose you know the forfeit of putting on a gentleman's hat?"

Apparently she did, for she suddenly made a warning

gesture, and said, "Not here! It would be a bigger forfeit than you 'd keer fo'." Before he could reply she turned aside as if quite innocently, and passed into the shade of a fringe of buckeyes. He followed quickly. "I did n't mean that," she said; but in the mean time he had kissed the pink tip of her ear under its brown coils. He was, nevertheless, somewhat discomfited by her undisturbed manner and serene face. "Ye don't seem to mind bein' shot at," she said, with an odd smile, "but it won't do for you to kalkilate that *everybody* shoots as keerfully as uncle Harry."

"I don't understand," he replied, struck by her manner.

"Ye ain't very complimentary, or you 'd allow that other folks might be wantin' what you took just now, and might consider you was poachin'," she returned gravely. "My best and strongest holt among those men is that uncle Harry would kill the first one who tried anything like that on — and they know it. That 's how I get all the liberty I want here, and can come and go alone as I like."

Brice's face flushed quickly with genuine shame and remorse. "Do forgive me," he said hurriedly. "I did n't think — I 'm a brute and a fool!"

"Uncle Harry allowed you was either drunk or a born idiot when you was promenadin' into the valley just now," she said, with a smile.

"And what did you think?" he asked a little uneasily.

"I thought you did n't look like a drinkin' man," she answered audaciously.

Brice bit his lip and walked on silently, at which she cast a sidelong glance under her widely spaced heavy lashes and said demurely, "I thought last night it was mighty good for you to stand up for your frien' Yuba Bill, and then, after ye knew who *I* was, to let the folks see you kinder cottoned to me too. Not in the style o' that land-grabber Heckshill, nor that peart newspaper man, neither. Of course I gave them as good as they sent," she went on, with a little laugh, but Brice could see that her sensitive lip in profile had the tremulous and resentful curve of one who was accustomed to slight and annoyance. Was it possible that this reckless, self-contained girl felt her position keenly?

"I am proud to have your good opinion," he said, with a certain respect mingled with his admiring glance, "even if I have not your uncle's."

"Oh, he likes you well enough, or he wouldn't have hearkened to you a minute," she said quickly. "When you opened out about them greenbacks, I jes' clutched my cheer so," — she illustrated her words with a gesture of her hands, and her face actually seemed to grow pale at the recollection, — "and I nigh started up to stop ye; but that idea of Yuba Bill bein' robbed *twice* I think tickled him awful. But it was lucky none o' the gang heard ye or suspected anything. I reckon that's why he sent me with you, — to keep them from doggin' you and askin' questions that a straight man like you would be sure to answer. But they daren't come nigh ye as long as I'm with you!" She threw back her head and rose-crested hat with a mock air of protection that, however, had a certain real pride in it.

"I am very glad of that, if it gives me the chance of having your company alone," returned Brice, smiling, "and very grateful to your uncle, whatever were his reasons for making you my guide. But you have already been that to me," and he told her of the footprints. "But for you," he added, with gentle significance, "I should not have been here."

She was silent for a moment, and he could only see the back of her head and its heavy brown coils. After a pause she asked abruptly, "Where's your handkerchief?"

He took it from his pocket; her ingenious uncle's bullet had torn rather than pierced the cambric.

"I thought so," she said, gravely examining it, "but I kin mend it as good as new. I reckon you allow I can't sew," she continued, "but I do heaps of mendin', as the digger squaw and Chinamen we have here do only the coarser work. I 'll send it back to you, and meanwhiles you keep mine."

She drew a handkerchief from her pocket and handed it to him. To his great surprise it was a delicate one, beautifully embroidered, and utterly incongruous to her station. The idea that flashed upon him, it is to be feared, showed itself momentarily in his hesitation and embarrassment.

She gave a quick laugh. "Don't be frightened. It's bought and paid for. Uncle Harry don't touch passengers' fixin's; that ain't his style. You oughter know that." Yet in spite of her laugh, he could see the sensitive pout of her lower lip.

"I was only thinking," he said hurriedly and sympathetically, "that it was too fine for me. But I will be proud to keep it as a souvenir of you. It 's not too pretty for *that!* "

"Uncle gets me these things. He don't keer what they cost," she went on, ignoring the compliment. "Why, I 've got awfully fine gowns up there that I only wear when I go to Marysville oncet in a while."

"Does he take you there?" asked Brice.

"No!" she answered quietly. "Not" — a little defiantly — "that he 's afeard, for they can't prove anything against him; no man kin swear to him, and thar ain't an officer that keers to go for him. But he 's that shy for *me* he don't keer to have me mixed with him."

"But nobody recognizes you?"

"Sometimes — but I don't keer for that." She cocked her hat a little audaciously, but Brice noticed that her arms afterwards dropped at her side with the same weary gesture he had observed before. "Whenever I go into shops it 's always 'Yes, miss,' and 'No, miss,' and 'Certainly, Miss Dimwood.' Oh, they 're mighty respectful. I reckon they allow that Snapshot Harry's rifle carries far."

Presently she faced him again, for their conversation had been carried on in profile. There was a critical, searching look in her brown eyes.

"Here I 'm talkin' to you as if you were one" — Mr. Brice was positive she was going to say "one of the gang," but she hesitated and concluded, "one of my relations — like cousin Hiram."

"I wish you would think of me as being as true a friend," said the young man earnestly.

She did not reply immediately, but seemed to be examining the distance. They were not far from the cañon now, and the river bank. A fringe of buckeyes hid the base of the mountain, which had begun to tower up above them to the invisible stage road overhead. "I am going to be a real guide to you now," she said suddenly. "When we reach that buckeye corner and are out of sight, we will turn into it instead of going through the cañon. You shall go up the mountain to the stage road from *this* side."

"But it is impossible!" he exclaimed, in astonishment. "Your uncle said so."

"Coming *down*, but not going up," she returned, with a laugh. "I found it, and no one knows it but myself."

He glanced up at the towering cliff; its nearly perpendicular flanks were seamed with fissures, some clefts deeply set with stunted growths of thorn and "scrub," but still sheer and forbidding, and then glanced back at her incredulously. "I will show you," she said, answering his look with a smile of triumph. "I have n't tramped over this whole valley for nothing! But wait until we reach the river bank. They must think that we 've gone through the cañon."

"They ? "

"Yes — any one who is watching us," said the girl dryly.

A few steps further on brought them to the buckeye thicket, which extended to the river bank and mouth of the cañon. The girl lingered for a moment ostentatiously before it, and then, saying "Come," suddenly turned at right angles into the thicket. Brice followed, and the next moment they were hidden by its friendly screen from the valley. On the other side rose the mountain wall, leaving a narrow trail before them. It was composed of the rocky débris and fallen trees of the cliff, from which buckeyes and larches were now springing. It was uneven, irregular, and slowly ascending; but the young girl led the way with the free footstep of a mountaineer, and yet a grace that was akin to delicacy. Nor could he fail to notice that, after the Western girl's fashion, she was shod more elegantly and lightly than was consistent with the rude and rustic surroundings. It was the same slim shoe-print which had guided him that morning. Presently she stopped, and seemed to be gazing curiously at the cliff side. Brice followed the direction of her eyes. On a protruding bush at the edge of one of the wooded clefts of the mountain flank something was hanging, and in the freshening southerly wind was flapping heavily, like a raven's wing, or as if still saturated with the last night's rain. "That's mighty queer!" said Flo, gazing intently at the unsightly and incongruous attachment to the shrub, which had a vague, weird suggestion. "It was n't there yesterday."

"It looks like a man's coat," remarked Brice uneasily.

"Whew!" said the girl. "Then somebody has come down who won't go up again! There's a lot of fresh rocks and brush here, too. What's that?" She was pointing to a spot some yards before them where there had been a recent precipitation of débris and uprooted shrubs. But mingled with it lay a mass of rags strangely akin to the tattered remnant that flagged from the bush a hundred feet above them. The girl suddenly uttered a sharp feminine cry of mingled horror and disgust, — the first weakness of sex she had shown, — and, recoiling, grasped Brice's arm. "Don't go there! Come away!"

But Brice had already seen that which, while it shocked him, was urging him forward with an invincible fascination. Gently releasing himself, and bidding the girl stand back, he moved toward the unsightly heap. Gradually it disclosed a grotesque caricature of a human figure, but so maimed and doubled up that it seemed a stuffed and fallen scarecrow. As is common in men stricken suddenly down by accident in the fullness of life, the clothes asserted themselves before all else with a hideous ludicrousness, obliterating even the majesty of death in their helpless yet ironical incongruity. The garments seemed to have never fitted the wearer, but to have been assumed in ghastly jocularity, — a boot half off the swollen foot, a ripped waistcoat thrown over the shoulder, were like the properties of some low comedian. At first the body appeared to be headless; but as Brice cleared away the débris and lifted it, he saw with horror that the head was twisted under the shoulder, and swung helplessly from the dislocated neck. But that horror gave way to a more intense and thrilling emotion as he saw the face — although strangely free from laceration or disfigurement, and impurpled and distended into the simulation of a self-complacent smile — was a face he recognized! It was the face of the cynical traveler in the coach — the man who he was now satisfied had robbed it.

A strange and selfish resentment took possession of him. Here was the man through whom he had suffered shame and peril, and who even now seemed complacently victorious in death. He examined him closely; his coat and waistcoat had been partly torn away in his fall; his shirt still clung to him, but through its torn front could be seen a heavy treasure belt encircling his waist. Forgetting his disgust, Brice tore away the shirt and unloosed the belt. It was saturated with water like the rest of the clothing, but its pocket seemed heavy and distended. In another instant he had opened it, and discovered the envelope containing the packet of greenbacks, its seal still inviolate and unbroken. It was the stolen treasure!

A faint sigh recalled him to himself. The girl was standing a few feet from him, regarding him curiously.

"It's the thief himself!" he said, in a breathless explanation. "In trying to escape he must have fallen from the road above. But here are the greenbacks safe! We must go back to your uncle at once," he said excitedly. "Come!"

"Are you mad?" she cried, in astonishment.

"No," returned Brice, in equal astonishment, "but you know I agreed with him that we should work together to recover the money, and I must show him our good luck."

"He told you that if you met the thief and could get the money from him, you were welcome to it," said the girl gravely, "and you *have* got it."

"But not in the way he meant," returned Brice hurriedly. "This man's death is the result of his attempting to escape from your uncle's guards along the road; the merit of it belongs to them and your uncle. It would be cowardly and mean of me to take advantage of it."

The girl looked at him with an expression of mingled admiration and pity. "But the guards were placed there before he ever saw you," said she impatiently. "And whatever uncle Harry may want to do, he must do what the gang says. And with the money once in their possession, or even in yours, if they knew it, I would n't give much for its chances — or *yours* either — for gettin' out o' this hollow again."

"But if *they* are treacherous, that is no reason why I should be so," protested Brice stoutly.

"You've no right to say they were treacherous when they knew nothing of your plans," said the girl sharply. "Your company would have more call to say *you* were treacherous to it for making a plan without consultin' them." Brice winced, for he had never thought of that before. "You can offer that reward *after* you get away from here with the greenbacks. But," she added proudly, with a toss of her head, "go back if you want to! Tell him all! Tell him where you found it — tell him I did not take you through the cañon, but was showin' you a new trail I had never shown to *them!* Tell him that I am a traitor, for I have given them and him away to you, a stranger, and that you consider yourself the only straight and honest one about here!"

Brice flushed with shame. "Forgive me," he said hurriedly; "you are right and I am wrong again. I will do just what you say. I will first place these greenbacks in a secure place — and then " —

"Get away first — that's your only holt," she interrupted him quickly, her eyes still flashing through indignant tears. "Come quick, for I must put you on the trail before they miss me."

She darted forward; he followed, but she kept the lead, as much, he fancied, to evade his observation as to expedite his going. Presently they stopped before the sloping trunk of a huge pine that had long since fallen from the height above, but, although splintered where it had broken ground, had preserved some fifty feet of its straight trunk erect and leaning like a ladder against the mountain wall. "There," she said, hurriedly pointing to its decaying but still projecting lateral branches, "you climb it — I have. At the top you 'll find it 's stuck in a cleft among the brush. There 's a little hollow and an old waterway from a spring above which makes a trail through the brush. It 's as good as the trail you took from the stage road this mornin', but

it 's not as safe comin' down. Keep along it to the spring,
and it will land ye jest the other side of uncle Hiram's
cabin.   Go quick!   I 'll wait here until ye 've reached the
cleft."

"But you," he said, turning toward her, "how can I ever
thank you ? "

As if anticipating a leavetaking, the girl had already
withdrawn herself a few yards away, and simply made an
upward gesture with her hand. "Quick! Up with you!
Every minute now is a risk to me."

Thus appealed to, Brice could only comply. Perhaps
he was a little hurt at the girl's evident desire to avoid a
gentler parting.   Securing his prized envelope within his
breast, he began to ascend the tree.   Its inclination, and
the aid offered by the broken stumps of branches, made this
comparatively easy, and in a few moments he reached its top,
and stood upon a little ledge in the wall.   A swift glance
around him revealed the whole waterway or fissure slanting
upward along the mountain face.   Then he turned quickly
to look down the dizzy height.   At first he could distinguish
nothing but the top of the buckeyes and their white clustering blossoms.   Then something fluttered, — the torn white
handkerchief of his that she had kept.   And then he caught
a single glimpse of the flower-plumed hat receding rapidly
among the trees, and Flora Dimwood was gone.

III

In twenty-four hours Edward Brice was in San Francisco.
But although successful and the bearer of the treasure, it is
doubtful if he approached this end of his journey with the
temerity he had shown on entering the robbers' valley.   A
consciousness that the methods he had employed might excite the ridicule, if not the censure, of his principals, or

that he might have compromised them in his meeting with Snapshot Harry, considerably modified his youthful exultation. It is possible that Flora's reproach, which still rankled in his mind, may have quickened his sensitiveness on that point. However, he had resolved to tell the whole truth, except his episode with Flora, and to place the conduct of Snapshot Harry and the Tarboxes in as favorable a light as possible. But first he had recourse to the manager, a man of shrewd worldly experience, who had recommended him to his place. When he had finished and handed him the treasured envelope, the man looked at him with a critical and yet not unkindly expression. "Perhaps it's just as well, Brice, that you did come to me at first, and did not make your report to the president and directors."

"I suppose," said Brice diffidently, "that they would n't have liked my communicating with the highwayman without their knowledge?"

" More than that — they would n't have believed your story."

" Not believe it?" cried Brice, flushing quickly. "Do you think "—

The manager checked him with a laugh. " Hold on! I believe every word of it, and why? Because you 've added nothing to it to make yourself the regular hero. Why, with your opportunity, and no one able to contradict you, you might have told me you had a hand-to-hand fight with the thief, and had to kill him to recover the money, and even brought your handkerchief and hat back with the bullet holes to prove it." Brice winked as he thought of the fair possessor of those articles. " But as a story for general circulation, it won't do. Have you told it to any one else? Does any one know what happened but yourself?"

Brice thought of Flora, but he had resolved not to compromise her, and he had a consciousness that she would be equally loyal to him. " No one," he answered boldly.

" Very good.   And I suppose you would n't mind if it
were kept out of the newspapers?   You 're not hankering
after a reputation as a hero?"

" Certainly not," said Brice indignantly.

" Well, then, we 'll keep it where it is.   You will say
nothing.   I will hand over the greenbacks to the company,
but only as much of your story as I think they 'll stand.
You 're all right as it is.   Yuba Bill has already set you up
in his report to the company, and the recovery of this money
will put you higher!   Only, the *public* need know nothing
about it."

" But," asked Brice amazedly, " how can it be prevented?
The shippers who lost the money will have to know that it
has been recovered."

" Why should they?   The company will assume the risk,
and repay them just the same.   It 's a great deal better to
have the reputation for accepting the responsibility than for
the shippers to think that they only get their money through
the accident of its recovery."

Brice gasped at this large business truth.   Besides, it
occurred to him that it kept the secret, and Flora's partici-
pation in it, from Snapshot Harry and the gang.   He had
not thought of that before.

" Come," continued the manager, with official curtness,
" what do you say?   Are you willing to leave it to me?"

Brice hesitated a moment.   It was not what his impulsive,
truthful nature had suggested.   It was not what his youthful fancy had imagined.   He had not worked upon the sympathies of the company on behalf of Snapshot Harry as he
believed he would do.   He had not even impressed the manager.   His story, far from exciting a chivalrous sentiment,
had been pronounced improbable.   Yet he reflected he had
so far protected *her*, and he consented with a sigh.

Nevertheless, the result ought to have satisfied him.   A
dazzling check, inclosed in a letter of thanks from the com-

pany the next day, and his promotion from "the road" to the San Francisco office, would have been quite enough for any one but Edward Brice. Yet he was grateful, albeit a little frightened and remorseful over his luck. He could not help thinking of the kindly tolerance of the highway man, the miserable death of the actual thief, which had proved his own salvation, and above all, the generous, high-spirited girl who had aided his escape. While on his way to San Francisco, and yet in the first glow of his success, he had written her a few lines from Marysville, inclosed in a letter to Mr. Tarbox. He had received no reply.

Then a week passed. He wrote again, and still no reply. Then a vague feeling of jealousy took possession of him as he remembered her warning hint of the attentions to which she was subjected, and he became singularly appreciative of Snapshot Harry's proficiency as a marksman. Then, cruel-est of all, for your impassioned lover is no lover at all if not cruel in his imaginings, he remembered how she had evaded her uncle's espionage with *him ;* could she not equally with *another?* Perhaps that was why she had hurried him away, — why she had prevented his returning to her uncle. Fol-lowing this came another week of disappointment and equally miserable cynical philosophy, in which he persuaded himself he was perfectly satisfied with his material advancement, that it was the only outcome of his adventure to be recog-nized; and he was more miserable than ever.

A month had passed, when one morning he received a small package by post. The address was in a handwriting unknown to him, but opening the parcel he was surprised to find only a handkerchief neatly folded. Examining it closely, he found it was his own, — the one he had given her, the rent made by her uncle's bullet so ingeniously and delicately mended as to almost simulate embroidery. The joy that suddenly filled him at this proof of her remembrance showed him too plainly how hollow had been his cynicism and how lasting his hope! Turning over the wrapper eagerly, he discovered what he had at first thought was some business card. It was, indeed, printed and not engraved, in some common newspaper type, and bore the address, " Hiram Tarbox, Land and Timber Agent, 1101 California Street." He again examined the parcel; there was nothing else, — not a line from *her!* But it was a clue at last, and she had not forgotten him! He seized his hat, and ten minutes later was breasting the steep sand hill into which California Street in those days plunged, and again emerged at its crest, with a few struggling houses.

But when he reached the summit he could see that the outline of the street was still plainly marked along the distance by cottages and new suburban villa-like blocks of houses. No. 1101 was in one of these blocks, a small tenement enough, but a palace compared to Mr. Tarbox's Sierran cabin. He impetuously rang the bell, and without waiting to be announced dashed into the little drawing-room and Mr. Tarbox's presence. That had changed too; Mr. Tarbox was arrayed in a suit of clothes as new, as cheaply decorative, as fresh and, apparently, as damp as his own drawing-room.

" Did you get my letter? Did you give her the one I inclosed? Why did n't you answer?" burst out Brice, after his first breathless greeting.

Mr. Tarbox's face here changed so suddenly into his old dejected doggedness that Brice could have imagined himself back in the Sierran cabin. The man straightened and bowed himself at Brice's questions, and then replied with bold, deliberate emphasis: —

" Yes, I *did* get your letter. I *did n't* give no letter o' yours to her. And I did n't answer your letter *before*, for I did n't propose to answer it *at all.*"

" Why?" demanded Brice indignantly.

" I did n't give her your letter because I did n't kalkilate

to be any go-between 'twixt you and Snapshot Harry's
niece. Look yar, Mr. Brice. Sense I read that 'ar paragraph in that paper you gave me, I allowed to myself that
it was n't the square thing for me to have any more doin's
with him, and I quit it. I jest chucked your letter in the
fire. I did n't answer you because I reckoned I 'd no call
to correspond with ye, and when I showed ye that trail over
to Harry's camp, it was ended. I 've got a house and business to look arter, and it don't jibe with keepin' company
with 'road agents.' That 's what I got outer that paper
you gave me, Mr. Brice."

Rage and disgust filled Brice at the man's utter selfishness and shameless desertion of his kindred, none the less
powerfully that he remembered the part he himself had
played in concocting the paragraph. " Do you mean to
say," he demanded passionately, " that for the sake of that
foolish paragraph you gave up your own kindred? That
you truckled to the mean prejudices of your neighbors and
kept that poor, defenseless girl from the only honest roof
she could find refuge under? That you dared to destroy
my letter to her, and make her believe I was as selfish and
ungrateful as yourself? "

" Young feller," said Mr. Tarbox still more deliberately,
yet with a certain dignity that Brice had never noticed before, " what 's between you and Flo, and what rights she
has fer thinkin' ye ' ez selfish ' and ' ez ongrateful ' ez me —
ef she does, I dunno! — but when ye talk o' me givin' up
my kindred, and sling such hogwash ez ' ongrateful ' and
' selfish ' round this yer sittin'-room, mebbe it mout occur to
ye that Harry Dimwood might hev *his* opinion o' what was
' ongrateful ' and ' selfish ' ef I 'd played in between his
niece and a young man o' the express company, his nat'ral
enemy. It 's one thing to hev helped ye to see her in her
uncle's own camp, but another to help ye by makin' a clan-
decent post-offis o' my cabin. Ef, instead o' writin', you 'd

hev posted yourself by comin' to me, you mout hev found out that when I broke with Harry I offered to take Flo with me for good and all — ef he 'd keep away from us. And that 's the kind o' ' honest roof ' that that thar ' poor defenseless girl ' got under when her crippled mother died three weeks ago, and left Harry free. It was by ' trucklin'" to them ' mean prejudices,' and readin' that thar ' foolish paragraph,' that I settled tnis thing then and thar ! "

Brice's revulsion of sentiment was so complete, and the gratitude that beamed in his eyes was so sincere, that Mr. Tarbox hardly needed the profuse apologies which broke from him. " Forgive me ! " he continued to stammer, " I have wronged you, wronged *her* — everybody. But as you know, Mr. Tarbox, how I have felt over this, how deeply — how passionately " —

" It *does* make a man loony sometimes," said Mr. Tarbox, relaxing into demure dryness again, "so I reckon you *did !* Mebbe she reckoned so, too, for she asked me to give you the handkercher I sent ye. It looked as if she 'd been doin' some fancy work on it. "

Brice glanced quickly at Mr. Tarbox's face. It was stolid and imperturbable. She had evidently kept the secret of what passed in the hollow to herself. For the first time he looked around the room curiously. " I did n't know you were a land agent before, " he said.

" No more I was ! All that kem out o' that paragraph, Mr. Brice. That man Heckshill, who was so mighty perlite that night, wrote to me afterwards that he did n't know my name till he 'd seed that paragraph, and he wanted to know ef, ez a ' well-known citizen,' I could recommend him some timber lands. I recommended him half o' my own quarter section, and he took it. He 's puttin' up a mill thar, and that 's another reason why we want peace and quietness up thar. I 'm tryin' (betwixt and between us, Mr. Brice) to get Harry to cl'ar out and sell his rights in

the valley and the water power on the Fork to Heckshill
and me. I'm opening a business here."

"Then you've left Mrs. Tarbox with Miss Flora in your
cabin while you attend to business here," said Brice tentatively.

"Not exactly, Mr. Brice. The old woman thought it a
good chance to come to 'Frisco and put Flo in one o' them
Catholic convent schools — that asks no questions whar the
raw logs come from, and turns 'em out first-class plank all
round. You foller me, Mr. Brice? But Mrs. Tarbox is
jest in the next room, and would admire to tell ye all this
— and I'll go in and send her to you." And with a pat-
ronizing wave of the hand, Mr. Tarbox complacently disappeared in the hall.

Mr. Brice was not sorry to be left to himself in his utter
bewilderment! Flo, separated from her detrimental uncle,
and placed in a convent school! Tarbox, the obscure pioneer, a shrewd speculator emerging into success, and taking
the uncle's place! And all this within that month which
he had wasted with absurd repinings. How feeble seemed
his own adventure and advancement; how even ludicrous
his pretensions to any patronage and superiority. How this
common backwoodsman had set him in his place as easily as
she had evaded the advances of the journalist and Heckshill! They had taught him a lesson; perhaps even the
sending back of his handkerchief was part of it! His heart
grew heavy; he walked to the window and gazed out with
a long sigh.

A light laugh, that might have been an echo of the one
which had attracted him that night in Tarbox's cabin, fell
upon his ear. He turned quickly to meet Flora Dimwood's
laughing eyes shining upon him as she stood in the doorway.

Many a time during that month he had thought of this
meeting — had imagined what it would be like — what

would be his manner towards her — what would be her
greeting, and what they would say. He would be cold, gentle, formal, gallant, gay, sad, trustful, reproachful, even as
the moods in which he thought of her came to his foolish
brain. He would always begin with respectful seriousness,
or a frankness equal to her own, but never, never again
would he offend as he had offended under the buckeyes!
And now, with her pretty face shining upon him, all his
plans, his speeches, his preparations vanished, and left him
dumb. Yet he moved towards her with a brief articulate
something on his lips, — something between a laugh and a
sigh, — but that really was a kiss, and — in point of fact —
promptly folded her in his arms.

Yet it was certainly direct, and perhaps the best that could
be done, for the young lady did not emerge from it as coolly,
as unemotionally, nor possibly as quickly as she had under
the shade of the buckeyes. But she persuaded him — by
still holding his hand — to sit beside her on the chilly,
highly varnished "green rep" sofa, albeit to him it was a
bank in a bower of enchantment. Then she said, with
adorable reproachfulness, " You don't ask what I did with
the body."

Mr. Edward Brice started. He was young, and unfamiliar with the evasive expansiveness of the female mind at
such supreme moments.

" The body — oh, yes — certainly."

" I buried it myself — it was suthin too awful! — and
the gang would have been sure to have found it, and the
empty belt. I burned *that*. So that nobody knows
nothin'."

It was not a time for strictly grammatical negatives, and
I am afraid that the girl's characteristically familiar speech,
even when pathetically corrected here and there by the influence of the convent, endeared her the more to him. And
when she said, " And now, Mr. Edward Brice, sit over at

that end of the sofy and let 's talk," they talked.   They talked for an hour, more or less continuously, until they were surprised by a discreet cough and the entrance of Mrs. Tarbox.   Then there was more talk, and the discovery that Mr. Brice was long due at the office.

"Ye might drop in, now and then, whenever ye feel like it, and Flo is at home," suggested Mrs. Tarbox at parting.

Mr. Brice *did* drop in frequently during the next month. On one of these occasions Mr. Tarbox accompanied him to the door.   "And now — ez everything is settled and in order, Mr. Brice, and ef you should be wantin' to say anything about it to your bosses at the office, ye may mention *my* name ez Flo Dimwood's second cousin, and say I 'm a depositor in their bank.   And," with greater deliberation, "ef anything at any time should be thrown up at ye for marryin' a niece o' Snapshot Harry's, ye might mention, keerless like, that Snapshot Harry, under the name o' Henry J. Dimwood, has held shares in their old bank for years!"

WHAT HAPPENED AT THE FONDA

PART I

" WELL! " said the editor of the " Mountain Clarion, " looking up impatiently from his copy. " What 's the matter now ? "

The intruder in his sanctum was his foreman. He was also acting as pressman, as might be seen from his shirt-sleeves spattered with ink, rolled up over the arm that had just been working " the Archimedean lever that moves the world, " which was the editor's favorite allusion to the hand-press that strict economy obliged the " Clarion " to use. His braces, slipped from his shoulders during his work, were looped negligently on either side, their functions being replaced by one hand, which occasionally hitched up his trousers to a securer position. A pair of down-at-heel slippers — dear to the country printer — completed his négligée.

But the editor knew that the ink-spattered arm was sinewy and ready, that a stout and loyal heart beat under the soiled shirt, and that the slipshod slippers did not prevent its owner's foot from being " put down " very firmly on occasion. He accordingly met the shrewd, good-humored blue eyes of his faithful henchman with an interrogating smile.

" I won't keep you long, " said the foreman, glancing at the editor's copy with his habitual half humorous toleration of that work, it being his general conviction that news and advertisements were the only valuable features of a newspaper, " I only wanted to talk to you a minute about makin' suthin more o' this yer accident to Colonel Starbottle. "

"Well, we 've a full report of it in, have n't we?" said the editor wonderingly. "I have even made an editorial para. about the frequency of these accidents, and called attention to the danger of riding those half broken Spanish mustangs."

"Yes, ye did that," said the foreman tolerantly; "but ye see, thar 's some folks around here that allow it warn't no accident. There 's a heap of them believe that no runaway hoss ever mauled the colonel ez *he* got mauled."

"But I heard it from the colonel's own lips," said the editor, " and *he* surely ought to know."

"He mout know and he mout n't, and if he *did* know, he would n't tell," said the foreman musingly, rubbing his chin with the cleaner side of his arm. "Ye did n't see him when he was picked up, did ye?"

"No," said the editor. "Only after the doctor had attended him. Why?"

"Jake Parmlee, ez picked him up outer the ditch, says that he was half choked, and his black silk neck-handkercher was pulled tight around his throat. There was a mark on his nose ez ef some one had tried to gouge out his eye, and his left ear was chawed ez ef he 'd been down in a reg-'lar rough-and-tumble clinch."

"He told me his horse bolted, buck-jumped, threw him, and he lost consciousness," said the editor positively. "He had no reason for lying, and a man like Starbottle, who carries a Derringer and is a dead shot, would have left his mark on somebody if he 'd been attacked."

"That 's what the boys say is just the reason why he lied. He was *took suddent,* don't ye see, — he 'd no show — and don't like to confess it. See? A man like *him* ain't goin' to advertise that he kin be tackled and left senseless and no one else got hurt by it! His political influence would be ruined here!"

The editor was momentarily staggered at this large truth.

"Nonsense!" he said, with a laugh. "Who would attack Colonel Starbottle in that fashion? He might have been shot on sight by some political enemy with whom he had quarreled — but not *beaten*."

"S'pose it warn't no political enemy?" said the foreman doggedly.

"Then who else could it be?" demanded the editor impatiently.

"That's jest for the press to find out and expose," returned the foreman, with a significant glance at the editor's desk. "I reckon that's whar the 'Clarion' ought to come in."

"In a matter of this kind," said the editor promptly, "the paper has no business to interfere with a man's statement. The colonel has a perfect right to his own secret — if there is one, which I very much doubt. But," he added, in laughing recognition of the half reproachful, half humorous discontent on the foreman's face, "what dreadful theory have *you* and the boys got about it — and what do *you* expect to expose?"

"Well," said the foreman very seriously, "it's jest this: You see, the colonel is mighty sweet on that Spanish woman Ramierez up on the hill yonder. It was her mustang he was ridin' when the row happened near her house."

"Well?" said the editor, with disconcerting placidity.

"Well," — hesitated the foreman, "you see, they're a bad lot, those Greasers, especially the Ramierez, her husband."

The editor knew that the foreman was only echoing the provincial prejudice against this race, which he himself had always combated. Ramierez kept a fonda or hostelry on a small estate, — the last of many leagues formerly owned by the Spanish grantee, his landlord, — and had a wife of some small coquetries and redundant charms. Gambling took place at the fonda, and it was said the common prejudice against the Mexican did not, however, prevent the American from trying to win his money.

" Then you think Ramierez was jealous of the colonel ? But in that case he would have knifed him, — Spanish fashion, — and not without a struggle."

" There 's more ways they have o' killin' a man than that; he might hev been dragged off his horse by a lasso and choked," said the foreman darkly.

The editor had heard of this vaquero method of putting an enemy *hors de combat ;* but it was a clumsy performance for the public road, and the brutality of its manner would have justified the colonel in exposing it.

The foreman saw the incredulity expressed in his face, and said somewhat aggressively, " Of course I know ye don't take no stock in what 's said agin the Greasers, and that 's what the boys know, and what they said, and that 's the reason why I thought I oughter tell ye, so that ye might n't seem to be always favorin' 'em."

The editor's face darkened slightly, but he kept his temper and his good humor. " So that to prove that the ' Clarion ' is unbiased where the Mexicans are concerned, I ought to make it their only accuser, and cast a doubt on the American's veracity ? " he said, with a smile.

" I don't mean that," said the foreman, reddening. " Only I thought ye might — as ye understand these folks' ways — ye might be able to get at them easy, and mebbe make some copy outer the blamed thing. It would just make a stir here, and be a big boom for the ' Clarion.' "

" I 've no doubt it would," said the editor dryly. " However, I 'll make some inquiries; but you might as well let ' the boys ' know that the ' Clarion ' will not publish the colonel's secret without his permission. Meanwhile," he continued, smiling, "if you are very anxious to add the functions of a reporter to your other duties and bring me any discoveries you may make, I 'll — look over your copy."

He good humoredly nodded, and took up his pen again, — a hint at which the embarrassed foreman, under cover of hitching up his trousers, awkwardly and reluctantly withdrew.

It was with some natural youthful curiosity, but no lack of loyalty to Colonel Starbottle, that the editor that evening sought this " war-horse of the Democracy," as he was familiarly known, in his invalid chamber at the Palmetto Hotel.   He found the hero with a bandaged ear — and perhaps it was fancy suggested by the story of the choking — cheeks more than usually suffused and apoplectic.   Nevertheless, he was seated by the table with a mint julep before him, and welcomed the editor by instantly ordering another.

The editor was glad to find him so much better.

" Gad, sir, no bones broken, but a good deal of 'possum scratching about the head for such a little throw like that. I must have slid a yard or two on my left ear before I brought up."

" You were unconscious from the fall, I believe."

" Only for an instant, sir — a single instant!   I recovered myself with the assistance of a No'the'n gentleman — a Mr. Parmlee — who was passing."

" Then you think your injuries were entirely due to your fall ? "

The colonel paused with the mint julep halfway to his lips, and set it down.   " Sir!" he ejaculated, with astounded indignation.

" You say you were unconscious," returned the editor lightly, " and some of your friends think the injuries inconsistent with what you believe to be the cause.   They are concerned lest you were unknowingly the victim of some foul play."

" Unknowingly!   Sir!   Do you take me for a chuckle-headed niggah, that I don't know when I'm thrown from a buck-jumping mustang? or do they think I'm a Chinaman

to be hustled and beaten by a gang of bullies? Do they
know, sir, that the account I have given I am responsible
for, sir? — personally responsible?"

There was no doubt to the editor that the colonel was
perfectly serious, and that the indignation arose from no
guilty consciousness of a secret. A man as peppery as the
colonel would have been equally alert in defense.

"They feared that you might have been ill used by some
evilly disposed person during your unconsciousness," explained the editor diplomatically; "but as you say *that* was
only for a moment, and that you were aware of everything
that happened" — He paused.

"Perfectly, sir! Perfectly! As plain as I see this julep before me. I had just left the Ramierez rancho. The
señora, — a devilish pretty woman, sir, — after a little playful badinage, had offered to lend me her daughter's mustang
if I could ride it home. You know what it is, Mr. Grey,"
he said gallantly. "I'm an older man than you, sir, but
a challenge from a d—d fascinating creature, I trust, sir, I
am not yet old enough to decline. Gad, sir, I mounted the
brute. I've ridden Morgan stock and Blue Grass thorough-
breds bareback, sir, but I've never thrown my leg over such
a blanked Chinese cracker before. After he bolted I held
my own fairly, but he buck-jumped before I could lock my
spurs under him, and the second jump landed me!"

"How far from the Ramierez fonda were you when you
were thrown?"

"A matter of four or five hundred yards, sir."

"Then your accident might have been seen from the
fonda?"

"Scarcely, sir. For in that case, I may say, without
vanity, that — er — the — er señora would have come to my
assistance."

"But not her husband?"

The old-fashioned shirt-frill which the colonel habitually

wore grew erectile with a swelling indignation, possibly half
assumed to conceal a certain conscious satisfaction beneath.
" Mr. Grey," he said, with pained severity, "as a personal
friend of mine, and a representative of the press, — a power
which I respect, — I overlook a disparaging reflection upon a
lady, which I can only attribute to the levity of youth and
thoughtlessness. At the same time, sir," he added, with
illogical sequence, "if Ramierez felt aggrieved at my attentions, he knew where I could be found, sir, and that it was
not my habit to decline giving gentlemen — of any nation-
ality — satisfaction — sir! — personal satisfaction."

He paused, and then added, with a singular blending of
anxiety and a certain natural dignity, "I trust, sir, that
nothing of this — er — kind will appear in your paper."

"It was to keep it out by learning the truth from you,
my dear colonel," said the editor lightly, "that I called to-
day. Why, it was even suggested," he added, with a laugh,
"that you were half strangled by a lasso."

To his surprise the colonel did not join in the laugh, but
brought his hand to his loose cravat with an uneasy gesture
and a somewhat disturbed face.

"I admit, sir," he said, with a forced smile, "that I
experienced a certain sensation of choking, and I may have
mentioned it to Mr. Parmlee; but it was due, I believe, sir,
to my cravat, which I always wear loosely, as you perceive,
becoming twisted in my fall, and in rolling over."

He extended his fat white hand to the editor, who shook
it cordially, and then withdrew. Nevertheless, although
perfectly satisfied with his mission, and firmly resolved to
prevent any further discussion on the subject, Mr. Grey's
curiosity was not wholly appeased. What were the relations of the colonel with the Ramierez family? From what
he himself had said, the theory of the foreman as to the motives of the attack might have been possible, and the assault
itself committed while the colonel was unconscious.

Mr. Grey, however, kept this to himself, briefly told his foreman that he found no reason to add to the account already in type, and dismissed the subject from his mind. The colonel left the town the next day.

One morning a week afterward, the foreman entered the sanctum cautiously, and, closing the door of the composing-room behind him, stood for a moment before the editor with a singular combination of irresolution, shamefacedness, and humorous discomfiture in his face.

Answering the editor's look of inquiry, he began slowly, "Mebbe ye remember when we was talkin' last week o' Colonel Starbottle's accident, I sorter allowed that he knew all the time *why* he was attacked that way, only he would n't tell."

"Yes, I remember you were incredulous," said the editor, smiling.

"Well, I take it all back! I reckon he told all he knew. I was wrong! I cave!"

"Why?" asked the editor wonderingly.

"Well, I have been through the mill myself!"

He unbuttoned his shirt collar, pointed to his neck, which showed a slight abrasion and a small livid mark of strangulation at the throat, and added, with a grim smile, "And I 've got about as much proof as I want."

The editor put down his pen and stared at him.

"You see, Mr. Grey, it was partly your fault! When you bedeviled me about gettin' that news, and allowed I might try my hand at reportin', I was fool enough to take up the challenge. So once or twice, when I was off duty here, I hung around the Ramierez shanty. Once I went in thar when they were gamblin'; thar war one or two Americans thar that war winnin' as far as I could see, and was pretty full o' that aguardiente that they sell thar — that kills at forty rods. You see, I had a kind o' suspicion that ef thar was any foul play goin' on it might be worked on these

fellers *arter* they were drunk, and war goin' home with thar
winnin's."

"So you gave up your theory of the colonel being attacked from jealousy ? " said the editor, smiling.

"Hol' on! I ain't through yet! I only reckoned that
ef thar was a gang of roughs kept thar on the premises they
might be used for that purpose, and I only wanted to ketch
'em at thar work. So I jest meandered into the road when
they war about comin' out, and kept my eye skinned for
what might happen. Thar was a kind o' corral about a
hundred yards down the road, half adobe wall, and a stockade o' palin's on top of it, about six feet high. Some of
the palin's were off, and I peeped through, but thar warn't
nobody thar. I stood thar, alongside the bank, leanin' my
back agin one o' them openin's, and jest watched and waited.

"All of a suddent I felt myself grabbed by my coat
collar behind, and my neck-handkercher and collar drawn
tight around my throat till I could n't breathe. The more
I twisted round, the tighter the clinch seemed to get. I
could n't holler nor speak, but thar I stood with my mouth
open, pinned back agin that cursed stockade, and my arms
and legs movin' up and down, like one o' them dancin'
jacks! It seems funny, Mr. Grey — I reckon I looked like
a darned fool — but I don't wanter feel ag'in as I did jest
then. The clinch o' my throat got tighter; everything got
black about me; I was jest goin' off and kalkilatin' it was
about time for you to advertise for another foreman, when
suthin broke — fetched away!

"It was my collar button, and I dropped like a shot. It
was a minute before I could get my breath ag'in, and when
I did and managed to climb that darned stockade, and drop
on the other side, thar warn't a soul to be seen! A few
hosses that stampeded in my gettin' over the fence war all
that was there! I was mighty shook up, you bet! — and
to make the hull thing perfectly ridic'lous, when I got back

to the road, after all I 'd got through, darn my skin ef thar
warn't that pesky lot o' drunken men staggerin' along, jin-
glin' the scads they had won, and enjoyin' themselves, and
nobody a-followin' 'em! I jined 'em jest for kempany's
sake, till we got back to town, but nothin' happened."

"But, my dear Richards," said the editor warmly, "this
is no longer a matter of mere reporting, but of business
for the police. You must see the deputy sheriff at once,
and bring your complaint — or shall I? It 's no joking
matter."

"Hol' on, Mr. Grey," replied Richards slowly. "I 've
told this to nobody but you — nor am I goin' to — *sabe?*
It 's an affair of my own — and I reckon I kin take care of
it without goin' to the Revised Statutes of the State of
California, or callin' out the sheriff's posse."

His humorous blue eyes just then had certain steely
points in them like glittering facets as he turned them away,
which the editor had seen before on momentous occasions,
and he was speaking slowly and composedly, which the editor also knew boded no good to an adversary.

"Don't be a fool, Richards," he said quietly. "Don't
take as a personal affront what was a common, vulgar crime.
You would undoubtedly have been robbed by that rascal had
not the others come along."

Richards shook his head. "I might hev been robbed a
dozen times afore *they* came along — ef that was the little
game. No, Mr. Grey, — it warn't no robbery."

"Had you been paying court to the Señora Ramierez,
like Colonel Starbottle?" asked the editor, with a smile.

"Not much," returned Richards scornfully; "she ain't
my style. But " — he hesitated, and then added, "thar
was a mighty purty gal thar — and her darter, I reckon —
a reg'lar pink fairy! She kem in only a minute, and they
sorter hustled her out ag'in — for darn my skin ef she
did n't look as much out o' place in that smoky old garlic-

smellin' room as an angel at a bull-fight. And what got me — she was ez white ez you or me, with blue eyes and a lot o' dark reddish hair in a long braid down her back. Why, only for her purty sing-song voice and her '*Gracias, señor,*' you 'd hev reckoned she was a Blue Grass girl jest fresh from across the plains."

A little amused at his foreman's enthusiasm, Mr. Grey gave an ostentatious whistle and said, " Come, now, Richards, look here! Really!"

"Only a little girl — a mere child, Mr. Grey — not more 'n fourteen if a day," responded Richards, in embarrassed depreciation.

"Yes, but those people marry at twelve," said the editor, with a laugh. "Look out! Your appreciation may have been noticed by some other admirer."

He half regretted this speech the next moment in the quick flush — the male instinct of rivalry — that brought back the glitter of Richards's eyes. "I reckon I kin take care of that, sir," he said slowly, "and I kalkilate that the next time I meet that chap — whoever he may be — he won't see so much of my back as he did."

The editor knew there was little doubt of this, and for an instant believed it his duty to put the matter in the hands of the police. Richards was too good and brave a man to be risked in a barroom fight. But reflecting that this might precipitate the scandal he wished to avoid, he concluded to make some personal investigation. A stronger curiosity than he had felt before was possessing him. It was singular, too, that Richards's description of the girl was that of a different and superior type — the hidalgo, or fair-skinned Spanish settler. If this was true, what was she doing there — and what were her relations to the Ramierez?

PART II

The next afternoon he went to the fonda. Situated on the outskirts of the town which had long outgrown it, it still bore traces of its former importance as a hacienda, or smaller farm, of one of the old Spanish landholders. The patio, or central courtyard, still existed as a stable-yard for carts, and even one or two horses were tethered to the railings of the inner corridor, which now served as an open veranda to the fonda or inn. The opposite wing was utilized as a tienda, or general shop, — a magazine for such goods as were used by the Mexican inhabitants, — and belonged also to Ramierez.

Ramierez himself — round-whiskered and Sancho Panza-like in build — welcomed the editor with fat, perfunctory urbanity. The fonda and all it contained was at his disposicion.

The señora coquettishly bewailed, in rising and falling inflections, his long absence, his infidelity, and general perfidiousness. Truly he was growing great in writing of the affairs of his nation — he could no longer see his humble friends! Yet not long ago — truly that very week — there was the head impresor of Don Pancho's imprenta himself who had been there!

A great man, of a certainty, and they must take what they could get! They were only poor innkeepers; when the governor came not they must welcome the alcalde. To which the editor — otherwise Don Pancho — replied with equal effusion. He had indeed recommended the fonda to his impresor, who was but a courier before him. But what was this? The impresor had been ravished at the sight of a beautiful girl — a mere muchacha — yet of a beauty that deprived the senses — this angel — clearly the daughter of his friend! Here was the old miracle of the orange in full fruition and the lovely fragrant blossom all on the same tree — at the fonda. And this had been kept from him!

"Yes, it was but a thing of yesterday," said the señora, obviously pleased. "The muchacha — for she was but that — had just returned from the convent at San José, where she had been for four years. Ah! what would you? The fonda was no place for the child, who should know only the litany of the Virgin — and they had kept her there. And now — that she was home again — she cared only for the horse. From morning to night! Caballeros might come and go! There might be a festival — all the same to her, it made nothing if she had the horse to ride! Even now she was with one in the fields. Would Don Pancho attend and see Cota and her horse?"

The editor smilingly assented, and accompanied his hostess along the corridor to a few steps which brought them to the level of the open meadows of the old farm inclosure. A slight white figure on horseback was careering in the distance. At a signal from Señora Ramierez it wheeled and came down rapidly toward them. But when within a hundred yards the horse was suddenly pulled up vaquero fashion, and the little figure leaped off and advanced toward them on foot, leading the horse.

To his surprise Mr. Grey saw that she had been riding bareback, and from her discreet halt at that distance he half suspected *astride!* His effusive compliments to the mother on this exhibition of skill were sincere, for he was struck by the girl's fearlessness. But when both horse and rider at last stood before him, he was speechless and embarrassed.

For Richards had not exaggerated the girl's charms. She was indeed dangerously pretty, from her tawny little head to her small feet, and her figure, although comparatively diminutive, was perfectly proportioned. Gray eyed and blonde as she was in color, her racial peculiarities were distinct, and only the good humored and enthusiastic Richards could have likened her to an American girl.

But he was the more astonished in noticing that her mustang was as distinct and peculiar as herself — a mongrel mare of the extraordinary type known as a "pinto," or "calico" horse, mottled in lavender and pink, Arabian in proportions, and half broken! Her greenish gray eyes, in which too much of the white was visible, had, he fancied, a singular similarity of expression to Cota's own!

Utterly confounded, and staring at the girl in her white, many flounced frock, bare head, and tawny braids, as she stood beside this incarnation of equine barbarism, Grey could remember nothing like it outside of a circus.

He stammered a few words of admiration of the mare. Miss Cota threw out her two arms with a graceful gesture and a profound curtsey, and said, —

"*Á la disposicion de usted, señor.*"

Grey was quick to understand the malicious mischief which underlay this formal curtsey and danced in the girl's eyes, and even fancied it shared by the animal itself. But he was a singularly good rider of untrained stock, and rather proud of his prowess. He bowed.

"I accept that I may have the honor of laying the señorita's gift again at her little feet."

But here the burly Ramierez intervened. "Ah, Mother of God! May the devil fly away with all this nonsense! I will have no more of it," he said impatiently to the girl. "Have a care, Don Pancho," he turned to the editor; "it is a trick!"

"One I think I know," said Grey sapiently. The girl looked at him curiously as he managed to edge between her and the mustang, under the pretense of stroking its glossy neck. "I shall keep *my own* spurs," he said to her in a lower voice, pointing to the sharp, small-roweled American spurs he wore, instead of the large, blunt, five-pointed star of the Mexican pattern.

The girl evidently did not understand him then — though she did a moment later! For, without attempting to catch hold of the mustang's mane, Grey in a single leap threw himself across its back. The animal, utterly unprepared, was at first stupefied. But by this time her rider had his seat. He felt her sensitive spine arch like a cat's beneath him as she sprang rocket-wise into the air.

But here she was mistaken! Instead of clinging tightly to her flanks with the inner side of his calves, after the old vaquero fashion to which she was accustomed, he dropped his spurred heels into her sides and allowed his body to rise with her spring, and the cruel spur to cut its track upward from her belly almost to her back.

She dropped like a shot, he dexterously withdrawing his spurs, and regaining his seat, jarred but not discomfited. Again she essayed a leap; the spur again marked its height in a scarifying track along her smooth barrel. She tried a third leap, but this time dropped halfway as she felt the steel scraping her side, and then stood still, trembling. Grey leaped off!

There was a sound of applause from the innkeeper and his wife, assisted by a lounging vaquero in the corridor. Ashamed of his victory, Grey turned apologetically to Cota. To his surprise she glanced indifferently at the trickling sides of her favorite, and only regarded him curiously.

"Ah," she said, drawing in her breath, "you are strong — and you comprehend!"

"It was only a trick for a trick, señorita," he replied, reddening; "let me look after those scratches in the stable," he added, as she was turning away, leading the agitated and excited animal toward a shed in the rear.

He would have taken the riata which she was still holding, but she motioned him to precede her. He did so by a few feet, but he had scarcely reached the stable-door before she suddenly caught him roughly by the shoulders, and, shoving him into the entrance, slammed the door upon him.

Amazed and a little indignant, he turned in time to hear a slight sound of scuffling outside, and to see Cota reënter with a flushed face.

"Pardon, señor," she said quickly, "but I feared she might have kicked you. Rest tranquil, however, for the servant he has taken her away."

She pointed to a slouching peon with a malevolent face, who was angrily driving the mustang toward the corral.

"Consider it no more! I was rude! Santa Maria! I almost threw you, too; but," she added, with a dazzling smile, "you must not punish me as you have her! For you are very strong — and you comprehend."

But Grey did not comprehend, and with a few hurried apologies he managed to escape his fair but uncanny tormentor. Besides, this unlooked-for incident had driven from his mind the more important object of his visit, — the discovery of the assailants of Richards and Colonel Starbottle.

His inquiries of the Ramierez produced no result. Señor Ramierez was not aware of any suspicious loiterers among the frequenters of the fonda, and except from some drunken American or Irish revelers he had been free of disturbance. Ah! the peon — an old vaquero — was not an angel, truly, but he was dangerous only to the bull and the wild horses — and he was afraid even of Cota! Mr. Grey was fain to ride home empty of information.

He was still more concerned a week later, on returning unexpectedly one afternoon to his sanctum, to hear a musical, childish voice in the composing-room.

It was Cota! She was there, as Richards explained, on his invitation, to view the marvels and mysteries of printing at a time when they would not be likely to "disturb Mr. Grey at his work." But the beaming face of Richards and the simple tenderness of his blue eyes plainly revealed the sudden growth of an evidently sincere passion, and the unwonted splendors of his best clothes showed how carefully he had prepared for the occasion.

Grey was worried and perplexed, believing the girl a malicious flirt. Yet nothing could be more captivating than her simple and childish curiosity, as she watched Richards swing the lever of the press, or stood by his side as he marshaled the type into files on his "composing-stick." He had even printed a card with her name, "Señorita Cota Ramierez," the type of which had been set up, to the accompaniment of ripples of musical laughter, by her little brown fingers.

The editor might have become quite sentimental and poetical had he not noticed that the gray eyes which often rested tentatively and meaningly on himself, even while apparently listening to Richards, were more than ever like the eyes of the mustang on whose scarred flanks her glance had wandered so coldly.

He withdrew presently so as not to interrupt his foreman's innocent téte-à-tête, but it was not very long after that Cota passed him on the highroad with the pinto horse in a gallop, and blew him an audacious kiss from the tips of her fingers.

For several days afterwards Richards's manner was tinged with a certain reserve on the subject of Cota which the editor attributed to the delicacy of a serious affection, but he was surprised also to find that his foreman's eagerness to discuss his unknown assailant had somewhat abated. Further discussion regarding it naturally dropped, and the editor was beginning to lose his curiosity when it was suddenly awakened by a chance incident.

An intimate friend and old companion of his — one Enriquez Saltillo — had diverged from a mountain trip especially to call upon him. Enriquez was a scion of one of the oldest Spanish-California families, and in addition to his friendship for the editor it pleased him also to affect an intense admiration of American ways and habits, and even to combine the current California slang with his native precision of speech — and a certain ironical levity still more his own.

It seemed, therefore, quite natural to Mr. Grey to find him seated with his feet on the editorial desk, his hat cocked on the back of his head, reading the "Clarion" exchanges. But he was up in a moment, and had embraced Grey with characteristic effusion.

"I find myself, my leetle brother, but an hour ago two leagues from this spot! I say to myself, 'Hola! It is the home of Don Pancho — my friend! I shall find him composing the magnificent editorial leader, collecting the subscription of the big pumpkin and the great gooseberry, or gouging out the eye of the rival editor, at which I shall assist!' I hesitate no longer; I fly on the instant, and I am here."

Grey was delighted. Saltillo knew the Spanish population thoroughly — his own superior race and their Mexican and Indian allies. If any one could solve the mystery of the Ramierez fonda, and discover Richards's unknown assailant, it was _he_! But Grey contented himself, at first, with a few brief inquiries concerning the beautiful Cota and her anonymous association with the Ramierez. Enriquez was as briefly communicative.

"Of your suspicions, my leetle brother, you are right — on the half! That leetle angel of a Cota is, without doubt, the daughter of the adorable Señora Ramierez, but not of the admirable señor — her husband. Ah! what would you? We are a simple, patriarchal race; thees Ramierez, he was the Mexican tenant of the old Spanish landlord — such as my father — and we are ever the fathers of the poor, and sometimes of their children. It is possible, therefore, that

the exquisite Cota resemble the Spanish landlord. Ah!
stop — remain tranquil! I remember," he went on, suddenly striking his forehead with a dramatic gesture, "the
old owner of thees ranch was my cousin Tiburcio. Of a
consequence, my friend, thees angel is my second cousin!
Behold! I shall call there on the instant. I shall embrace
my long-lost relation. I shall introduce my best friend,
Don Pancho, who lofe her. I shall say, ' Bless you, my
children,' and it is feenish! I go! I am gone even now!"
He started up and clapped on his hat, but Grey caught
him by the arm.

"For Heaven's sake, Enriquez, be serious for once," he
said, forcing him back into the chair. "And don't speak
so loud. The foreman in the other room is an enthusiastic
admirer of the girl. In fact, it is on his account that I am
making these inquiries."

"Ah, the gentleman of the pantuflos, whose trousers will
not remain! I have seen him, friend. Truly he has the
ambition excessif to arrive from the bed to go to the work
without the dress or the wash. But," in recognition of
Grey's half serious impatience, "remain tranquil. On him
I shall not go back! I have said! The friend of my friend
is ever the same as my friend! He is truly not seducing to
the eye, but without doubt he will arrive a governor or a
senator in good time. I shall gif to him my second cousin.
It is feenish! I will tell him now!"

He attempted to rise, but was held down and vigorously
shaken by Grey.

"I 've half a mind to let you do it, and get chucked
through the window for your pains," said the editor, with
a half laugh. "Listen to me. This is a more serious matter than you suppose."

And Grey briefly recounted the incident of the mysterious attacks on Starbottle and Richards. As he proceeded
he noticed, however, that the ironical light died out of En-

riquez's eyes, and a singular thoughtfulness, yet unlike his usual precise gravity, came over his face. He twirled the ends of his penciled mustache — an unfailing sign of Enriquez's emotion.

"The same accident that arrive to two men that shall be as opposite as the gallant Starbottle and the excellent Richards shall not prove that it come from Ramierez, though they both were at the fonda," he said gravely. "The cause of it have not come to-day, nor yesterday, nor last week. The cause of it have arrive before there was any gallant Starbottle or excellent Richards; before there was any American in California — before you and I, my leetle brother, have lif! The cause happen first — *two hundred years ago!*"

The editor's start of impatient incredulity was checked by the unmistakable sincerity of Enriquez's face. "It is so," he went on gravely; "it is an old story — it is a long story. I shall make him short — and new."

He stopped and lit a cigarette without changing his odd expression.

"It was when the padres first have the mission, and take the heathen and convert him — and save his soul. It was their business, you comprehend, my Pancho? The more heathen they convert, the more soul they save, the better business for their mission shop. But the heathen do not always wish to be 'convert;' the heathen fly, the heathen skedaddle, the heathen will not remain, or will backslide. What will you do? So the holy fathers make a little game. You do not of a possibility comprehend how the holy fathers make a convert, my leetle brother?" he added gravely.

"No," said the editor.

"I shall tell to you. They take from the presidio five or six dragons — you comprehend — the cavalry soldiers, — and they pursue the heathen from his little hut. When

they cannot surround him and he fly, they catch him with
the lasso, like the wild hoss. The lasso catch him around
the neck; he is obliged to remain. Sometime he is strangle. Sometime he is dead, but the soul is save! You believe not, Pancho? I see you wrinkle the brow — you flash
the eye; you like it not? Believe me, I like it not, neither, but it is so!"

He shrugged his shoulders, threw away his half smoked
cigarette, and went on.

"One time a padre who have the zeal excessif for the
saving of soul, when he find the heathen, who is a young
girl, have escape the soldiers, he of himself have seize the
lasso and flung it! He is lucky; he catch her — but look
you! She stop not — she still fly! She not only fly, but
of a surety she drag the good padre with her! He cannot
loose himself, for his riata is fast to the saddle; the dragons
cannot help, for he is drag so fast. On the instant she
have gone — and so have the padre. For why? It is not
a young girl he have lasso, but the devil! You comprehend — it is a punishment — a retribution — he is feenish!
And forever!

"For every year he must come back a spirit — on a spirit
hoss — and swing the lasso, and make as if to catch the
heathen. He is condemn ever to play his little game; now
there is no heathen more to convert, he catch what he can.
My grandfather have once seen him — it is night and a
storm, and he pass by like a flash! My grandfather like it
not — he is much dissatisfied! My uncle have seen him,
too, but he make the sign of the cross, and the lasso have
fall to the side, and my uncle have much gratification. A
vaquero of my father and a peon of my cousin have both
been picked up, lassoed, and dragged dead.

"Many peoples have died of him in the strangling.
Sometime he is seen, sometime it is the woman only that
one sees — sometime it is but the hoss. But ever some-

body is dead — strangle! Of a truth, my friend, the gallant Starbottle and the ambitious Richards have just escaped! "

The editor looked curiously at his friend. There was not the slightest suggestion of mischief or irony in his tone or manner; nothing, indeed, but a sincerity and anxiety usually rare with his temperament. It struck him also that his speech had but little of the odd California slang which was always a part of his imitative levity. He was puzzled.

"Do you mean to say that this superstition is well known?" he asked, after a pause.

"Among my people — yes."

"And do *you* believe in it?"

Enriquez was silent. Then he arose, and shrugged his shoulders. "*Quien sabe?* It is not more difficult to comprehend than your story."

He gravely put on his hat. With it he seemed to have put on his old levity. "Come, behold, it is a long time between drinks! Let us to the hotel and the bar-keep, who shall give up the smash of brandy and the julep of mints before the lasso of Friar Pedro shall prevent us the swallow! Let us skedaddle!"

Mr. Grey returned to the "Clarion" office in a much more satisfied condition of mind. Whatever faith he held in Enriquez's sincerity, for the first time since the attack on Colonel Starbottle he believed he had found a really legitimate journalistic opportunity in the incident. The legend and its singular coincidence with the outrages would make capital "copy."

No names would be mentioned, yet even if Colonel Starbottle recognized his own adventure, he could not possibly object to this interpretation of it. The editor had found that few people objected to be the hero of a ghost story, or the favored witness of a spiritual manifestation. Nor could

Richards find fault with this view of his own experience, hitherto kept a secret, so long as it did not refer to his relations with the fair Cota. Summoning him at once to his sanctum, he briefly repeated the story he had just heard, and his purpose of using it. To his surprise, Richards's face assumed a seriousness and anxiety equal to Enriquez's own.

"It's a good story, Mr. Grey," he said awkwardly, "and I ain't sayin' it ain't mighty good newspaper stuff, but it won't do *now*, for the whole mystery's up and the assailant found."

"Found! When? Why did n't you tell me before?" exclaimed Grey, in astonishment.

"I did n't reckon ye were so keen on it," said Richards embarrassedly, "and — and — it was n't my own secret altogether."

"Go on," said the editor impatiently.

"Well," said Richards slowly and doggedly, "ye see there was a fool that was sweet on Cota, and he allowed himself to be bedeviled by her to ride her cursed pink and yaller mustang. Naturally the beast bolted at once, but he managed to hang on by the mane for half a mile or so, when it took to buck-jumpin'. The first ' buck ' threw him clean into the road, but did n't stun him, yet when he tried to rise, the first thing he knowed he was grabbed from behind and half choked by somebody. He was held so tight that he could n't turn, but he managed to get out his revolver and fire two shots under his arm. The grip held on for a minute, and then loosened, and the somethin' slumped down on top o' him, but he managed to work himself around. And then — what do you think he saw? — why, that thar hoss! with two bullet holes in his neck, lyin' beside him, but still grippin' his coat collar and neck-handkercher in his teeth! Yes, sir! the rough that attacked Colonel Starbottle, the villain that took me behind when I was leanin' agin that cursed fence, was that same God-forsaken, hell-invented pinto hoss!"

In a flash of recollection the editor remembered his own experience, and the singular scuffle outside the stable-door of tho fonda. Undoubtedly Cota had saved him from a similar attack.

"But why not tell this story with the other?" said the editor, returning to his first idea. "It 's tremendously interesting."

"It won't do," said Richards, with dogged resolution.

"Why?"

"Because, Mr. Grey — that fool was myself!"

"You! Again attacked!"

"Yes," said Richards, with a darkening face. "Again attacked, and by the same hoss! Cota's hoss! Whether Cota was or was not knowin' its tricks, she was actually furious at me for killin' it — and it 's all over 'twixt me and her."

"Nonsense," said the editor impulsively. "She will forgive you! You did n't know your assailant was a horse *when you fired*. Look at the attack on you in the road!"

Richards shook his head with dogged hopelessness.

"It 's no use, Mr. Grey. I oughter guessed it was a hoss then — thar was nothin' else in that corral. No! Cota 's already gone away back to San José, and I reckon the Ramierez has got scared of her and packed her off. So on account of it 's bein' *her* hoss, and what happened betwixt me and her, you see my mouth is shut."

"And the columns of the 'Clarion' too," said the editor with a sigh.

"I know it 's hard, sir, but it 's better so. I 've reckoned mebbe she was a little crazy, and since you 've told me that Spanish yarn, it mout be that she was sort o' playin' she was that priest, and trained that mustang ez she did."

After a pause, something of his old self came back into his blue eyes as he sadly hitched up his braces and passed them over his broad shoulders. "Yes, sir, I was a fool, for we 've lost the only bit of real sensation news that ever came in the way of the ' Clarion.' "

MR. BILSON'S HOUSEKEEPER

I

WHEN Joshua Bilson, of the Summit House, Buckeye Hill, lost his wife, it became necessary for him to take a housekeeper to assist him in the management of the hotel. Already all Buckeye had considered this a mere preliminary to taking another wife, after a decent probation, as the relations of housekeeper and landlord were confidential and delicate, and Bilson was a man, and not above female influence. There was, however, some change of opinion on that point when Miss Euphemia Trotter was engaged for that position. Buckeye Hill, which had confidently looked forward to a buxom widow or, with equal confidence, to the promotion of some pretty but inefficient chambermaid, was startled by the selection of a maiden lady of middle age, and above the medium height, at once serious, precise, and masterful, and to all appearances outrageously competent. More carefully "taking stock" of her, it was accepted she had three good points, — dark, serious eyes, a trim but somewhat thin figure, and well-kept hands and feet. These, which in so susceptible a community would have been enough, in the words of one critic, "to have married her to three men," she seemed to make of little account herself, and her attitude toward those who were inclined to make them of account was ceremonious and frigid. Indeed, she seemed to occupy herself entirely with looking after the servants, Chinese and Europeans, examining the bills and stores of traders and shopkeepers, in a fashion that made her respected and — feared. It was whispered, in fact, that Bilson stood in awe of her as he never had of his wife, and that he was "henpecked in his own farmyard by a strange pullet."

Nevertheless, he always spoke of her with a respect and even a reverence that seemed incompatible with their relative positions. It gave rise to surmises more or less ingenious and conflicting: Miss Trotter had a secret interest in the hotel, and represented a San Francisco syndicate; Miss Trotter was a woman of independent property, and had advanced large sums to Bilson; Miss Trotter was a woman of no property, but she was the only daughter of — variously — a late distinguished nobleman, a ruined millionaire, and a foreign statesman, bent on making her own living.

Alas, for romance! Miss Euphemia Trotter, or "Miss E. Trotter," as she preferred to sign herself, loathing her sentimental prefix, was really a poor girl who had been educated in an Eastern seminary, where she eventually became a teacher. She had survived her parents and a neglected childhood, and had worked hard for her living since she was fourteen. She had been a nurse in a hospital, an assistant in a reformatory, had observed men and women under conditions of pain and weakness, and had known the body only as a tabernacle of helplessness and suffering; yet had brought out of her experience a hard philosophy which she used equally to herself as to others. That she had ever indulged in any romance of human existence, I greatly doubt; the lanky girl teacher at the Vermont academy had enough to do to push herself forward without entangling girl friendships or confidences, and so became a prematurely hard duenna, paid to look out for, restrain, and report, if necessary, any vagrant flirtation or small intrigue of her companions. A pronounced "old maid" at fifteen, she had nothing to forget or forgive in others, and still less to learn from them.

It was spring, and down the long slopes of Buckeye Hill the flowers were already effacing the last dented footprints of the winter rains, and the winds no longer brought their

monotonous patter. In the pine woods there were the song
and flash of birds, and the quickening stimulus of the stirring aromatic sap. Miners and tunnelmen were already for-
saking the direct road for a ramble through the woodland
trail and its sylvan charms, and occasionally breaking into
shouts and horseplay like great boys. The school children
were disporting there; there were some older couples senti-
mentally gathering flowers side by side. Miss Trotter was
also there, but making a short cut from the bank and express office, and by no means disturbed by any gentle reminiscence of her girlhood or any other instinctive participa-
tion in the wanton season. Spring came, she knew, regularly
every year, and brought "spring cleaning" and other necessary changes and rehabilitations. This year it had brought
also a considerable increase in the sum she was putting by,
and she was, perhaps, satisfied in a practical way, if not
with the blind instinctiveness of others. She was walking
leisurely, holding her gray skirt well over her slim ankles
and smartly booted feet, and clear of the brushing of daisies
and buttercups, when suddenly she stopped. A few paces
before her, partly concealed by a myrtle, a young woman,
startled at her approach, had just withdrawn herself from
the embrace of a young man and slipped into the shadow.
Nevertheless, in that moment, Miss Trotter's keen eyes had
recognized her as a very pretty Swedish girl, one of her
chambermaids at the hotel. Miss Trotter passed without
a word, but gravely. She was not shocked nor surprised,
but it struck her practical mind at once that if this were an
affair with impending matrimony, it meant the loss of a
valuable and attractive servant; if otherwise, a serious disturbance of that servant's duties. She must look out for
another girl to take the place of Frida Pauline Jansen, that
was all. It is possible, therefore, that Miss Jansen's criticism of Miss Trotter to her companion as a "spying, jealous
old cat" was unfair. This companion Miss Trotter had

noticed, only to observe that his face and figure were unfamiliar to her. His red shirt and heavy boots gave no indication of his social condition in that locality. He seemed more startled and disturbed at her intrusion than the girl had been, but that was more a condition of sex than of degree, she also knew. In such circumstances it is the woman always who is the most composed and self-possessed.

A few days after this, Miss Trotter was summoned in some haste to the office. Chris Calton, a young man of twenty-six, partner in the Roanoke Ledge, had fractured his arm and collar-bone by a fall, and had been brought to the hotel for that rest and attention, under medical advice, which he could not procure in the Roanoke company's cabin. She had a retired, quiet room made ready. When he was installed there by the doctor she went to see him, and found a good-looking, curly headed young fellow, even boyish in appearance and manner, who received her with that air of deference and timidity which she was accustomed to excite in the masculine breast — when it was not accompanied with distrust. It struck her that he was somewhat emotional, and had the expression of one who had been spoiled and petted by women, a rather unusual circumstance among the men of the locality. Perhaps it would be unfair to her to say that a disposition to show him that he could expect no such "nonsense" *there* sprang up in her heart at that moment, for she never had understood any tolerance of such weakness, but a certain precision and dryness of manner was the only result of her observation. She adjusted his pillow, asked him if there was anything that he wanted, but took her directions from the doctor, rather than from himself, with a practical insight and minuteness that was as appalling to the patient as it was an unexpected delight to Dr. Duchesne. "I see you quite understand me, Miss Trotter," he said, with great relief.

"I ought to," responded the lady dryly. "I had a dozen

such cases, some of them with complications, while I was
assistant at the Sacramento Hospital."

"Ah, then!" returned the doctor, dropping gladly into
purely professional detail, "you'll see this is very simple,
not a comminuted fracture; constitution and blood healthy;
all you've to do is to see that he eats properly, keeps free
from excitement and worry, but does not get despondent;
a little company; his partners and some of the boys from
the Ledge will drop in occasionally; not too much of *them*,
you know; and of course, absolute immobility of the injured
parts." The lady nodded; the patient lifted his blue eyes
for an instant to hers with a look of tentative appeal, but it
slipped off Miss Trotter's dark pupils — which were as abstractedly critical as the doctor's — without being absorbed
by them. When the door closed behind her, the doctor
exclaimed: "By Jove! you're in luck, Chris! That's a
splendid woman! Just the one to look after you!" The
patient groaned slightly. "Do what she says, and we'll
pull you through in no time. Why! she's able to adjust
those bandages herself!"

This, indeed, she did a week later, when the surgeon had
failed to call, unveiling his neck and arm with professional
coolness, and supporting him in her slim arms against her
stiff, erect, buckramed breast, while she replaced the splints
with masculine firmness of touch and serene and sexless indifference. His stammered embarrassed thanks at the relief — for he had been in considerable pain — she accepted
with a certain pride as a tribute to her skill, a tribute which
Dr. Duchesne himself afterward fully indorsed.

On reëntering his room the third or fourth morning after
his advent at the Summit House, she noticed with some
concern that there was a slight flush on his cheek and a
certain exaltation which she at first thought presaged fever.
But an examination of his pulse and temperature dispelled
that fear, and his talkativeness and good spirits convinced

her that it was only his youthful vigor at last overcoming
his despondency. A few days later, this cheerfulness not
being continued, Dr. Duchesne followed Miss Trotter into
the hall. "We must try to keep our patient from moping
in his confinement, you know," he began, with a slight
smile, "and he seems to be somewhat of an emotional nature,
accustomed to be amused and — er — er — petted."

"His friends were here yesterday," returned Miss Trotter
dryly, "but I did not interfere with them until I thought
they had stayed long enough to suit your wishes."

"I am not referring to *them*," said the doctor, still smiling; "but you know a woman's sympathy and presence in
a sick-room is often the best of tonics or sedatives."

Miss Trotter raised her eyes to the speaker with a half
critical impatience.

"The fact is," the doctor went on, "I have a favor to
ask of you for our patient. It seems that the other morning a new chambermaid waited upon him, whom he found
much more gentle and sympathetic in her manner than the
others, and more submissive and quiet in her ways — possibly because she is a foreigner, and accustomed to servitude.
I suppose you have no objection to *her* taking charge of
his room?"

Miss Trotter's cheek slightly flushed. Not from wounded
vanity, but from the consciousness of some want of acumen
that had made her make a mistake. She had really believed,
from her knowledge of the patient's character and the doctor's preamble, that he wished *her* to show some more kindness and personal sympathy to the young man, and had even
been prepared to question its utility! She saw her blunder
quickly, and at once remembering that the pretty Swedish
girl had one morning taken the place of an absent fellow
servant, in the rebound from her error, she said quietly:
"You mean Frida! Certainly! she can look after his room,
if he prefers her." But for her blunder she might have

added conscientiously that she thought the girl would prove inefficient, but she did not. She remembered the incident of the wood; yet if the girl had a lover in the wood, she could not urge it as a proof of incapacity. She gave the necessary orders, and the incident passed.

Visiting the patient a few days afterward, she could not help noticing a certain shy gratitude in Mr. Calton's greeting of her, which she quietly ignored. This forced the ingenuous Chris to more positive speech. He dwelt with great simplicity and enthusiasm on the Swedish girl's gentleness and sympathy. "You have no idea of — her — natural tenderness, Miss Trotter," he stammered naïvely. Miss Trotter, remembering the wood, thought to herself that she had some faint idea of it, but did not impart what it was. He spoke also of her beauty, not being clever enough to affect an indifference or ignorance of it, which made Miss Trotter respect him and smile an unqualified acquiescence. Frida certainly was pretty! But when he spoke of her as "Miss Jansen," and said she was so much more "ladylike and refined than the other servants," she replied by asking him if his bandages hurt him, and, receiving a negative answer, graciously withdrew.

Indeed, his bandages gave him little trouble now, and his improvement was so marked and sustained that the doctor was greatly gratified, and, indeed, expressed as much to Miss Trotter, with the conscientious addition that he believed the greater part of it was due to her capable nursing! "Yes, ma'am, he has to thank *you* for it, and no one else!"

Miss Trotter raised her dark eyes and looked steadily at him. Accustomed as he was to men and women, the look strongly held him. He saw in her eyes an intelligence equal to his own, a knowledge of good and evil, and a toleration and philosophy, equal to his own, but a something else that was as distinct and different as their sex. And therein lay its charm, for it merely translated itself in his

mind that she had very pretty eyes, which he had never
noticed before, without any aggressive intellectual quality.
And with this, alas! came the man's propensity to reason.
It meant of course but *one* thing; he saw it all now! If
he, in his preoccupation and coolness, had noticed her eyes,
so also had the younger and emotional Chris. The young
fellow was in love with her! It was that which had stimulated his recovery, and she was wondering if he, the doctor,
had observed it. He smiled back the superior smile of our
sex in moments of great inanity, and poor Miss Trotter
believed he understood her. A few days after this, she
noticed that Frida Jansen was wearing a pearl ring and a
somewhat ostentatious locket. She remembered now that
Mr. Bilson had told her that the Roanoke Ledge was very
rich, and that Calton was likely to prove a profitable guest.
But it was not *her* business.

It became her business, however, some days later, when
Mr. Calton was so much better that he could sit in a chair,
or even lounge listlessly in the hall and corridor. It so
chanced that she was passing along the upper hall when she
saw Frida's pink cotton skirt disappear in an adjacent room,
and heard her light laugh as the door closed. But the room
happened to be a card-room reserved exclusively for gentlemen's poker or euchre parties, and the chambermaids had
no business there. Miss Trotter had no doubt that Mr.
Calton was there, and that Frida knew it; but as this was
an indiscretion so open, flagrant, and likely to be discovered
by the first passing guest, she called to her sharply. She
was astonished, however, at the same moment to see Mr.
Calton walking in the corridor at some distance from the
room in question. Indeed, she was so confounded that
when Frida appeared from the room a little flurried, but
with a certain audacity new to her, Miss Trotter withheld
her rebuke, and sent her off on an imaginary errand, while
she herself opened the card-room door. It contained simply

Mr. Bilson, her employer; his explanation was glaringly embarrassed and unreal! Miss Trotter affected obliviousness, but was silent; perhaps she thought her employer was better able to take care of himself than Mr. Calton.

A week later this tension terminated by the return of Calton to Roanoke Lodge, a convalescent man. A very pretty watch and chain afterward were received by Miss Trotter, with a few lines expressing the gratitude of the ex-patient. Mr. Bilson was highly delighted, and frequently borrowed the watch to show to his guests as an advertisement of the healing powers of the Summit Hotel. What Mr. Calton sent to the more attractive and flirtatious Frida did not as publicly appear, and possibly Mr. Bilson did not know it. The incident of the card-room was forgotten. Since that discovery, Miss Trotter had felt herself debarred from taking the girl's conduct into serious account, and it did not interfere with her work.

II

One afternoon Miss Trotter received a message that Mr. Calton desired a few moments' private conversation with her. A little curious, she had him shown into one of the sitting-rooms, but was surprised on entering to find that she was in the presence of an utter stranger! This was explained by the visitor saying briefly that he was Chris's elder brother, and that he presumed the name would be sufficient introduction. Miss Trotter smiled doubtfully, for a more distinct opposite to Chris could not be conceived. The stranger was apparently strong, practical, and masterful in all those qualities in which his brother was charmingly weak. Miss Trotter, for no reason whatever, felt herself inclined to resent them.

"I reckon, Miss Trotter," he said bluntly, "that you

don't know anything of this business that brings me here. At least," he hesitated, with a certain rough courtesy, "I should judge from your general style and gait that you would n't have let it go on so far if you had, but the fact is, that darned fool brother of mine — beg your pardon! — has gone and got himself engaged to one of the girls that help here, — a yellow-haired foreigner, called Frida Jansen."

"I was not aware that it had gone so far as that," said Miss Trotter quietly, "although his admiration for her was well known, especially to his doctor, at whose request I selected her to especially attend to your brother."

"The doctor is a fool," broke in Mr. Calton abruptly. "He only thought of keeping Chris quiet while he finished his job."

"And really, Mr. Calton," continued Miss Trotter, ignoring the interruption, "I do not see what right *I* have to interfere with the matrimonial intentions of any guest in this house, even though or — as you seem to put it — *because* the object of his attentions is in its employ."

Mr. Calton stared — angrily at first, and then with a kind of wondering amazement that any woman — above all, a housekeeper — should take such a view. "But," he stammered, "I thought you — you — looked after the conduct of those girls."

"I 'm afraid you 've assumed too much," said Miss Trotter placidly. "My business is to see that they attend to their duties here. Frida Jansen's duty was — as I have just told you — to look after your brother's room. And as far as I understand you, you are not here to complain of her inattention to that duty, but of its resulting in an attachment on your brother's part, and, as you tell me, an intention as to her future, which is really the one thing that would make my ' looking after her conduct ' an impertinence and interference! If you had come to tell me that he did *not* intend to marry her, but was hurting her reputation, I could have understood and respected your motives."

Mr. Calton felt his face grow red and himself discomfited. He had come there with the firm belief that he would convict Miss Trotter of a grave fault, and that in her penitence she would be glad to assist him in breaking off the match. On the contrary, to find himself arraigned and put on his defense by this tall, slim woman, erect and smartly buckramed in logic and whalebone, was preposterous! But it had the effect of subduing his tone.

"You don't understand," he said awkwardly yet pleadingly. "My brother is a fool, and any woman could wind him round her finger. *She* knows it. She knows he is rich and a partner in the Roanoke Ledge. That's all she wants. She is not a fit match for him. I 've said he was a fool — but, hang it all! that 's no reason why he should marry an ignorant girl — a foreigner and a servant — when he could do better elsewhere."

"This would seem to be a matter between you and your brother, and not between myself and my servant," said Miss Trotter coldly. "If you cannot convince *him*, your own brother, I do not see how you expect me to convince *her*, a servant, over whom I have no control except as a mistress of her *work*, when, on your own showing, she has everything to gain by the marriage. If you wish Mr. Bilson, the proprietor, to threaten her with dismissal unless she gives up your brother" — Miss Trotter smiled inwardly at the thought of the card-room incident — "it seems to me you might only precipitate the marriage."

Mr. Calton looked utterly blank and hopeless. His reason told him that she was right. More than that, a certain admiration for her clear-sightedness began to possess him, with the feeling that he would like to have "shown up" a little better than he had in this interview. If Chris had fallen in love with *her* — but Chris was a fool and would n't have appreciated her!

"But you might talk with her, Miss Trotter," he said, now completely subdued. "Even if you could not reason her out of it, you might find out what she expects from this marriage. If you would talk to her as sensibly as you have to me " —

"It is not likely that she will seek my assistance as you have," said Miss Trotter, with a faint smile which Mr. Calton thought quite pretty, "but I will see about it."

Whatever Miss Trotter intended to do did not transpire. She certainly was in no hurry about it, as she did not say anything to Frida that day, and the next afternoon it so chanced that business took her to the bank and post office. Her way home again lay through the Summit woods. It recalled to her the memorable occasion when she was first a witness to Frida's flirtations. Neither that nor Mr. Bilson's presumed gallantries, however, seemed inconsistent, in Miss Trotter's knowledge of the world, with a serious engagement with young Calton. She was neither shocked nor horrified by it, and for that reason she had not thought it necessary to speak of it to the elder Mr. Calton.

Her path wound through a thicket fragrant with syringa and southernwood; the faint perfume was reminiscent of Atlantic hillsides, where, long ago, a girl teacher, she had walked with the girl pupils of the Vermont academy and kept them from the shy advances of the local swains. She smiled — a little sadly — as the thought occurred to her that after this interval of years it was again her business to restrain the callow affections. Should she never have the match-making instincts of her sex? never become the trusted confidante of youthful passion? Young Calton had not confessed his passion to *her*, nor had Frida revealed her secret. Only the elder brother had appealed to her hard, practical common sense against such sentiment. Was there something in her manner that forbade it? She wondered if it was some uneasy consciousness of this quality which had impelled her to snub the elder Calton, and rebelled against it.

It was quite warm; she had been walking a little faster than her usual deliberate gait, and checked herself, halting in the warm breath of the syringas. Here she heard her name called in a voice that she recognized, but in tones so faint and subdued that it seemed to her part of her thoughts. She turned quickly and beheld Chris Calton a few feet from her, panting, partly from running and partly from some nervous embarrassment. His handsome but weak mouth was expanded in an apologetic smile; his blue eyes shone with a kind of youthful appeal so inconsistent with his long brown mustache and broad shoulders that she was divided between a laugh and serious concern.

"I saw you — go into the wood — but I lost you," he said, breathing quickly, "and then when I did see you again — you were walking so fast I had to run after you. I wanted — to speak — to you — if you 'll let me. I won't detain you — I can walk your way."

Miss Trotter was a little softened, but not so much as to help him out with his explanation. She drew her neat skirts aside, and made way for him on the path beside her.

"You see," he went on nervously, taking long strides to her shorter ones, and occasionally changing sides in his embarrassment, "my brother Jim has been talking to you about my engagement to Frida, and trying to put you against her and me. He said as much to me, and added you half promised to help him! But I did n't believe him — Miss Trotter! — I know you would n't do it — you have n't got it in your heart to hurt a poor girl! He says he has every confidence in you — that you 're worth a dozen such girls as she is, and that I 'm a big fool or I 'd see it. I don't say you 're not all he says, Miss Trotter; but I 'm not such a fool as he thinks, for I know your *goodness* too. I know how you tended me when I was ill, and how you

sent Frida to comfort me. You know, too, — for you 're
a woman yourself, — that all you could say, or anybody
could, would n't separate two people who loved each other."

Miss Trotter for the first time felt embarrassed, and this
made her a little angry. "I don't think I gave your brother any right to speak for me or of me in this matter,"
she said icily; "and if you are quite satisfied, as you say
you are, of your own affection and Frida's, I do not see
why you should care for anybody's interference."

"Now you are angry with me," he said in a doleful voice
which at any other time would have excited her mirth;
"and I 've just done it. Oh, Miss Trotter, don't! Please
forgive me! I did n't mean to say your talk was no good.
I did n't mean to say you could n't help us. Please don't
be mad at me!"

He reached out his hand, grasped her slim fingers in his
own, and pressed them, holding them and even arresting her
passage. The act was without familiarity or boldness, and
she felt that to snatch her hand away would be an imputation of that meaning, instead of the boyish impulse that
prompted it. She gently withdrew her hand as if to continue her walk, and said, with a smile: —

"Then you confess you need help — in what way?"

"With her!"

Miss Trotter stared. "With *her!*" she repeated. This
was a new idea. Was it possible that this common, ignorant girl was playing and trifling with her golden opportunity? "Then you are not quite sure of her?" she said a
little coldly.

"She 's so high spirited, you know," he said humbly,
"and so attractive, and if she thought my friends objected
and were saying unkind things of her, — well!" — he threw
out his hands with a suggestion of hopeless despair —
"there 's no knowing what she might do."

Miss Trotter's obvious thought was that Frida knew on

which side her bread was buttered; but remembering that
the proprietor was a widower, it occurred to her that the
young woman might also have it buttered on both sides.
Her momentary fancy of uniting two lovers somehow weakened at this suggestion, and there was a hardening of her
face as she said, "Well, if *you* can't trust her, perhaps your
brother may be right."

"I don't say that, Miss Trotter," said Chris pleadingly,
yet with a slight wincing at her words; "*you* could convince her, if you would only try. Only let her see that she
has some other friends beside myself. Look! Miss Trotter,
I'll leave it all to you — there! If you will only help me,
I will promise not to see her — not to go near her again —
until you have talked with her. There! Even my brother
would not object to that. And if he has every confidence
in you, I'm showing you I've more — don't you see?
Come, now, promise — won't you, dear Miss Trotter?"
He again took her hand, and this time pressed a kiss upon
her slim fingers. And this time she did not withdraw them.
Indeed, it seemed to her, in the quick recurrence of her
previous sympathy, as if a hand had been put into her love-
less past, grasping and seeking hers in its loneliness. None
of her school friends had ever appealed to her like this simple, weak, and loving young man. Perhaps it was because
they were of her own sex, and she distrusted them.

Nevertheless, this momentary weakness did not disturb
her good common sense. She looked at him fixedly for a
moment and then said, with a faint smile, "Perhaps she
does not trust *you*. Perhaps you cannot trust yourself."

He felt himself reddening with a strange embarrassment.
It was not so much the question that disturbed him as the
eyes of Miss Trotter; eyes that he had never before noticed
as being so beautiful in their color, clearness, and half
tender insight. He dropped her hand with a new-found
timidity, and yet with a feeling that he would like to hold
it longer.

"I mean," she said, stopping short in the trail at a point where a fringe of almost impenetrable "buckeyes" marked the extreme edge of the woods, — "I mean that you are still very young, and as Frida is nearly your own age," — she could not resist this peculiarly feminine innuendo, — "she may doubt your ability to marry her in the face of opposition; she may even think my interference is a proof of it; but," she added quickly, to relieve his embarrassment and a certain abstracted look with which he was beginning to regard her, "I will speak to her, and," she concluded playfully, "you must take the consequences."

He said "Thank you," but not so earnestly as his previous appeal might have suggested, and with the same awkward abstraction in his eyes. Miss Trotter did not notice it, as her own eyes were at that moment fixed upon a point on the trail a few rods away. "Look," she said in a lower voice, "I may have the opportunity now, for there is Frida herself passing." Chris turned in the direction of her glance. It was indeed the young girl walking leisurely ahead of them. There was no mistaking the smart pink calico gown in which Frida was wont to array her rather generous figure, nor the long yellow braids that hung Marguerite-wise down her back. With the consciousness of good looks which she always carried, there was, in spite of her affected ease, a slight furtiveness in the occasional swift turn of her head, as if evading or seeking observation.

"I will overtake her and speak to her now," continued Miss Trotter. "I may not have so good a chance again to see her alone. You can wait here for my return, if you like."

Chris started out of his abstraction. "Stay!" he stammered, with a faint, tentative smile. "Perhaps — don't you think? — I had better go first and tell her you want to see her. I can send her here. You see, she might" — He stopped.

Miss Trotter smiled. "It was part of your promise, you know, that you were *not* to see her again until I had spoken. But no matter! Have it as you wish. I will wait here. Only be quick. She has just gone into the grove."

Without another word the young man turned away, and she presently saw him walking toward the pine grove into which Frida had disappeared. Then she cleared a space among the matted moss and chickweed, and, gathering her skirts about her, sat down to wait. The unwonted attitude, the whole situation, and the part that she seemed destined to take in this sentimental comedy affected her like some quaint child's play out of her lost youth, and she smiled, albeit with a little heightening of color and lively brightening of her eyes. Indeed, as she sat there listlessly probing the roots of the mosses with the point of her parasol, the casual passer-by might have taken herself for the heroine of some love tryst. She had a faint consciousness of this as she glanced to the right and left, wondering what any one from the hotel who saw her would think of her sylvan rendezvous; and as the recollection of Chris kissing her hand suddenly came back to her, her smile became a nervous laugh, and she found herself actually blushing!

But she was recalled to herself as suddenly. Chris was returning. He was walking directly towards her with slow, determined steps, quite different from his previous nervous agitation, and as he drew nearer she saw with some concern an equally strange change in his appearance: his colorful face was pale, his eyes fixed, and he looked ten years older. She rose quickly.

"I came back to tell you," he said, in a voice from which all trace of his former agitation had passed, "that I relieve you of your promise. It won't be necessary for you to see — Frida. I thank you all the same, Miss Trotter," he said, avoiding her eyes with a slight return to his boyish manner. "It was kind of you to promise to undertake a

foolish errand for me, and to wait here, and the best thing
I can do is to take myself off now and keep you no longer.
Please don't ask me *why*. Sometime I may tell you, but
not now."

"Then you have seen her?" asked Miss Trotter quickly,
premising Frida's refusal from his face.

He hesitated a moment, then he said gravely, "Yes.
Don't ask me any more, Miss Trotter, please. Good-by!"
He paused, and then, with a slight, uneasy glance toward
the pine grove, "Don't let me keep you waiting here any
longer." He took her hand, held it lightly for a moment,
and said, "Go, now."

Miss Trotter, slightly bewildered and unsatisfied, nevertheless passed obediently out into the trail. He gazed after
her for a moment, and then turned and began rapidly to
ascend the slope where he had first overtaken her, and was
soon out of sight. Miss Trotter continued her way home;
but when she had reached the confines of the wood she
turned, as if taking some sudden resolution, and began
slowly to retrace her steps in the direction of the pine grove.
What she expected to see there possibly she could not have
explained; what she actually saw after a moment's waiting
were the figures of Frida and Mr. Bilson issuing from the
shade! Her respected employer wore an air of somewhat
ostentatious importance mingled with rustic gallantry.
Frida's manner was also conscious with gratified vanity;
and although they believed themselves alone, her voice was
already pitched into a high key of nervous affectation, in-
dicative of the peasant. But there was nothing to suggest
that Chris had disturbed them in their privacy and confidences. Yet he had evidently seen enough to satisfy himself of her faithlessness. Had he ever suspected it before?

Miss Trotter waited only until they had well preceded
her, and then took a shorter cut home. She was quite
prepared that evening for an interview which Mr. Bilson

" Please don't ask me why "

requested. She found him awkward and embarrassed in her cool, self-possessed presence. He said he deemed it his duty to inform her of his approaching marriage with Miss Jansen; but it was because he wished distinctly to assure her that it would make no difference in Miss Trotter's position in the hotel, except to promote her to the entire control of the establishment. He was to be married in San Francisco at once, and he and his wife were to go abroad for a year or two; indeed, he contemplated eventually retiring from business. If Mr. Bilson was uneasily conscious during this interview that he had once paid attentions to Miss Trotter, which she had ignored, she never betrayed the least recollection of it. She thanked him for his confidence and wished him happiness.

Sudden as was this good fortune to Miss Trotter, an independence she had so often deservedly looked forward to, she was, nevertheless, keenly alive to the fact that she had attained it partly through Chris's disappointment and unhappiness. Her sane mind taught her that it was better for him; that he had been saved an ill-assorted marriage; that the girl had virtually rejected him for Bilson before he had asked her mediation that morning. Yet these reasons failed to satisfy her feelings. It seemed cruel to her that the interest which she had suddenly taken in poor Chris should end so ironically in disaster to her sentiment and success to her material prosperity. She thought of his boyish appeal to her; of what must have been his utter discomfiture in the discovery of Frida's relations to Mr. Bilson that afternoon, but more particularly of the singular change it had effected in him. How nobly and gently he had taken his loss! How much more like a man he looked in his defeat than in his passion! The element of respect which had been wanting in her previous interest in him was now present in her thoughts. It prevented her seeking him with perfunctory sympathy and worldly counsel; it made her feel strangely and unaccountably shy of any other expression.

As Mr. Bilson evidently desired to avoid local gossip until after his marriage, he had enjoined secrecy upon her, and she was also debarred from any news of Chris through his brother, who, had he known of Frida's engagement, would have naturally come to her for explanation. It also convinced her that Chris himself had not revealed anything to his brother.

III

When the news of the marriage reached Buckeye Hill, it did not, however, make much scandal, owing, possibly, to the scant number of the sex who are apt to disseminate it, and to many the name of Miss Jansen was unknown. The intelligence that Mr. Bilson would be absent for a year, and that the superior control of the Summit Hotel would devolve upon Miss Trotter, *did*, however, create a stir in that practical business community. No one doubted the wisdom of the selection. Every one knew that to Miss Trotter's tact and intellect the success of the hotel had been mainly due. Possibly, the satisfaction of Buckeye Hill was due to something else. Slowly and insensibly Miss Trotter had achieved a social distinction; the wives and daughters of the banker, the lawyer, and the pastor, had made much of her, and now, as an independent woman of means, she stood first in the district. Guests deemed it an honor to have a personal interview with her. The governor of the State and the Supreme Court judges treated her like a private hostess; middle-aged Miss Trotter was considered as eligible a match as the proudest heiress in California. The old romantic fiction of her past was revived again, — they had known she was a "real lady" from the first! She received these attentions, as became her sane intellect and cool temperament, without pride, affectation, or hesitation. Only her dark eyes brightened on the day when Mr. Bilson's marriage was made known, and she was called upon by James Calton.

"I did you a great injustice," he said with a smile.

"I don't understand you," she replied a little coldly.

"Why, this woman and her marriage," he said; "you must have known something of it all the time, and perhaps helped it along to save Chris."

"You are mistaken," returned Miss Trotter truthfully. "I knew nothing of Mr. Bilson's intentions."

"Then I have wronged you still more," he said briskly; "for I thought at first that you were inclined to help Chris in his foolishness. Now I see it was your persuasions that changed him."

"Let me tell you once for all, Mr. Calton," she returned with an impulsive heat which she regretted, "that I did not interfere in any way with your brother's suit. He spoke to me of it, and I promised to see Frida, but he afterwards asked me not to. I know nothing of the matter."

"Well," laughed Mr. Calton, "*whatever* you did, it was most efficacious, and you did it so graciously and tactfully that it has not altered his high opinion of you, if, indeed, he has n't really transferred his affections to you."

Luckily Miss Trotter had her face turned from him at the beginning of the sentence, or he would have noticed the quick flush that suddenly came to her cheek and eyes. Yet for an instant this calm, collected woman trembled, not at what Mr. Calton might have noticed, but at what *she* had noticed in *herself*. Mr. Calton, construing her silence and averted head into some resentment of his familiar speech, continued hurriedly: —

"I mean, don't you see, that I believe no other woman could have influenced my brother as you have."

"You mean, I think, that he has taken his broken heart

very lightly," said Miss Trotter with a bitter little laugh, so unlike herself that Mr. Calton was quite concerned at it. "No," he said gravely. "I can't say *that!* He 's regularly cut up, you know! And changed; you 'd hardly know him. More like a gloomy crank than the easy fool he used to be," he went on, with brotherly directness. "It would n't be a bad thing, you know, if you could manage to see him, Miss Trotter! In fact, as he 's off his feed, and has some trouble with his arm again, owing to all this I reckon, I 've been thinking of advising him to come up to the hotel once more till he 's better. So long as *she 's* gone it would be all right, you know!"

By this time Miss Trotter was herself again. She reasoned, or thought she did, that this was a question of the business of the hotel, and it was clearly her duty to assent to Chris's coming. The strange yet pleasurable timidity which possessed her at the thought she ignored completely.

He came the next day. Luckily, she was so much shocked by the change in his appearance that it left no room for any other embarrassment in the meeting. His face had lost its fresh color and round outline; the lines of his mouth were drawn with pain and accented by his drooping mustache; his eyes, which had sought hers with a singular seriousness, no longer wore the look of sympathetic appeal which had once so exasperated her, but were filled with an older experience. Indeed, he seemed to have approximated so near to her own age that, by one of those paradoxes of the emotions, she felt herself much younger, and in smile and eye showed it; at which he colored faintly. But she kept her sympathy and inquiries limited to his physical health, and made no allusion to his past experiences; indeed, ignoring any connection between the two. He had been shockingly careless in his convalescence, had had a relapse in consequence, and deserved a good scolding! His relapse was a reflection upon the efficacy of the hotel as a perfect cure! She should treat him more severely now, and allow him no indulgences! I do not know that Miss Trotter intended anything covert, but their eyes met and he colored again. Ignoring this also, and promising to look after him occasionally, she quietly withdrew.

But about this time it was noticed that a change took place in Miss Trotter. Always scrupulously correct, and even severe in her dress, she allowed herself certain privileges of color, style, and material. She, who had always affected dark shades and stiff white cuffs and collars, came out in delicate tints and laces, which lent a brilliancy to her dark eyes and short crisp black curls, slightly tinged with gray. One warm summer evening she startled every one by appearing in white, possibly a reminiscence of her youth at the Vermont academy. The masculine guests thought it pretty and attractive; even the women forgave her what they believed a natural expression of her prosperity and new condition, but regretted a taste so inconsistent with her age. For all that, Miss Trotter had never looked so charming, and the faint autumnal glow in her face made no one regret her passing summer.

One evening she found Chris so much better that he was sitting on the balcony, but still so depressed that she was compelled so far to overcome the singular timidity she had felt in his presence as to ask him to come into her own little drawing-room, ostensibly to avoid the cool night air. It was the former "card-room" of the hotel, but now fitted with feminine taste and prettiness. She arranged a seat for him on the sofa, which he took with a certain brusque boyish surliness, the last vestige of his youth.

"It's very kind of you to invite me in here," he began bitterly, "when you are so run after by every one, and to leave Judge Fletcher just now to talk to me; but I suppose you are simply pitying me for being a fool!"

"I thought you were imprudent in exposing yourself to

the night air on the balcony, and I think Judge Fletcher is old enough to take care of himself," she returned, with the faintest touch of coquetry, and a smile which was quite as much an amused recognition of that quality in herself as anything else.

"And I'm a baby who can't," he said angrily. After a pause he burst out abruptly: "Miss Trotter, will you answer me one question?"

"Go on," she said smilingly.

"Did you know — that — woman was engaged to Bilson when I spoke to you in the wood?"

"No!" she answered quickly, but without the sharp resentment she had shown at his brother's suggestion. "I only knew it when Mr. Bilson told me the same evening."

"And *I* only knew it when news came of their marriage," he said bitterly.

"But you must have suspected something when you saw them together in the wood," she responded.

"When I saw them together in the wood?" he repeated dazedly.

Miss Trotter was startled, and stopped short. Was it possible he had not seen them together? She was shocked that she had spoken; but it was too late to withdraw her words. "Yes," she went on hurriedly, "I thought that was why you came back to say that I was not to speak to her."

He looked at her fixedly, and said slowly: "You thought that? Well, listen to me. I saw *no one!* I knew nothing of this! I suspected nothing! I returned before I had reached the wood — because — because — I had changed my mind!"

"Changed your mind!" she repeated wonderingly.

"Yes! Changed my mind! I couldn't stand it any longer! I did not love the girl — I never loved her — I was sick of my folly. Sick of deceiving you and myself any

longer. Now you know why I did n't go into the wood, and
why I did n't care where she was nor who was with her!"

"I don't understand," she said, lifting her clear eyes to
his coldly.

"Of course you don't," he said bitterly.   "I did n't understand myself!   And when you do understand you will
hate and despise me — if you do not laugh at me for a con-
ceited fool! Hear me out, Miss Trotter, for I am speaking
the truth to you now, if I never spoke it before.   I never
asked the girl to marry me!   I never said to *her* half what
I told to *you ;* and when I asked you to intercede with her,
I never wanted you to do it — and never expected you
would."

"May I ask *why* you did it, then?" said Miss Trotter,
with an acerbity which she put on to hide a vague, tan-
talizing consciousness.

"You would not believe me if I told you, and you would
hate me if you did."   He stopped, and, locking his fingers
together, threw his hands over the back of the sofa and
leaned toward her.   "You never liked me, Miss Trotter,"
he said more quietly; "not from the first!   From the day
that I was brought to the hotel, when you came to see me,
I could see that you looked upon me as a foolish, petted
boy.   When I tried to catch your eye, you looked at the
doctor, and took your speech from him.   And yet I thought
I had never seen a woman so great and perfect as you were,
and whose sympathy I longed so much to have.   You may
not believe me, but I thought you were a queen, for you
were the first lady I had ever seen, and you were so different from the other girls I knew, or the women who had been
kind to me.   You may laugh, but it 's the truth I 'm telling
you, Miss Trotter!"

He had relapsed completely into his old pleading, boyish way — it had struck her even as he had pleaded to her
for Frida!

"I knew you did n't like me that day you came to change the bandages. Although every touch of your hands seemed to ease my pain, you did it so coldly and precisely; and although I longed to keep you there with me, you scarcely waited to take my thanks, but left me as if you had only done your duty to a stranger. And worst of all," he went on more bitterly, "the doctor knew it too — guessed how I felt toward you, and laughed at me for my hopelessness! That made me desperate, and put me up to act the fool. I did! Yes, Miss Trotter; I thought it mighty clever to appear to be in love with Frida, and to get him to ask to have her attend me regularly. And when you simply consented, without a word or thought about it and me, I knew I was nothing to you."

Miss Trotter felt a sudden thrill. The recollection of Dr. Duchesne's strange scrutiny of her, of her own mistake, which she now knew might have been the truth — flashed across her confused consciousness in swift corroboration of his words. It was a *double* revelation to her; for what else was the meaning of this subtle, insidious, benumbing sweetness that was now creeping over her sense and spirit and holding her fast. She felt she ought to listen no longer — to speak — to say something — to get up — to turn and confront him coldly — but she was powerless. Her reason told her that she had been the victim of a trick — that having deceived her once, he might be doing so again; but she could not break the spell that was upon her, nor did she want to. She must know the culmination of this confession, whose preamble thrilled her so strangely.

"The girl was kind and sympathetic," he went on, "but I was not so great a fool as not to know that she was a flirt and accustomed to attention. I suppose it was in my desperation that I told my brother, thinking he would tell you, as he did. He would not tell me what you said to him, except that you seemed to be indignant at the thought that

I was only flirting with Frida. Then I resolved to speak with you myself — and I did. I know it was a stupid, clumsy contrivance. It never seemed so stupid before I spoke to you. It never seemed so wicked as when you promised to help me, and your eyes shone on me for the first time with kindness. And it never seemed so hopeless as when I found you touched with my love for another. You wonder why I kept up this deceit until you promised. Well, I had prepared the bitter cup myself — I thought I ought to drink it to the dregs."

She turned quietly, passionately, and, standing up, faced him with a little cry. "Why are you telling me this *now?*"

He rose too, and catching her hands in his, said, with a white face, "Because I love you."

.   .   .   .

Half an hour later, when the under-housekeeper was summoned to receive Miss Trotter's orders, she found that lady quietly writing at the table. Among the orders she received was the notification that Mr. Calton's rooms would be vacated the next day. When the servant, who, like most of her class, was devoted to the good-natured, good-looking, liberal Chris, asked with some concern if the young gentleman was no better, Miss Trotter, with equal placidity, answered that it was his intention to put himself under the care of a specialist in San Francisco, and that she, Miss Trotter, fully approved of his course. She finished her letter, — the servant noticed that it was addressed to Mr. Bilson at Paris, — and, handing it to her, bade that it should be given to a groom, with orders to ride over to the Summit post office at once to catch the last post. As the housekeeper turned to go, she again referred to the departing guest. "It seems such a pity, ma'am, that Mr. Calton could n't stay, as he always said you did him so much good." Miss Trotter smiled affably. But when the door closed she

gave a hysterical little laugh, and then, dropping her handsome gray-streaked head in her slim hands, cried like a girl
— or, indeed, as she had never cried when a girl.

When the news of Mr. Calton's departure became known
the next day, some lady guests regretted the loss of this
most eligible young bachelor. Miss Trotter agreed with
them, with the consoling suggestion that he might return
for a day or two. He did return for a day; it was thought
that the change to San Francisco had greatly benefited him,
though some believed he would be an invalid all his life.

Meantime Miss Trotter attended regularly to her duties,
with the difference, perhaps, that she became daily more
socially popular and perhaps less severe in her reception of
the attentions of the masculine guests. It was finally whispered that the great Judge Boompointer was a serious rival
of Judge Fletcher for her hand. When, three months later,
some excitement was caused by the intelligence that Mr.
Bilson was returning to take charge of his hotel, owing to
the resignation of Miss Trotter, who needed a complete
change, everybody knew what that meant. A few were
ready to name the day when she would become Mrs. Boompointer; others had seen the engagement ring of Judge
Fletcher on her slim finger.

Nevertheless, Miss Trotter married neither, and by the
time Mr. and Mrs. Bilson had returned she had taken her
holiday, and the Summit House knew her no more.

Three years later, and at a foreign Spa, thousands of miles
distant from the scene of her former triumphs, Miss Trotter
reappeared as a handsome, stately, gray-haired stranger,
whose aristocratic bearing deeply impressed a few of her
own countrymen who witnessed her arrival, and believed
her to be a grand duchess at the least. They were still more
convinced of her superiority when they saw her welcomed
by the well-known Baroness X., and afterwards engaged in
a very confidential conversation with that lady. But they

would have been still more surprised had they known the tenor of that conversation.

"I am afraid you will find the Spa very empty just now," said the baroness critically. "But there are a few of your compatriots here, however, and they are always amusing. You see that somewhat faded blonde sitting quite alone in that arbor? That is her position day after day, while her husband openly flirts or is flirted with by half the women here. Quite the opposite experience one has of American women, where it's all the other way, is it not? And there is an odd story about her which may account for, if it does not excuse, her husband's neglect. They're very rich, but they say she was originally a mere servant in a hotel."

"You forget that I told you I was once only a housekeeper in one," said Miss Trotter, smiling.

"Nonsense. I mean that this woman was a mere peasant, and frightfully ignorant at that!"

Miss Trotter put up her eyeglass, and, after a moment's scrutiny, said gently, "I think you are a little severe. I know her; it's a Mrs. Bilson."

"No, my dear. You are quite wrong. That was the name of her *first* husband. I am told she was a widow who married again — quite a fascinating young man, and evidently her superior — that is what is so funny. She is a Mrs. Calton — 'Mrs. Chris Calton,' as she calls herself."

"Is her husband — Mr. Calton — here?" said Miss Trotter after a pause, in a still gentler voice.

"Naturally not. He has gone on an excursion with a party of ladies to the Schwartzberg. He returns to-morrow. You will find *her* very stupid, but *he* is very jolly, though a little spoiled by women. Why do we always spoil them?"

Miss Trotter smiled, and presently turned the subject. But the baroness was greatly disappointed to find the next day that an unexpected telegram had obliged Miss Trotter to leave the Spa without meeting the Caltons.

JIMMY'S BIG BROTHER FROM CALIFORNIA

As night crept up from the valley that stormy afternoon, Sawyer's Ledge was at first quite blotted out by wind and rain, but presently reappeared in little nebulous star-like points along the mountain side, as the straggling cabins of the settlement were one by one lit up by the miners returning from tunnel and claim. These stars were of varying brilliancy that evening, two notably so — one that eventually resolved itself into a many-candled illumination of a cabin of evident festivity; the other into a glimmering taper in the window of a silent one. They might have represented the extreme mutations of fortune in the settlement that night: the celebration of a strike by Robert Falloner, a lucky miner; and the sick-bed of Dick Lasham, an unlucky one.

The latter was, however, not quite alone. He was ministered to by Daddy Folsom, a weak but emotional and aggressively hopeful neighbor, who was sitting beside the wooden bunk whereon the invalid lay. Yet there was something perfunctory in his attitude: his eyes were continually straying to the window, whence the illuminated Falloner festivities could be seen between the trees, and his ears were more intent on the songs and laughter that came faintly from the distance than on the feverish breathing and unintelligible moans of the sufferer.

Nevertheless, he looked troubled equally by the condition of his charge and by his own enforced absence from the revels. A more impatient moan from the sick man, however, brought a change to his abstracted face, and he turned to him with an exaggerated expression of sympathy.

"In course! Lordy! I know jest what those pains are: kinder ez ef you was havin' a tooth pulled that had roots branchin' all over ye! My! I 've jest had 'em so bad I could n't keep from yellin'! That 's hot rheumatics! Yes, sir, I oughter know! And " (confidentially) "the sing'ler thing about 'em is that they get worse jest as they 're going off — sorter wringin' yer hand and punchin' ye in the back to say ' Good-by.' There!" he continued, as the man sank exhaustedly back on his rude pillow of flour-sacks. "There! did n't I tell ye? Ye 'll be all right in a minit, and ez chipper ez a jay bird in the mornin'. Oh, don't tell me about rheumatics — I 've bin thar! On'y mine was the cold kind — that hangs on longest — yours is the hot, that burns itself up in no time!"

If the flushed face and bright eyes of Lasham were not enough to corroborate this symptom of high fever, the quick, wandering laugh he gave would have indicated the point of delirium. But the too optimistic Daddy Folsom referred this act to improvement, and went on cheerfully: "Yes, sir, you 're better now, and " — here he assumed an air of cautious deliberation, extravagant, as all his assumptions were — "I ain't sayin' that — ef — you — was — to — rise — up " (very slowly) "and heave a blanket or two over your shoulders — jest by way o' caution, you know — and leanin' on me, kinder meander over to Bob Falloner's cabin and the boys, it would n't do you a heap o' good. Changes o' this kind is often prescribed by the faculty." Another moan from the sufferer, however, here apparently corrected Daddy's too favorable prognosis. "Oh, all right! Well, perhaps ye know best; and I 'll jest run over to Bob's and say how as ye ain't comin', and will be back in a jiffy!"

"The letter," said the sick man hurriedly, "the letter, the letter!"

Daddy leaned suddenly over the bed. It was impossible

for even his hopefulness to avoid the fact that Lasham was delirious.   It was a strong factor in the case — one that would certainly justify his going over to Falloner's with the news.   For the present moment, however, this aberration was to be accepted cheerfully and humored after Daddy's own fashion.   "Of course — the letter, the letter," he said convincingly; "that's what the boys hev bin singin' jest now —

> 'Good-by, Charley; when you are away,
> Write me a letter, love; send me a letter, love!'

That's what you heard, and a mighty purty song it is too, and kinder clings to you.   It's wonderful how these things gets in your head."

"The letter — write — send money — money — money, and the photograph — the photograph — photograph — money," continued the sick man, in the rapid reiteration of delirium.

"In course you will — to-morrow — when the mail goes," returned Daddy soothingly; "plenty of them.   Jest now you try to get a snooze, will ye?   Hol' on! — take some o' this."

There was an anodyne mixture on the rude shelf, which the doctor had left on his morning visit.   Daddy had a comfortable belief that what would relieve pain would also check delirium, and he accordingly measured out a dose with a liberal margin to allow of waste by the patient in swallowing in his semi-conscious state.   As he lay more quiet, muttering still, but now unintelligibly, Daddy, waiting for a more complete unconsciousness and the opportunity to slip away to Falloner's, cast his eyes around the cabin.   He noticed now for the first time since his entrance that a crumpled envelope bearing a Western postmark was lying at the foot of the bed.   Daddy knew that the tri-weekly post had arrived an hour before he came, and that Lasham had evidently received a letter.   Sure enough the letter it-

self was lying against the wall beside him.   It was open.
Daddy felt justified in reading it.

It was curt and business-like, stating that unless Lasham
at once sent a remittance for the support of his brother and
sister — two children in charge of the writer — they must
find a home elsewhere; that the arrears were long standing, and the repeated promises of Lasham to send money
had been unfulfilled; that the writer could stand it no
longer.   This would be his last communication unless the
money were sent forthwith.

It was by no means a novel or, under the circumstances,
a shocking disclosure to Daddy.   He had seen similar mis-
sives from daughters, and even wives, consequent on the
varying fortunes of his neighbors; no one knew better than
he the uncertainties of a miner's prospects, and yet the inevitable hopefulness that buoyed him up.   He tossed it
aside impatiently, when his eye caught a strip of paper he
had overlooked lying upon the blanket near the envelope.
It contained a few lines in an unformed boyish hand addressed to "my brother," and evidently slipped into the
letter after it was written.   By the uncertain candlelight
Daddy read as follows: —

DEAR BROTHER, Rite to me and Cissy rite off.   Why aint
you done it?   It's so long since you rote any.   Mister
Recketts ses you dont care any more.   Wen you rite send
your fotograff.   Folks here ses I aint got no big bruther
any way, as I disremember his looks, and cant say wots like
him.   Cissy's kryin' all along of it.   I've got a hedake.
William Walker make it ake by a blo.   So no more at
present from your loving little bruther Jim.

The quick, hysteric laugh with which Daddy read this
was quite consistent with his responsive, emotional nature:
so, too, were the ready tears that sprang to his eyes.   He

put the candle down unsteadily, with a casual glance at the sick man.   It was notable, however, that this look contained less sympathy for the ailing "big brother" than his emotion might have suggested.   For Daddy was carried quite away by his own mental picture of the helpless children, and eager only to relate his impressions of the incident.   He cast another glance at the invalid, thrust the papers into his pocket, and clapping on his hat slipped from the cabin and ran to the house of festivity.   Yet it was characteristic of the man, and so engrossed was he by his one idea, that to the usual inquiries regarding his patient he answered, "He's all right," and plunged at once into the incident of the dunning letter, reserving — with the instinct of an emotional artist — the child's missive until the last.   As he expected, the money demand was received with indignant criticisms of the writer.

"That's just like 'em in the States," said Captain Fletcher; "darned if they don't believe we've only got to bore a hole in the ground and snake out a hundred dollars. Why, there's my wife — with a heap of hoss sense in everything else — is allus wonderin' why I can't rake in a cool fifty betwixt one steamer day and another."

"That's nothin' to my old dad," interrupted Gus Houston, the "infant" of the camp, a bright-eyed young fellow of twenty; "why, he wrote to me yesterday that if I'd only pick up a single piece of gold every day and just put it aside, sayin' 'That's for popper and mommer,' and not fool it away — it would be all they'd ask of me."

"That's so," added another; "these ignorant relations is just the ruin o' the mining industry.   Bob Falloner hez bin lucky in his strike to-day, but he's a darned sight luckier in being without kith or kin that he knows of."

Daddy waited until the momentary irritation had subsided, and then drew the other letter from his pocket. "That ain't all, boys," he began in a faltering voice, but gradually working himself up to a pitch of pathos; "just as I was thinking all them very things, I kinder noticed this yer poor little bit o' paper lyin' thar lonesome like and forgotten, and I — read it — and well — gentlemen — it just choked me right up!" He stopped, and his voice faltered.

"Go slow, Daddy, go slow!" said an auditor smilingly. It was evident that Daddy's sympathetic weakness was well known.

Daddy read the child's letter. But, unfortunately, what with his real emotion and the intoxication of an audience, he read it extravagantly, and interpolated a child's lisp (on no authority whatever), and a simulated infantile delivery, which, I fear, at first provoked the smiles rather than the tears of his audience. Nevertheless, at its conclusion the little note was handed round the party, and then there was a moment of thoughtful silence.

"Tell you what it is, boys," said Fletcher, looking around the table, "we ought to be doin' suthin' for them kids right off! Did you," turning to Daddy, "say anythin' about this to Dick?"

"Nary — why, he's clean off his head with fever — don't understand a word — and just babbles," returned Daddy, forgetful of his roseate diagnosis a moment ago, "and has n't got a cent."

"We must make up what we can amongst us afore the mail goes to-night," said the "infant," feeling hurriedly in his pockets. "Come, ante up, gentlemen," he added, laying the contents of his buckskin purse upon the table.

"Hold on, boys," said a quiet voice. It was their host Falloner, who had just risen and was slipping on his oilskin coat. "You 've got enough to do, I reckon, to look after your own folks. I 've none! Let this be my affair. I 've got to go to the Express Office anyhow to see about my passage home, and I 'll just get a draft for a hundred dollars for that old skeesicks — what 's his blamed name? Oh,

Ricketts " — he made a memorandum from the letter — "and I 'll send it by express. Meantime, you fellows sit down there and write something — you know what — saying that Dick 's hurt his hand and can't write — you know ; but asked you to send a draft, which you 're doing. Sabe ? That 's all ! I 'll skip over to the express now and get the draft off, and you can mail the letter an hour later. So put your dust back in your pockets and help yourselves to the whiskey while I 'm gone." He clapped his hat on his head and disappeared.

"There goes a white man, you bet ! " said Fletcher admiringly, as the door closed behind their host. "Now, boys," he added, drawing a chair to the table, "let 's get this yer letter off, and then go back to our game."

Pens and ink were produced, and an animated discussion ensued as to the matter to be conveyed. Daddy's plea for an extended explanatory and sympathetic communication was overruled, and the letter was written to Ricketts on the simple lines suggested by Falloner.

"But what about poor little Jim's letter ? That ought to be answered," said Daddy pathetically.

"If Dick hurt his hand so he can't write to Ricketts, how in thunder is he goin' to write to Jim ? " was the reply.

"But suthin' oughter be said to the poor kid," urged Daddy piteously.

"Well, write it yourself — you and Gus Houston make up somethin' together. I 'm going to win some money," retorted Fletcher, returning to the card-table, where he was presently followed by all but Daddy and Houston.

"Ye can't write it in Dick's name, because that little brother knows Dick's handwriting, even if he don't remember his face. See ? " suggested Houston.

"That 's so," said Daddy dubiously; "but," he added, with elastic cheerfulness, "we can write that Dick ' says.' See ? "

"Your head's level, old man! Just you wade in on that."

Daddy seized the pen and "waded in." Into somewhat deep and difficult water, I fancy, for some of it splashed into his eyes, and he sniffed once or twice as he wrote. "Suthin' like this," he said, after a pause: —

DEAR LITTLE JIMMIE, — Your big brother havin' hurt his hand, wants me to tell you that otherways he is all hunky and A1. He says he don't forget you and little Cissy, you bet! and he's sendin' money to old Ricketts straight off. He says don't you and Cissy mind whether school keeps or not as long as big Brother Dick holds the lines. He says he'd have written before, but he's bin follerin' up a lead mighty close, and expects to strike it rich in a few days.

"You ain't got no sabe about kids," said Daddy imperturbably; "they've got to be humored like sick folks. And they want everythin' big — they don't take no stock in things ez they are — even ef they hev 'em worse than they are. 'So,'" continued Daddy, reading to prevent further interruption, "' he says you're just to keep your eyes skinned lookin' out for him comin' home any time — day or night. All you've got to do is to sit up and wait. He might come and even snake you out of your beds! He might come with four white horses and a nigger driver, or he might come disguised as an ornary tramp. Only you've got to be keen on watchin'.' Ye see," interrupted Daddy explanatorily, "that 'll jest keep them kids lively. 'He says Cissy's to stop cryin' right off, and if Willie Walker hits yer on the right cheek you just slug out with your left fist, 'cordin' to Scripter.' Gosh," ejaculated Daddy, stopping suddenly and gazing anxiously at Houston, "there's that blamed photograph — I clean forgot that."

"And Dick has n't got one in the shop, and never had," returned Houston emphatically. "Golly! that stumps us! Unless," he added, with diabolical thoughtfulness, "we take Bob's? The kids don't remember Dick's face, and Bob's about the same age. And it's a regular star picture — you bet! Bob had it taken in Sacramento — in all his war paint. See!" He indicated a photograph pinned against the wall — a really striking likeness which did full justice to Bob's long silken mustache and large brown determined eyes. "I 'll snake it off while they ain't lookin', and you jam it in the letter. Bob won't miss it, and we can fix it up with Dick after he 's well, and send another."

Daddy silently grasped the "infant's" hand, who presently secured the photograph without attracting attention from the card-players. It was promptly inclosed in the letter, addressed to Master James Lasham. The "infant" started with it to the post office, and Daddy Folsom returned to Lasham's cabin to relieve the watcher that had been detached from Falloner's to take his place beside the sick man.

Meanwhile the rain fell steadily and the shadows crept higher and higher up the mountain. Towards midnight the star points faded out one by one over Sawyer's Ledge even as they had come, with the difference that the illumination of Falloner's cabin was extinguished first, while the dim light of Lasham's increased in number. Later, two stars seemed to shoot from the centre of the ledge, trailing along the descent, until they were lost in the obscurity of the slope — the lights of the stage-coach to Sacramento carrying the mail and Robert Falloner. They met and passed two fainter lights toiling up the road — the buggy lights of the doctor, hastily summoned from Carterville to the bedside of the dying Dick Lasham.

The slowing up of his train caused Bob Falloner to start from a half doze in a Western Pullman car. As he glanced

from his window he could see that the blinding snowstorm
which had followed him for the past six hours had at last
hopelessly blocked the line.   There was no prospect beyond
the interminable snowy level, the whirling flakes, and the
monotonous palisades of leafless trees seen through it to
the distant banks of the Missouri.   It was a prospect that
the mountain-bred Falloner was beginning to loathe, and
although it was scarcely six weeks since he left California,
he was already looking back regretfully to the deep slopes
and the free song of the serried ranks of pines.

The intense cold had chilled his temperate blood, even
as the rigors and conventions of Eastern life had checked
his sincerity and spontaneous flow of animal spirits begotten
in the frank intercourse and brotherhood of camps.   He
had just fled from the artificialities of the great Atlantic
cities to seek out some Western farming lands in which he
might put his capital and energies.   The unlooked-for interruption of his progress by a long-forgotten climate only
deepened his discontent.   And now — that train was actually backing!   It appeared they must return to the last station to wait for a snow-plough to clear the line.   It was,
explained the conductor, barely a mile from Shepherdstown,
where there was a good hotel and a chance of breaking the
journey for the night.

Shepherdstown!   The name touched some dim chord in
Bob Falloner's memory and conscience — yet one that was
vague.   Then he suddenly remembered that before leaving
New York he had received a letter from Houston informing
him of Lasham's death, reminding him of his previous
bounty, and begging him — if he went West — to break the
news to the Lasham family.   There was also some allusion
to a joke about his (Bob's) photograph, which he had dismissed as unimportant, and even now could not remember
clearly.   For a few moments his conscience pricked him
that he should have forgotten it all, but now he could make

amends by this providential delay. It was not a task to his liking; in any other circumstances he would have written, but he would not shirk it now.

Shepherdstown was on the main line of the Kansas Pacific Road, and as he alighted at its station, the big through trains from San Francisco swept out of the stormy distance and stopped also. He remembered, as he mingled with the passengers, hearing a childish voice ask if this was the California train. He remembered hearing the amused and patient reply of the station-master: "Yes, sonny — here she is again, and here's her passengers," as he got into the omnibus and drove to the hotel. Here he resolved to perform his disagreeable duty as quickly as possible, and on his way to his room stopped for a moment at the office to ask for Ricketts' address. The clerk, after a quick glance of curiosity at his new guest, gave it to him readily, with a somewhat familiar smile. It struck Falloner also as being odd that he had not been asked to write his name on the hotel register, but this was a saving of time he was not disposed to question, as he had already determined to make his visit to Ricketts at once, before dinner. It was still early evening.

He was washing his hands in his bedroom when there came a light tap at his sitting-room door. Falloner quickly resumed his coat and entered the sitting-room as the porter ushered in a young lady holding a small boy by the hand. But to Falloner's utter consternation, no sooner had the door closed on the servant than the boy, with a half-apologetic glance at the young lady, uttered a childish cry, broke from her, and calling, "Dick! Dick!" ran forward and leaped into Falloner's arms.

The mere shock of the onset and his own amazement left Bob without breath for words. The boy, with arms convulsively clasping his body, was imprinting kisses on Bob's waistcoat in default of reaching his face. At last Falloner

managed gently but firmly to free himself, and turned a
half-appealing, half-embarrassed look upon the young lady,
whose own face, however, suddenly flushed pink.   To add
to the confusion, the boy, in some reaction of instinct, suddenly ran back to her, frantically clutched at her skirts,
and tried to bury his head in their folds.

"He don't love me," he sobbed.   "He don't care for
me any more."

The face of the young girl changed.   It was a pretty face
in its flushing; in the paleness and thoughtfulness that
overcast it, it was a striking face, and Bob's attention was
for a moment distracted from the grotesqueness of the situation.   Leaning over the boy she said in a caressing yet
authoritative voice, "Run away for a moment, dear, until
I call you," opening the door for him in a maternal way so
inconsistent with the youthfulness of her figure that it
struck him even in his confusion.   There was something
also in her dress and carriage that equally affected him: her
garments were somewhat old-fashioned in style, yet of good
material, with an odd incongruity to the climate and season.

Under her rough outer cloak she wore a polka jacket and
the thinnest of summer blouses; and her hat, though dark,
was of rough straw, plainly trimmed.   Nevertheless, these
peculiarities were carried off with an air of breeding and
self-possession that was unmistakable.   It was possible that
her cool self-possession might have been due to some instinctive antagonism, for as she came a step forward with
coldly and clearly-opened gray eyes, he was vaguely conscious that she did n't like him.   Nevertheless, her manner was formally polite, even, as he fancied, to the point of
irony, as she began, in a voice that occasionally dropped
into the lazy Southern intonation, and a speech that easily
slipped at times into Southern dialect: —

"I sent the child out of the room, as I could see that his
advances were annoying to you, and a good deal, I reckon,

because I knew your reception of them was still more painful to him. It is quite natural, I dare say, you should feel as you do, and I reckon consistent with your attitude towards him. But you must make some allowance for the depth of his feelings, and how he has looked forward to this meeting. When I tell you that ever since he received your last letter, he and his sister — until her illness kept her home — have gone every day when the Pacific train was due to the station to meet you; that they have taken literally as gospel truth every word of your letter " —

"My letter?" interrupted Falloner.

The young girl's scarlet lip curled slightly. "I beg your pardon — I should have said the letter you dictated. Of course it was n't in your handwriting — you had hurt your hand, you know," she added ironically. "At all events, they believed it all — that you were coming at any moment; they lived in that belief, and the poor things went to the station with your photograph in their hands so that they might be the first to recognize and greet you."

"With my photograph?" interrupted Falloner again.

The young girl's clear eyes darkened ominously. "I reckon," she said deliberately, as she slowly drew from her pocket the photograph Daddy Folsom had sent, "that that is your photograph. It certainly seems an excellent likeness," she added, regarding him with a slight suggestion of contemptuous triumph.

In an instant the revelation of the whole mystery flashed upon him! The forgotten passage in Houston's letter about the stolen photograph stood clearly before him; the coincidence of his appearance in Shepherdstown, and the natural mistake of the children and their fair protector, were made perfectly plain. But with this relief and the certainty that he could confound her with an explanation came a certain mischievous desire to prolong the situation and increase his triumph. She certainly had not shown him any favor.

"Have you got the letter also?" he asked quietly.

She whisked it impatiently from her pocket and handed it to him. As he read Daddy's characteristic extravagance and recognized the familiar idiosyncrasies of his old companions, he was unable to restrain a smile. He raised his eyes, to meet with surprise the fair stranger's leveled eye brows and brightly indignant eyes, in which, however, the rain was fast gathering with the lightning.

"It may be amusing to you, and I reckon likely it was all a California joke," she said with slightly trembling lips; "I don't know No'thern gentlemen and their ways, and you seem to have forgotten our ways as you have your kindred. Perhaps all this may seem funny to them: it may not seem so funny to that boy who is now crying his heart out in the hall; it may not be very amusing to that poor Cissy in her sick-bed longing to see her brother. It may be so far from amusing to her, that I should hesitate to bring you there in her excited condition and subject her to the pain that you have caused him. But I have promised her; she is already expecting us, and the disappointment may be dangerous, and I can only implore you — for a few moments at least — to show a little more affection than you feel." As he made an impulsive, deprecating gesture, yet without changing his look of restrained amusement, she stopped him hopelessly. "Oh, of course, yes, yes, I know it is years since you have seen them; they have no right to expect more; only — only — feeling as you do," she burst out impulsively, "why — oh, why did you come?"

Here was Bob's chance. He turned to her politely; began gravely, "I simply came to" — when suddenly his face changed; he stopped as if struck by a blow. His cheek flushed, and then paled! Good God! What had he come for? To tell them that this brother they were longing for — living for — perhaps even dying for — was dead! In his crass stupidity, his wounded vanity over the scorn of

the young girl, his anticipation of triumph, he had forgotten — totally forgotten — what that triumph meant! Perhaps if he had felt more keenly the death of Lasham the
thought of it would have been uppermost in his mind; but
Lasham was not his partner or associate, only a brother
miner, and his single act of generosity was in the ordinary
routine of camp life.   If she could think him cold and
heartless before, what would she think of him now? The
absurdity of her mistake had vanished in the grim tragedy
he had seemed to have cruelly prepared for her.   The
thought struck him so keenly that he stammered, faltered,
and sank helplessly into a chair.

The shock that he had received was so plain to her that
her own indignation went out in the breath of it.   Her lip
quivered.   "Don't you mind," she said hurriedly, dropping
into her Southern speech; "I did n't go to hurt you, but I
was just that mad with the thought of those pickaninnies,
and the easy way you took it, that I clean forgot I 'd no
call to catechise you!   And you don't know me from the
Queen of Sheba.   Well," she went on, still more rapidly,
and in odd distinction to her previous formal slow Southern
delivery, "I 'm the daughter of Colonel Boutelle, of Bayou
Sara, Louisiana; and his paw, and his paw before him, had
a plantation there since the time of Adam, but he lost it
and six hundred niggers during the Wah!   We were pooh
as pohverty — paw and maw and we four girls — and no
more idea of work than a baby.   But I had an education
at the convent at New Orleans, and could play, and speak
French, and I got a place as school-teacher here; I reckon
the first Southern woman that has taught school in the
No'th!   Ricketts, who used to be our steward at Bayou
Sara, told me about the pickaninnies, and how helpless they
were, with only a brother who occasionally sent them money
from California.   I suppose I cottoned to the pooh little
things at first because I knew what it was to be alone

amongst strangers, Mr. Lasham; I used to teach them at odd times, and look after them, and go with them to the train to look for you. Perhaps Ricketts made me think you did n't care for them; perhaps I was wrong in thinking it was true, from the way you met Jimmy just now. But I 've spoken my mind — and you know why." She ceased and walked to the window.

Falloner rose. The storm that had swept through him was over. The quick determination, resolute purpose, and infinite patience which had made him what he was, were all there, and with it a conscientiousness which his selfish independence had hitherto kept dormant. He accepted the situation, not passively — it was not in his nature — but threw himself into it with all his energy.

"You were quite right," he said, halting a moment beside her; "I don't blame you, and let me hope that later you may think me less to blame than you do now. Now, what 's to be done? Clearly, I 've first to make it right with Tommy — I mean Jimmy — and then we must make a straight dash over to the girl! Whoop!" Before she could understand from his face the strange change in his voice, he had dashed out of the room. In a moment he reappeared with the boy struggling in his arms. "Think of the little scamp not knowing his own brother!" he laughed, giving the boy a really affectionate, if slightly exaggerated hug, "and expecting me to open my arms to the first little boy who jumps into them! I 've a great mind not to give him the present I fetched all the way from California. Wait a moment." He dashed into the bedroom, opened his valise — where he providentially remembered he had kept with a miner's superstition the first little nugget of gold he had ever found — seized the tiny bit of quartz of gold, and dashed out again to display it before Jimmy's eager eyes.

If the heartiness, sympathy, and charming kindness of the man's whole manner and face convinced, even while it slightly startled, the young girl, it was still more effective with the boy. Children are quick to detect the false ring of affected emotion, and Bob's was so genuine — whatever its cause — that it might have easily passed for a fraternal expression with harder critics. The child trustfully nestled against him and would have grasped the gold, but the young man whisked it into his pocket. "Not until we 've shown it to our little sister — where we 're going now! I 'm off to order a sleigh." He dashed out again to the office as if he found some relief in action, or, as it seemed to Miss Boutelle, to avoid embarrassing conversation. When he came back again he was carrying an immense bearskin from his luggage. He cast a critical look at the girl's unseasonable attire.

"I shall wrap you and Jimmy in this — you know it 's snowing frightfully."

Miss Boutelle flushed a little. "I 'm warm enough when walking," she said coldly. Bob glanced at her smart little French shoes, and thought otherwise. He said nothing, but hastily bundled his two guests downstairs and into the street. The whirlwind dance of the snow made the sleigh an indistinct bulk in the glittering darkness, and as the young girl for an instant stood dazedly still, Bob incontinently lifted her from her feet, deposited her in the vehicle, dropped Jimmy in her lap, and wrapped them both tightly in the bearskin. Her weight, which was scarcely more than a child's, struck him in that moment as being tantalizingly incongruous to the matronly severity of her manner and its strange effect upon him. He then jumped in himself, taking the direction from his companion, and drove off through the storm.

The wind and darkness were not favorable to conversation, and only once did he break the silence. "Is there any one who would be likely to remember — me — where we are going?" he asked, in a lull of the storm.

Miss Boutelle uncovered enough of her face to glance at him curiously. "Hardly! You know the children came here from the No'th after your mother's death, while you were in California."

"Of course," returned Bob hurriedly; "I was only thinking — you know that some of my old friends might have called," and then collapsed into silence.

After a pause a voice came icily, although under the furs: "Perhaps you 'd prefer that your arrival be kept secret from the public? But they seem to have already recognized you at the hotel from your inquiry about Ricketts, and the photograph Jimmy had already shown them two weeks ago." Bob remembered the clerk's familiar manner and the omission to ask him to register. "But it need go no further, if you like," she added, with a slight return of her previous scorn.

"I 've no reason for keeping it secret," said Bob stoutly.

No other words were exchanged until the sleigh drew up before a plain wooden house in the suburbs of the town. Bob could see at a glance that it represented the income of some careful artisan or small shopkeeper, and that it promised little for an invalid's luxurious comfort. They were ushered into a chilly sitting-room, and Miss Boutelle ran upstairs with Jimmy to prepare the invalid for Bob's appearance. He noticed that a word dropped by the woman who opened the door made the young girl's face grave again, and paled the color that the storm had buffeted to her cheek. He noticed also that these plain surroundings seemed only to enhance her own superiority, and that the woman treated her with a deference in odd contrast to the ill-concealed disfavor with which she regarded him. Strangely enough, this latter fact was a relief to his conscience. It would have been terrible to have received their kindness under false pretenses; to take their just blame of the man he personated seemed to mitigate the deceit.

The young girl rejoined him presently with troubled eyes. Cissy was worse, and only intermittently conscious, but had asked to see him. It was a short flight of stairs to the bedroom, but before he reached it Bob's heart beat faster than it had in any mountain climb. In one corner of the plainly furnished room stood a small truckle bed, and in it lay the invalid. It needed but a single glance at her flushed face in its aureole of yellow hair to recognize the likeness to Jimmy, although, added to that strange refinement produced by suffering, there was a spiritual exaltation in the child's look — possibly from delirium — that awed and frightened him; an awful feeling that he could not lie to this hopeless creature took possession of him, and his step faltered. But she lifted her small arms pathetically towards him as if she divined his trouble, and he sank on his knees beside her. With a tiny finger curled around his long mustache, she lay there silent. Her face was full of trustfulness, happiness, and consciousness — but she spoke no word.

There was a pause, and Falloner, slightly lifting his head without disturbing that faintly clasping finger, beckoned Miss Boutelle to his side. "Can you drive?" he said, in a low voice.

"Yes."

"Take my sleigh and get the best doctor in town to come here at once. Bring him with you if you can; if he can't come at once, drive home yourself. I will stay here."

"But" — hesitated Miss Boutelle.

"I will stay here," he repeated.

The door closed on the young girl, and Falloner, still bending over the child, presently heard the sleigh-bells pass away in the storm. He still sat with his bent head held by the tiny clasp of those thin fingers. But the child's eyes were fixed so intently upon him that Mrs. Ricketts leaned over the strangely assorted pair and said, —

"It's your brother Dick, dearie. Don't you know him?"

The child's lips moved faintly. "Dick 's dead," she whispered.

"She 's wandering," said Mrs. Ricketts. "Speak to her." But Bob, with his eyes on the child's, lifted a protesting hand. The little sufferer's lips moved again. "It is n't Dick — it 's the angel God sent to tell me."

She spoke no more. And when Miss Boutelle returned with the doctor she was beyond the reach of finite voices. Falloner would have remained all night with them, but he could see that his presence in the contracted household was not desired. Even his offer to take Jimmy with him to the hotel was declined, and at midnight he returned alone.

What his thoughts were that night may be easily imagined. Cissy's death had removed the only cause he had for concealing his real identity. There was nothing more to prevent his revealing all to Miss Boutelle and to offer to adopt the boy. But he reflected this could not be done until after the funeral, for it was only due to Cissy's memory that he should still keep up the rôle of Dick Lasham as chief mourner. If it seems strange that Bob did not at this crucial moment take Miss Boutelle into his confidence, I fear it was because he dreaded the personal effect of the deceit he had practiced upon her more than any ethical consideration; she had softened considerably in her attitude towards him that night; he was human, after all, and while he felt his conduct had been unselfish in the main, he dared not confess to himself how much her opinion had influenced him. He resolved that after the funeral he would continue his journey, and write to her, *en route*, a full explanation of his conduct, inclosing Daddy's letter as corroborative evidence. But on searching his letter-case he found that he had lost even that evidence, and he must trust solely at present to her faith in his improbable story.

It seemed as if his greatest sacrifice was demanded at the funeral! For it could not be disguised that the neighbors were strongly prejudiced against him.   Even the preacher improved the occasion to warn the congregation against the dangers of putting off duty until too late.   And when Robert Falloner, pale, but self-restrained, left the church with Miss Boutelle, equally pale and reserved, on his arm, he could with difficulty restrain his fury at the passing of a significant smile across the faces of a few curious bystanders. "It was Amy Boutelle that was the ' penitence ' that fetched him, you bet!" he overheard, a barely concealed whisper; and the reply, "And it 's a good thing she 's made out of it, too, for he 's mighty rich!"

At the church door he took her cold hand into his.   " I am leaving to-morrow morning with Jimmy," he said, with a white face.   "Good-by."

"You are quite right; good-by," she replied as briefly, but with the faintest color.   He wondered if she had heard it too.

Whether she had heard it or not, she went home with Mrs. Ricketts in some righteous indignation which found — after the young lady's habit — free expression.   Whatever were Mr. Lasham's faults of omission it was most un-Christian to allude to them there, and an insult to the poor little dear's memory who had forgiven them.   Were she in his shoes she would shake the dust of the town off her feet; and she hoped he would.   She was a little softened on arriving to find Jimmy in tears.   He had lost Dick's photograph — or Dick had forgotten to give it back at the hotel, for this was all he had in his pocket.   And he produced a letter — the missing letter of Daddy, which by mistake Falloner had handed back instead of the photograph.   Miss Boutelle saw the superscription and Californian postmark with a vague curiosity.

"Did you look inside, dear?   Perhaps it slipped in."

Jimmy had not.   Miss Boutelle did — and I grieve to say, ended by reading the whole letter.

Bob Falloner had finished packing his things the next morning, and was waiting for Mr. Ricketts and Jimmy. But when a tap came at the door, he opened it to find Miss Boutelle standing there. "I have sent Jimmy into the bedroom," she said with a faint smile, "to look for the photograph which you gave him in mistake for this. I think for the present he prefers his brother's picture to this letter, which I have not explained to him or any one." She stopped, and raising her eyes to his, said gently: "I think it would have only been a part of your goodness to have trusted me, Mr. Falloner."

"Then you will forgive me?" he said eagerly.

She looked at him frankly, yet with a faint trace of coquetry that the angels might have pardoned. "Do you want me to say to you what Mrs. Ricketts says were the last words of poor Cissy?"

A year later, when the darkness and rain were creeping up Sawyer's Ledge, and Houston and Daddy Folsom were sitting before their brushwood fire in the old Lasham cabin, the latter delivered himself oracularly.

"It's a mighty queer thing, that news about Bob! It's not that he's married, for that might happen to any one; but this yer account in the paper of his wedding being attended by his 'little brother.' That gets me! To think all the while he was here he was lettin' on to us that he had n't kith or kin! Well, sir, that accounts to me for one thing — the sing'ler way he tumbled to that letter of poor Dick Lasham's little brother and sent him that draft! Don't ye see? It was a feller feelin'! Knew how it was himself! I reckon ye all thought I was kinder soft reading that letter o' Dick Lasham's little brother to him, but ye see what it did."

THE YOUNGEST MISS PIPER

I DO not think that any of us who enjoyed the acquaintance of the Piper girls or the hospitality of Judge Piper, their father, ever cared for the youngest sister. Not on account of her extreme youth, for the eldest Miss Piper confessed to twenty-six — and the youth of the youngest sister was established solely, I think, by one big braid down her back. Neither was it because she was the plainest, for the beauty of the Piper girls was a recognized general distinction, and the youngest Miss Piper was not entirely devoid of the family charms. Nor was it from any lack of intelligence, nor from any defective social quality; for her precocity was astounding, and her good-humored frankness alarming. Neither do I think it could be said that a slight deafness, which might impart an embarrassing publicity to any statement — the reverse of our general feeling — that might be confided by any one to her private ear, was a sufficient reason; for it was pointed out that she always understood everything that Tom Sparrell told her in his ordinary tone of voice. Briefly, it was very possible that Delaware — the youngest Miss Piper — did not like us.

Yet it was fondly believed by us that the other sisters failed to show that indifference to our existence shown by Miss Delaware, although the heartburnings, misunderstandings, jealousies, hopes, and fears, and finally the chivalrous resignation with which we at last accepted the long foregone conclusion that they were not for us, and far beyond our reach, is not a part of this veracious chronicle. Enough that none of the flirtations of her elder sisters affected or were shared by the youngest Miss Piper. She moved in this heart-breaking atmosphere with sublime indifference, treating her sisters' affairs with what we considered rank simplicity or appalling frankness. Their few admirers who were weak enough to attempt to gain her mediation or confidence had reason to regret it.

"It's no kind o' use givin' me goodies," she said to a helpless suitor of Louisiana Piper's who had offered to bring her some sweets, "for I ain't got no influence with Lu, and if I don't give 'em up to her when she hears of it, she'll nag me and hate you like pizen. Unless," she added thoughtfully, "it was wintergreen lozenges; Lu can't stand them, or anybody who eats them within a mile." It is needless to add that the miserable man, thus put upon his gallantry, was obliged in honor to provide Del with the wintergreen lozenges that kept him in disfavor and at a distance. Unfortunately, too, any predilection or pity for any particular suitor of her sister's was attended by even more disastrous consequences. It was reported that while acting as "gooseberry" — a rôle usually assigned to her — between Virginia Piper and an exceptionally timid young surveyor, during a ramble she conceived a rare sentiment of humanity towards the unhappy man. After once or twice lingering behind in the ostentatious picking of a wayside flower, or "running on ahead" to look at a mountain view, without any apparent effect on the shy and speechless youth, she decoyed him aside while her elder sister rambled indifferently and somewhat scornfully on. The youngest Miss Piper leaped upon the rail of a fence, and with the stalk of a thimbleberry in her mouth swung her small feet to and fro and surveyed him dispassionately.

"Ye don't seem to be ketchin' on?" she said tentatively.

The young man smiled feebly and interrogatively.

"Don't seem to be either follering suit nor trumpin'," continued Del bluntly.

"I suppose so — that is, I fear that Miss Virginia " — he stammered.

"Speak up! I 'm a little deaf. Say it again! " said Del, screwing up her eyes and eyebrows.

The young man was obliged to admit in stentorian tones that his progress had been scarcely satisfactory.

"You 're goin' on too slow — that 's it," said Del critically. "Why, when Captain Savage meandered along here with Jinny " (Virginia) "last week, afore we got as far as this he 'd reeled off a heap of Byron and Jamieson " (Tennyson), "and sich; and only yesterday Jinny and Doctor Beveridge was blowin' thistletops to know which was a flirt all along the trail past the cross-roads. Why, ye ain't picked ez much as a single berry for Jinny, let alone Lad's Love or Johnny Jumpups and Kissme's, and ye keep talkin' across me, you two, till I 'm tired. Now look here," she burst out with sudden decision, "Jinny 's gone on ahead in a kind o' huff; but I reckon she 's done that afore too, and you 'll find her, jest as Spinner did, on the rise of the hill, sittin' on a pine stump and lookin' like this." (Here the youngest Miss Piper locked her fingers over her left knee, and drew it slightly up, — with a sublime indifference to the exposure of considerable small-ankled red stocking, — and with a far-off, plaintive stare, achieved a colorable imitation of her elder sister's probable attitude.) "Then you jest go up softly, like as you was a bear, and clap your hands on her eyes, and say in a disguised voice like this " (here Del turned on a high falsetto beyond any masculine compass), " 'Who 's who?' jest like in forfeits."

"But she 'll be sure to know me," said the surveyor timidly.

"She won't," said Del in scornful skepticism.

"I hardly think " — stammered the young man, with an awkward smile, "that I — in fact — she 'll discover me — before I can get beside her."

"Not if you go softly, for she 'll be sittin' back to the road, so — gazing away, so " — the youngest Miss Piper again stared dreamily in the distance, "and you 'll creep up just behind, like this."

"But won't she be angry ? I have n't known her long — that is — don't you see ? " He stopped embarrassedly.

"Can't hear a word you say," said Del, shaking her head decisively. "You 've got my deaf ear. Speak louder, or come closer."

But here the instruction suddenly ended, once and for all time ! For whether the young man was seriously anxious to perfect himself; whether he was truly grateful to the young girl and tried to show it; whether he was emboldened by the childish appeal of the long brown distinguishing braid down her back, or whether he suddenly found something peculiarly provocative in the reddish brown eyes between their thick-set hedge of lashes, and with the trim figure and piquant pose, and was seized with that hysteric desperation which sometimes attacks timidity itself, I cannot say ! Enough that he suddenly put his arm around her waist and his lips to her soft satin cheek, peppered and salted as it was by sun-freckles and mountain air, and received a sound box on the ear for his pains. The incident was closed. He did not repeat the experiment on either sister. The disclosure of his rebuff seemed, however, to give a singular satisfaction to Red Gulch.

While it may be gathered from this that the youngest Miss Piper was impervious to general masculine advances, it was not until later that Red Gulch was thrown into skeptical astonishment by the rumors that all this time she really had a lover ! Allusion has been made to the charge that her deafness did not prevent her from perfectly understanding the ordinary tone of voice of a certain Mr. Thomas Sparrell.

No undue significance was attached to this fact through

the very insignificance and "impossibility " of that individual, — a lanky, red-haired youth, incapacitated for manual
labor through lameness, — a clerk in a general store at the
cross-roads! He had never been the recipient of Judge
Piper's hospitality; he had never visited the house even
with parcels; apparently his only interviews with her or
any of the family had been over the counter. To do him
justice he certainly had never seemed to seek any nearer
acquaintance; he was not at the church door when her sisters, beautiful in their Sunday gowns, filed into the aisle,
with little Delaware bringing up the rear; he was not at
the Democratic barbecue, that we attended without reference
to our personal politics, and solely for the sake of Judge
Piper and the girls; nor did he go to the Agricultural Fair
Ball — open to all. His abstention we believed to be owing
to his lameness; to a wholesome consciousness of his own
social defects; or an inordinate passion for reading cheap
scientific text-books, which did not, however, add fluency
nor conviction to his speech. Neither had he the abstraction of a student, for his accounts were kept with an accuracy which struck us, who dealt at the store, as ignobly
practical, and even malignant. Possibly we might have
expressed this opinion more strongly but for a certain rude
vigor of repartee which he possessed, and a suggestion that
he might have a temper on occasion. "Them red-haired
chaps is like to be tetchy and to kinder see blood through
their eyelashes," had been suggested by an observing cus-
'omer.

In short, little as we knew of the youngest Miss Piper,
he was the last man we should have suspected her to select
as an admirer. What we did know of their public relations, purely commercial ones, implied the reverse of any
cordial understanding. The provisioning of the Piper
household was entrusted to Del, with other practical odds
and ends of housekeeping, not ornamental, and the follow-

ing is said to be a truthful record of one of their overheard interviews at the store: —

The youngest Miss Piper, entering, displacing a quantity of goods in the centre to make a sideways seat for herself, and looking around loftily as she took a memorandum-book and pencil from her pocket.

"Ahem! If I ain't taking you away from your studies, Mr. Sparrell, maybe you 'll be good enough to look here a minit; — but" (in affected politeness) "if I 'm disturbing you I can come another time."

Sparrell, placing the book he had been reading carefully under the counter, and advancing to Miss Delaware with a complete ignoring of her irony: "What can we do for you to-day, Miss Piper?"

Miss Delaware, with great suavity of manner, examining her memorandum-book: "I suppose it would n't be shocking your delicate feelings too much to inform you that the canned lobster and oysters you sent us yesterday was n't fit for hogs?"

Sparrell (blandly): "They were n't intended for them, Miss Piper. If we had known you were having company over from Red Gulch to dinner, we might have provided something more suitable for them. We have a fair quality of oil-cake and corncobs in stock, at reduced figures. But the canned provisions were for your own family."

Miss Delaware (secretly pleased at this sarcastic allusion to her sister's friends, but concealing her delight): "I admire to hear you talk that way, Mr. Sparrell; it 's better than minstrels or a circus. I suppose you get it outer that book," indicating the concealed volume. "What do you call it?"

Sparrell (politely): " 'The First Principles of Geology.' "

Miss Delaware, leaning sideways and curling her little fingers around her pink ear: "Did you say the first principles of 'geology' or 'politeness'? You know I am so deaf; but, of course, it could n't be that."

Sparrell (easily): "Oh, no, you seem to have that in your hand" — pointing to Miss Delaware's memorandum-book — "you were quoting from it when you came in."

Miss Delaware, after an affected silence of deep resignation: "Well! it 's too bad folks can't just spend their lives listenin' to such elegant talk; I 'd admire to do nothing else! But there 's my family up at Cottonwood — and they must eat. They 're that low that they expect me to waste my time getting food for 'em here, instead of drinking in the 'First Principles of the Grocery.' "

"Geology," suggested Sparrell blandly. "The history of rock formation."

"Geology," accepted Miss Delaware apologetically; "the history of rocks, which is so necessary for knowing just how much sand you can put in the sugar. So I reckon I 'll leave my list here, and you can have the things toted to Cottonwood when you 've got through with your 'First Principles.' "

She tore out a list of her commissions from a page of her memorandum-book, leaped lightly from the counter, threw her brown braid from her left shoulder to its proper place down her back, shook out her skirts deliberately, and saying, "Thank you for a most improvin' afternoon, Mr. Sparrell," sailed demurely out of the store.

A few auditors of this narrative thought it inconsistent that a daughter of Judge Piper and a sister of the angelic host should put up with a mere clerk's familiarity, but it was pointed out that "she gave him as good as he sent," and the story was generally credited. But certainly no one ever dreamed that it pointed to any more precious confidences between them.

I think the secret burst upon the family, with other things, at the big picnic at Reservoir Cañon. This festiv-

ity had been arranged for weeks previously, and was undertaken chiefly by the "Red Gulch Contingent," as we were
called, as a slight return to the Piper family for their frequent hospitality. The Piper sisters were expected to bring
nothing but their own personal graces and attend to the
ministration of such viands and delicacies as the boys had
profusely supplied.

The site selected was Reservoir Cañon, a beautiful, triangular valley with very steep sides, one of which was
crowned by the immense reservoir of the Pioneer Ditch
Company. The sheer flanks of the cañon descended in fur-
rowed lines of vines and clinging bushes, like folds of falling skirts, until they broke again into flounces of spangled
shrubbery over a broad level carpet of monkshood, mari-
posas, lupines, poppies, and daisies. Tempered and secluded
from the sun's rays by its lofty shadows, the delicious obscurity of the cañon was in sharp contrast to the fiery mountain trail that in the full glare of the noonday sky made its
tortuous way down the hillside, like a stream of lava, to
plunge suddenly into the valley and extinguish itself in its
coolness as in a lake. The heavy odors of wild honey-
suckle, syringa, and ceanothus that hung over it were light-
ened and freshened by the sharp spicing of pine and bay.
The mountain breeze which sometimes shook the serrated
tops of the large redwoods above with a chill from the remote snow peaks even in the heart of summer, never reached
the little valley.

It seemed an ideal place for a picnic. Everybody was
therefore astonished to hear that an objection was suddenly
raised to this perfect site. They were still more astonished
to know that the objector was the youngest Miss Piper!
Pressed to give her reasons, she had replied that the locality was dangerous; that the reservoir placed upon the
mountain, notoriously old and worn out, had been rendered
more unsafe by false economy in unskillful and hasty re-

pairs to satisfy speculating stockbrokers, and that it had
lately shown signs of leakage and sapping of its outer walls;
that, in the event of an outbreak, the little triangular valley, from which there was no outlet, would be instantly
flooded.   Asked still more pressingly to give her authority
for these details, she at first hesitated, and then gave the
name of Tom Sparrell.

The derision with which this statement was received by
us all, as the opinion of a sedentary clerk, was quite natural
and obvious, but not the anger which it excited in the
breast of Judge Piper; for it was not generally known that
the judge was the holder of a considerable number of shares
in the Pioneer Ditch Company, and that large dividends
had been lately kept up by a false economy of expenditure,
to expedite a "sharp deal" in the stock, by which the judge
and others could sell out of a failing company.   Rather, it
was believed, that the judge's anger was due only to the
discovery of Sparrell's influence over his daughter and his
interference with the social affairs of Cottonwood.   It was
said that there was a sharp scene between the youngest Miss
Piper and the combined forces of the judge and the elder
sisters, which ended in the former's resolute refusal to attend the picnic at all if that site was selected.

As Delaware was known to be fearless even to the point
of recklessness, and fond of gayety, her refusal only intensified the belief that she was merely "stickin' up for Sparrell's judgment" without any reference to her own personal
safety or that of her sisters.   The warning was laughed
away; the opinion of Sparrell treated with ridicule as the
dyspeptic and envious expression of an impractical man.
It was pointed out that the reservoir had lasted a long time
even in its alleged ruinous state; that only a miracle of coincidence could make it break down that particular afternoon
of the picnic; that even if it did happen, there was no direct proof that it would seriously flood the valley, or at best

add more than a spice of excitement to the affair. The "Red Gulch Contingent," who *would* be there, was quite as capable of taking care of the ladies, in case of any accident, as any lame crank who would n't, but could only croak a warning to them from a distance. A few even wished something might happen that they might have an opportunity of showing their superior devotion; indeed, the prospect of carrying the half-submerged sisters, in a condition of helpless loveliness, in their arms to a place of safety was a fascinating possibility. The warning was conspicuously ineffective; everybody looked eagerly forward to the day and the unchanged locality; to the greatest hopefulness and anticipation was added the stirring of defiance, and when at last the appointed hour had arrived, the picnic party passed down the twisting mountain trail through the heat and glare in a fever of enthusiasm.

It was a pretty sight to view this sparkling procession — the girls cool and radiant in their white, blue, and yellow muslins and flying ribbons, the "Contingent" in its cleanest ducks, and blue and red flannel shirts, the judge white-waistcoated and panama-hatted, with a new dignity borrowed from the previous circumstances, and three or four impressive Chinamen bringing up the rear with hampers — as it at last debouched into Reservoir Cañon.

Here they dispersed themselves over the limited area, scarcely half an acre, with the freedom of escaped school children. They were secure in their woodland privacy. They were overlooked by no high road and its passing teams; they were safe from accidental intrusion from the settlement; indeed, they went so far as to effect the exclusiveness of "clique." At first they amused themselves by casting humorously defiant eyes at the long, low Ditch Reservoir, which peeped over the green wall of the ridge, six hundred feet above them; at times they even simulated an exaggerated terror of it, and one recognized humorist declaimed a grotesque appeal to its forbearance, with delightful local allusions. Others pretended to discover near a woodman's hut, among the belt of pines at the top of the descending trail, the peeping figure of the ridiculous and envious Sparrell. But all this was presently forgotten in the actual festivity. Small as was the range of the valley, it still allowed retreats during the dances for waiting couples among the convenient laurel and manzanita bushes which flounced the mountain side. After the dancing, old-fashioned children's games were revived with great laughter and half-hearted and coy protests from the ladies; notably one pastime known as "I 'm a-pinin'," in which ingenious performance the victim was obliged to stand in the centre of a circle and publicly "pine" for a member of the opposite sex. Some hilarity was occasioned by the mischievous Miss "Georgy" Piper declaring, when it came to her turn, that she was "pinin'" for a look at the face of Tom Sparrell just now!

In this local trifling two hours passed, until the party sat down to the long-looked-for repast. It was here that the health of Judge Piper was neatly proposed by the editor of the "Argus." The judge responded with great dignity and some emotion. He reminded them that it had been his humble endeavor to promote harmony — that harmony so characteristic of American principles — in social as he had in political circles, and particularly among the strangely constituted yet purely American elements of frontier life. He accepted the present festivity with its overflowing hospitalities, not in recognition of himself — ("yes! yes!") — nor of his family — (enthusiastic protests) — but of that American principle! If at one time it seemed probable that these festivities might be marred by the machinations of envy — (groans) — or that harmony interrupted by the importation of low-toned material interests — (groans) — he could say that, looking around him, he had never before felt — er — that — Here the judge stopped short, reeled slightly forward, caught at a camp-stool, recovered himself with an apologetic smile, and turned inquiringly to his neighbor.

A light laugh — instantly suppressed — at what was at first supposed to be the effect of the "overflowing hospitality" upon the speaker himself, went around the male circle until it suddenly appeared that half a dozen others had started to their feet at the same time, with white faces, and that one of the ladies had screamed.

"What is it?" everybody was asking with interrogatory smiles.

It was Judge Piper who replied.

"A little shock of earthquake," he said blandly; "a mere thrill! I think," he added with a faint smile, "we may say that Nature herself has applauded our efforts in good old Californian fashion, and signified her assent. What are you saying, Fludder?"

"I was thinking, sir," said Fludder deferentially, in a lower voice, "that if anything was wrong in the reservoir, this shock, you know, might" —

He was interrupted by a faint crashing and crackling sound, and looking up, beheld a good-sized boulder, evidently detached from some greater height, strike the upland plateau at the left of the trail and bound into the fringe of forest beside it. A slight cloud of dust marked its course, and then lazily floated away in mid air. But it had been watched agitatedly, and it was evident that that singular loss of nervous balance which is apt to affect all those who go through the slightest earthquake experience was felt by all. But some sense of humor, however, remained.

"Looks as if the water risks we took ain't goin' to cover earthquakes," drawled Dick Frisney; "still that was n't a bad shot, if we only knew what they were aiming at."

"Do be quiet," said Virginia Piper, her cheeks pink with

excitement. "Listen, can't you? What's that funny murmuring you hear now and then up there?"

"It's only the snow-wind playin' with the pines on the summit. You girls won't allow anybody any fun but yourselves."

But here a scream from "Georgy," who, assisted by Captain Fairfax, had mounted a camp-stool at the mouth of the valley, attracted everybody's attention. She was standing upright, with dilated eyes, staring at the top of the trail. "Look!" she said excitedly, "if the trail isn't moving!"

Everybody faced in that direction. At the first glance it seemed indeed as if the trail was actually moving; wriggling and undulating its tortuous way down the mountain like a huge snake, only swollen to twice its usual size. But the second glance showed it to be no longer a trail but a channel of water, whose stream, lifted in a bore-like wall four or five feet high, was plunging down into the devoted valley.

For an instant they were unable to comprehend even the nature of the catastrophe. The reservoir was directly over their heads; the bursting of its wall they had imagined would naturally bring down the water in a dozen trickling streams or falls over the cliff above them and along the flanks of the mountain. But that its suddenly liberated volume should overflow the upland beyond and then descend in a pent-up flood by their own trail and their only avenue of escape, had been beyond their wildest fancy.

They met this smiting truth with that characteristic short laugh with which the American usually receives the blow of Fate or the unexpected — as if he recognized only the absurdity of the situation. Then they ran to the women, collected them together, and dragged them to vantages of fancied security among the bushes which flounced the long skirts of the mountain walls. But I leave this part of the description to the characteristic language of one of the party : —

"When the flood struck us, it did not seem to take any stock of us in particular, but laid itself out to ' go for ' that picnic for all it was worth! It wiped it off the face of the earth in about twenty-five seconds! It first made a clean break from stem to stern, carrying everything along with it. The first thing I saw was old Judge Piper, puttin' on his best licks to get away from a big can of strawberry ice cream that was trundling after him and trying to empty itself on his collar, whenever a bigger wave lifted it. He was followed by what was left of the brass band; the big drum just humpin' itself to keep abreast o' the ice cream, mixed up with camp-stools, music-stands, a few Chinamen, and then what they call in them big San Francisco processions ' citizens generally.' The hull thing swept up the cañon inside o' thirty seconds. Then, what Captain Fairfax called ' the reflex action in the laws o' motion ' happened, and darned if the hull blamed procession did n't sweep back again — this time all the heavy artillery, such as camp-kettles, lager beer kegs, bottles, glasses, and crockery that was left behind takin' the lead now, and Jedge Piper ar. ' that ice cream can bringin' up the rear. As the jedge passed us the second time, we noticed that that ice cream can — hevin' swallowed water — was kinder losing its wind, and we encouraged the old man by shoutin' out, ' Five to one on him!' And then, you would n't believe what followed. Why, darn my skin, when that ' reflex ' met the current at the other end, it just swirled around again in what Captain Fairfax called the ' centrifugal curve,' and just went round and round the cañon like ez when yer washin' the dirt out o' a prospectin' pan — every now and then washin' some one of the boys that was in it, like scum, up ag'in the banks.

"We managed in this way to snake out the jedge, jest ez he was sailin' round on the home stretch, passin' the quarter post two lengths ahead o' the can. A good deal o' the ice cream had washed away, but it took us ten minutes to shake the cracked ice and powdered salt out o' the old man's clothes, and warm him up again in the laurel bush where he was clinging. This sort o' ' Here we go round the mulberry bush ' kep' on until most o' the humans was got out, and only the furniture o' the picnic was left in the race. Then it got kinder mixed up, and went sloshin' round here and there, ez the water kep' comin' down by the trail. Then Lulu Piper, what I was holdin' up all the time in a laurel bush, gets an idea, for all she was wet and draggled; and ez the things went bobbin' round, she calls out the figures o' a cotillon to 'em. ' Two camp-stools forward.' ' Sashay and back to your places.' ' Change partners.' ' Hands all round.'

"She was clear grit, you bet! And the joke caught on and the other girls jined in, and it kinder cheered 'em, for they was wantin' it. Then Fludder allowed to pacify 'em by sayin' he just figured up the size o' the reservoir and the size o' the cañon, and he kalkilated that the cube was about ekal, and the cañon could n't flood any more. And then Lulu — who was peart as a jay and could n't be fooled — speaks up and says, ' What 's the matter with the ditch, Dick ? '

"Lord! then we knew that she knew the worst; for of course all the water in the ditch itself — fifty miles of it! — was drainin' now into that reservoir and was bound to come down to the cañon."

It was at this point that the situation became really desperate, for they had now crawled up the steep sides as far as the bushes afforded foothold, and the water was still rising. The chatter of the girls ceased, there were long silences, in which the men discussed the wildest plans, and proposed to tear their shirts into strips to make ropes to support the girls by sticks driven into the mountain side. It was in one of those intervals that the distinct strokes of a woodman's axe were heard high on the upland at the point where the trail descended to the cañon. Every ear was alert, but only those on one side of the cañon could get a fair view of the spot. This was the good fortune of Captain Fairfax and Georgy Piper, who had climbed to the highest bush on that side, and were now standing up, gazing excitedly in that direction.

"Some one is cutting down a tree at the head of the trail," shouted Fairfax. The response and joyful explanation, "for a dam across the trail," was on everybody's lips at the same time.

But the strokes of the axe were slow and painfully intermittent. Impatience burst out.

"Yell to him to hurry up! Why have n't they brought two men?"

"It 's only one man," shouted the captain, "and he seems to be a cripple. By Jiminy! — it is — yes! — it 's Tom Sparrell!"

There was a dead silence. Then, I grieve to say, shame and its twin brother rage took possession of their weak humanity. Oh, yes! It was all of a piece! Why in the name of Folly had n't he sent for an able-bodied man? Were they to be drowned through his cranky obstinacy?

The blows still went on slowly. Presently, however, they seemed to alternate with other blows — but alas! they were slower, and if possible feebler!

"Have they got another cripple to work?" roared the Contingent in one furious voice.

"No — it 's a woman — a little one — yes! a girl. Hello! Why, sure as you live, it 's Delaware!"

A spontaneous cheer burst from the Contingent, partly as a rebuke to Sparrell, I think, partly from some shame over their previous rage. He could take it as he liked.

Still the blows went on distressingly slow. The girls were hoisted on the men's shoulders; the men were half submerged. Then there was a painful pause; then a crumbling crash. Another cheer went up from the cañon.

"It's down! straight across the trail," shouted Fairfax, "and a part of the bank on the top of it."

There was another moment of suspense. Would it hold or be carried away by the momentum of the flood? It held! In a few moments Fairfax again gave voice to the cheering news that the flow had stopped and the submerged trail was reappearing. In twenty minutes it was clear — a muddy river bed, but possible of ascent! Of course there was no diminution of the water in the cañon, which had no outlet, yet it now was possible for the party to swing from bush to bush along the mountain side until the foot of the trail — no longer an opposing one — was reached. There were some missteps and mishaps, — flounderings in the water, and some dangerous rescues, — but in half an hour the whole concourse stood upon the trail and commenced the ascent. It was a slow, difficult, and lugubrious procession — I fear not the best-tempered one, now that the stimulus of danger and chivalry was past. When they reached the dam made by the fallen tree, although they were obliged to make a long detour to avoid its steep sides, they could see how successfully it had diverted the current to a declivity on the other side.

But strangely enough they were greeted by nothing else! Sparrell and the youngest Miss Piper were gone; and when they at last reached the high road, they were astounded to hear from a passing teamster that no one in the settlement knew anything of the disaster!

This was the last drop in their cup of bitterness! They who had expected that the settlement was waiting breathlessly for their rescue, who anticipated that they would be welcomed as heroes, were obliged to meet the ill-concealed amusement of passengers and friends at their disheveled and bedraggled appearance, which suggested only the blun-

dering mishaps of an ordinary summer outing! "Boatin'
in the reservoir, and fell in?" "Playing at canal-boat in
the Ditch?" were some of the cheerful hypotheses. The
fleeting sense of gratitude they had felt for their deliverers
was dissipated by the time they had reached their homes,
and their rancor increased by the information that when
the earthquake occurred Mr. Tom Sparrell and Miss Delaware were enjoying a "pasear" in the forest — he having
a half holiday by virtue of the festival — and that the
earthquake had revived his fears of a catastrophe. The two
had procured axes in the woodman's hut and did what they
thought was necessary to relieve the situation of the picnickers. But the very modesty of this account of their own performance had the effect of belittling the catastrophe itself,
and the picnickers' report of their exceeding peril was received with incredulous laughter.

For the first time in the history of Red Gulch there was
a serious division between the Piper family, supported by
the Contingent and the rest of the settlement. Tom Sparrell's warning was remembered by the latter, and the in-
gratitude of the picnickers to their rescuers commented
upon; the actual calamity to the reservoir was more or less
attributed to the imprudent and reckless contiguity of the
revelers on that day, and there were not wanting those who
referred the accident itself to the machinations of the schem-
ing Ditch Director Piper!

It was said that there was a stormy scene in the Piper
household that evening. The judge had demanded that
Delaware should break off her acquaintance with Sparrell,
and she had refused; the judge had demanded of Sparrell's
employer that he should discharge him, and had been met
with the astounding information that Sparrell was already
a silent partner in the concern. At this revelation Judge
Piper was alarmed; while he might object to a clerk who
could not support a wife, as a consistent democrat he could

not oppose a fairly prosperous tradesman. A final appeal was made to Delaware; she was implored to consider the situation of her sisters, who had all made more ambitious marriages or were about to make them. Why should she now degrade the family by marrying a country storekeeper?

It is said that here the youngest Miss Piper made a memorable reply, and a revelation the truth of which was never gainsaid: —

"You all wanter know why I'm going to marry Tom Sparrell?" she queried, standing up and facing the whole family circle.

"Yes."

"Why I prefer him to the hull caboodle that you girls have married or are going to marry?" she continued, meditatively biting the end of her braid.

"Yes."

"Well, he's the only man of the whole lot that hasn't proposed to me first."

It is presumed that Sparrell made good the omission, or that the family were glad to get rid of her, for they were married that autumn. And really a later comparison of the family records shows that while Captain Fairfax remained "Captain Fairfax," and the other sons-in-law did not advance proportionately in standing or riches, the lame storekeeper of Red Gulch became the Hon. Senator Tom Sparrell.

A WIDOW OF THE SANTA ANA VALLEY

THE Widow Wade was standing at her bedroom window staring out, in that vague instinct which compels humanity in moments of doubt and perplexity to seek this change of observation or superior illumination. Not that Mrs. Wade's disturbance was of a serious character. She had passed the acute stage of widowhood by at least two years, and the slight redness of her soft eyelids as well as the droop of her pretty mouth were merely the recognized outward and visible signs of the grievously minded religious community in which she lived. The mourning she still wore was also partly in conformity with the sad-colored garments of her neighbors, and the necessities of the rainy season. She was in comfortable circumstances, the mistress of a large ranch in the valley, which had lately become more valuable by the extension of a wagon road through its centre. She was simply worrying whether she should go to a "sociable" ending with a "dance" — a daring innovation of some strangers — at the new hotel, or continue to eschew such follies, that were, according to local belief, unsuited to a "vale of tears."

Indeed, at this moment the prospect she gazed abstractedly upon seemed to justify that lugubrious description. The Santa Ana Valley — a long, monotonous level — was dimly visible through moving curtains of rain or veils of mist, to the black mourning edge of the horizon, and had looked like that for months. The valley — in some remote epoch an arm of the San Francisco Bay — every rainy season seemed to be trying to revert to its original condition, and, long after the early spring had laid on its liberal color in strips, bands, and patches of blue and yellow, the blossoms of mustard and lupine glistened like wet paint. Nevertheless, on that rich alluvial soil Nature's tears seemed only to fatten the widow's acres and increase her crops. Her neighbors, too, were equally prosperous. Yet for six months of the year the recognized expression of Santa Ana was one of sadness, and for the other six months — of resignation. Mrs. Wade had yielded early to this influence, as she had to others, in the weakness of her gentle nature, and partly as it was more becoming the singular tragedy that had made her a widow.

The late Mr. Wade had been found dead with a bullet through his head in a secluded part of the road over Heavy Tree Hill in Sonora County. Near him lay two other bodies, one afterwards identified as John Stubbs, a resident of the Hill, and probably a traveling companion of Wade's, and the other a noted desperado and highwayman, still masked, as at the moment of the attack. Wade and his companion had probably sold their lives dearly, and against odds, for another mask was found on the ground, indicating that the attack was not single-handed, and as Wade's body had not yet been rifled, it was evident that the remaining highwayman had fled in haste. The hue and cry had been given by apparently the only one of the travelers who escaped, but as he was hastening to take the overland coach to the East at the time, his testimony could not be submitted to the coroner's deliberation. The facts, however, were sufficiently plain for a verdict of willful murder against the highwayman, although it was believed that the absent witness had basely deserted his companion and left him to his fate, or, as was suggested by others, that he might even have been an accomplice. It was this circumstance which protracted comment on the incident, and the sufferings of the widow, far beyond that rapid ob-

literation which usually overtook such affairs in the feverish haste of the early days. It caused her to remove to
Santa Ana, where her old father had feebly ranched a
"quarter section" in the valley. He survived her husband only a few months, leaving her the property, and once
more in mourning. Perhaps this continuity of woe endeared her to a neighborhood where distinctive ravages of
diphtheria or scarlet fever gave a kind of social preëminence
to any household, and she was so sympathetically assisted by
her neighbors in the management of the ranch that, from
an unkempt and wasteful wilderness, it became paying property. The slim, willowy figure, soft red-lidded eyes, and
deep crape of "Sister Wade" at church or prayer-meeting
were grateful to the souls of these gloomy worshipers, and
in time she herself found that the arm of these dyspeptics
of mind and body was nevertheless strong and sustaining.
Small wonder that she should hesitate to-night about plunging into inconsistent, even though trifling, frivolities.

But apart from this superficial reason, there was another
instinctive one deep down in the recesses of Mrs. Wade's
timid heart which she had kept to herself, and indeed
would have tearfully resented had it been offered by another. The late Mr. Wade had been, in fact, a singular
example of this kind of frivolous existence carried to a
man-like excess. Besides being a patron of amusements,
Mr. Wade gambled, raced, and drank. He was often home
late, and sometimes not at all. Not that this conduct was
exceptional in the "roaring days" of Heavy Tree Hill, but
it had given Mrs. Wade perhaps an undue preference for a
less uncertain, even if a more serious life. His tragic death
was, of course, a kind of martyrdom, which exalted him in
the feminine mind to a saintly memory; yet Mrs. Wade
was not without a certain relief in that. It was voiced,
perhaps crudely, by the widow of Abner Drake in a visit
of condolence to the tearful Mrs. Wade a few days after

Wade's death. "It's a vale o' sorrow, Mrs. Wade," said the sympathizer, "but it has its ups and downs, and I recken ye 'll be feelin' soon pretty much as I did about Abner when *he* was took. It was mighty soothin' and comfortin' to feel that whatever might happen now, I always knew just whar Abner was passin' his nights." Poor slim Mrs. Wade had no disquieting sense of humor to interfere with her reception of this large truth, and she accepted it with a burst of reminiscent tears.

A long volleying shower had just passed down the level landscape, and was followed by a rolling mist from the warm saturated soil like the smoke of the discharge. Through it she could see a faint lightening of the hidden sun, again darkening through a sudden onset of rain, and changing as with her conflicting doubts and resolutions. Thus gazing, she was vaguely conscious of an addition to the landscape in the shape of a man who was passing down the road with a pack on his back like the tramping "prospectors" she had often seen at Heavy Tree Hill. That memory apparently settled her vacillating mind; she determined she would *not* go to the dance. But as she was turning away from the window a second figure, a horseman, appeared in another direction by a cross-road, a shorter cut through her domain. This she had no difficulty in recognizing as one of the strangers who were getting up the dance. She had noticed him at church on the previous Sunday. As he passed the house he appeared to be gazing at it so earnestly that she drew back from the window lest she should be seen. And then, for no reason whatever, she changed her mind once more, and resolved to go to the dance. Gravely announcing this fact to the wife of her superintendent, who kept house with her in her loneliness, she thought nothing more about it. She should go in her mourning, with perhaps the addition of a white collar and frill.

It was evident, however, that Santa Ana thought a good deal more than she did of this new idea, which seemed a part of the innovation already begun by the building up of the new hotel. It was argued by some that as the new church and new schoolhouse had been opened by prayer, it was only natural that a lighter festivity should inaugurate the opening of the hotel. "I reckon that dancin' is about the next thing to travelin' for gettin' up an appetite for refreshments, and that 's what the landlord is kalkilatin' to sarve," was the remark of a gloomy but practical citizen on the veranda of "The Valley Emporium." "That 's so," rejoined a bystander; "and I notice on that last box o' pills I got for chills the directions say that a little 'agreeable exercise' — not too violent — is a great assistance to the working o' the pills."

"I reckon that that Mr. Brooks who 's down here lookin' arter mill property, got up the dance. He 's bin round town canvassin' all the women folks and drummin' up likely gals for it. They say he actooally sent an invite to the Widder Wade," remarked another lounger. "Gosh! he 's got cheek!"

"Well, gentlemen," said the proprietor judicially, "while we don't intend to hev any minin' camp fandangoes or 'Frisco falals round Santa Any" (Santa Ana was proud of its simple agricultural virtues) "I ain't so hard-shelled as not to give new things a fair trial. And, after all, it 's the women folk that has the say about it. Why, there 's old Miss Ford sez she has n't kicked a fut sence she left Mizoori, but would n't mind trying it ag'in. Ez to Brooks takin' that trouble — well, I suppose it 's along o' his bein' *healthy!*" He heaved a deep dyspeptic sigh, which was faintly echoed by the others. "Why, look at him now, ridin' round on that black hoss o' his, in the wet since daylight and not carin' for blind chills or rheumatiz!"

He was looking at a serape-draped horseman, the one the

widow had seen on the previous night, who was now cantering slowly up the street.   Seeing the group on the veranda, he rode up, threw himself lightly from his saddle, and joined them.   He was an alert, determined, good-looking fellow of about thirty-five, whose smooth, smiling face hardly commended itself to Santa Ana, though his eyes were distinctly sympathetic.   He glanced at the depressed group around him and became ominously serious.

"When did it happen?" he asked gravely.

"What happen?" said the nearest bystander.

"The Funeral, Flood, Fight, or Fire.   Which of the four F's was it?"

"What are ye talkin' about?" said the proprietor stiffly, scenting some dangerous humor.

"*You,*" said Brooks promptly.   "You 're all standing here, croaking like crows, this fine morning.   I passed *your* farm, Johnson, not an hour ago; the wheat just climbing out of the black adobe mud as thick as rows of pins on paper — what have *you* to grumble at?   I saw *your* stock, Briggs, over on Two-Mile Bottom, waddling along, fat as the adobe they were sticking in, their coats shining like fresh paint — what 's the matter with *you?* And," turning to the proprietor, "there 's *your* shed, Saunders, over on the creek, just bursting with last year's grain that you know has gone up two hundred per cent. since you bought it at a bargain — what are *you* growling at?   It 's enough to provoke a fire or a famine to hear you groaning — and take care it don't, some day, as a lesson to you."

All this was so perfectly true of the prosperous burghers that they could not for a moment reply.   But Briggs had recourse to what he believed to be a retaliatory taunt.

"I heard you 've been askin' Widow Wade to come to your dance," he said, with a wink at the others.   "Of course she said ' Yes.' "

A serape-draped horseman

"Of course she did," returned Brooks coolly. "I 've just got her note."

"What?" ejaculated the three men together. "Mrs. Wade comin' ?"

"Certainly! Why should n't she? And it would do *you* good to come too, and shake the limp dampness out o' you," returned Brooks, as he quietly remounted his horse and cantered away.

"Darned ef I don't think he 's got his eye on the widder," said Johnson faintly.

"Or the quarter section," added Briggs gloomily.

For all that, the eventful evening came, with many lights in the staring, undraped windows of the hotel, coldly bright bunting on the still damp walls of the long dining-room, and a gentle downpour from the hidden skies above. A close carryall was especially selected to bring Mrs. Wade and her housekeeper. The widow arrived, looking a little slimmer than usual in her closely buttoned black dress, white collar and cuffs, very glistening in eye and in hair, — whose glossy black ringlets were perhaps more elaborately arranged than was her custom, — and with a faint coming and going of color, due perhaps to her agitation at this tentative reëntering into worldly life, which was nevertheless quite virginal in effect. A vague solemnity pervaded the introductory proceedings, and a singular want of sociability was visible in the "sociable" part of the entertainment. People talked in whispers or with that grave precision which indicates good manners in rural communities; conversed painfully with other people whom they did not want to talk to rather than appear to be alone, or rushed aimlessly together like water drops, and then floated in broken, adherent masses over the floor. The widow became a helpless, religious centre of deacons and Sunday-school teachers, which Brooks, untiring, yet fruitless, in his attempt to produce gayety, tried in vain to break. To this gloom the untried dangers of the impending dance, duly prefigured by a lonely cottage piano and two violins in a desert of expanse, added a nervous chill. When at last the music struck up — somewhat hesitatingly and protestingly, from the circumstance that the player was the church organist, and fumbled mechanically for his stops, the attempt to make up a cotillion set was left to the heroic Brooks. Yet he barely escaped disaster when, in posing the couples, he incautiously begged them to look a little less as if they were waiting for the coffin to be borne down the aisle between them, and was rewarded by a burst of tears from Mrs. Johnson, who had lost a child two years before, and who had to be led away, while her place in the set was taken by another. Yet the cotillion passed off; a Spanish dance succeeded; "Moneymusk," with the Virginia Reel, put a slight intoxicating vibration into the air, and healthy youth at last asserted itself in a score of freckled but buxom girls in white muslin, with romping figures and laughter, at the lower end of the room. Still a rigid decorum reigned among the elder dancers, and the figures were called out in grave formality, as if, to Brooks's fancy, they were hymns given from the pulpit, until at the close of the set, in half-real, half-mock despair, he turned desperately to Mrs. Wade, his partner: —

"Do you waltz?"

Mrs. Wade hesitated. She *had*, before marriage, and was a good waltzer. "I do," she said timidly, "but do you think they " —

But before the poor widow could formulate her fears as to the reception of "round dances," Brooks had darted to the piano, and the next moment she heard with a "fearful joy" the opening bars of a waltz. It was an old Julien waltz, fresh still in the fifties, daring, provocative to foot, swamping to intellect, arresting to judgment, irresistible, supreme! Before Mrs. Wade could protest, Brooks's arm

had gathered up her slim figure, and with one quick backward sweep and swirl they were off! The floor was cleared
for them in a sudden bewilderment of alarm — a suspense
of burning curiosity. The widow's little feet tripped
quickly, her long black skirt swung out; as she turned the
corner there was not only a sudden revelation of her pretty
ankles, but, what was more startling, a dazzling flash of
frilled and laced petticoat, which at once convinced every
woman in the room that the act had been premeditated for
days! Yet even that criticism was presently forgotten in
the pervading intoxication of the music and the movement.
The younger people fell into it with wild rompings, whirl-
ings, and clasping of hands and waists. And stranger than
all, a corybantic enthusiasm seized upon the emotionally
religious, and those priests and priestesses of Cybele who
were famous for their frenzy and passion in camp-meeting
devotions seemed to find an equal expression that night in
the waltz. And when, flushed and panting, Mrs. Wade
at last halted on the arm of her partner, they were nearly
knocked over by the revolving Johnson and Mrs. Stubbs
in a whirl of gloomy exultation! Deacons and Sunday-
school teachers waltzed together until the long room shook,
and the very bunting on the walls waved and fluttered with
the gyrations of those religious dervishes. Nobody knew
— nobody cared — how long this frenzy lasted; it ceased
only with the collapse of the musicians. Then, with much
vague bewilderment, inward trepidation, awkward and in-
coherent partings, everybody went dazedly home; there
was no other dancing after that — the waltz was the one
event of the festival and of the history of Santa Ana. And
later that night, when the timid Mrs. Wade, in the seclusion of her own room and the disrobing of her slim figure,
glanced at her spotless frilled and laced petticoat lying on a
chair, a faint smile — the first of her widowhood — curved
the corners of her pretty mouth.

A week of ominous silence regarding the festival succeeded in Santa Ana.   The local paper gave the fullest
particulars of the opening of the hotel, but contented itself
with saying: "The entertainment concluded with a dance."
Mr. Brooks, who felt himself compelled to call upon his
late charming partner twice during the week, characteristically soothed her anxieties as to the result.   "The fact of it
is, Mrs. Wade, there 's really nobody in particular to blame
— and that 's what gets them.   They 're all mixed up in
it, deacons and Sunday-school teachers; and when old
Johnson tried to be nasty the other evening and hoped you
had n't suffered from your exertions that night, I told him
you had n't quite recovered yet from the physical shock of
having been run into by him and Mrs. Stubbs, but that,
you being a lady, you did n't tell just how you felt at the
exhibition he and she made of themselves.   That shut him
up."

"But you should n't have said that," said Mrs. Wade
with a frightened little smile.

"No matter," returned Brooks cheerfully.   "I 'll take
the blame of it with the others.   You see they 'll have to
have a scapegoat — and I 'm just the man, for I got up the
dance!   And as I 'm going away, I suppose I shall bear off
the sin with me into the wilderness."

"You 're going away?" repeated Mrs. Wade in more
genuine concern.

"Not for long," returned Brooks laughingly.   "I came
here to look up a mill site, and I 've found it.   Meantime
I think I 've opened their eyes."

"You have opened mine," said the widow with timid
frankness.

They were soft pretty eyes when opened, in spite of
their heavy red lids, and Mr. Brooks thought that Santa
Ana would be no worse if they remained open.   Possibly
he looked it, for Mrs. Wade said hurriedly, "I mean — that

is — I 've been thinking that life need n't *always* be as gloomy as we make it here. And even *here*, you know, Mr. Brooks, we have six months' sunshine — though we always forget it in the rainy season."

"That 's so," said Brooks cheerfully. "I once lost a heap of money through my own foolishness, and I 've managed to forget it, and I even reckon to get it back again out of Santa Ana if my mill speculation holds good. So good-by, Mrs. Wade — but not for long." He shook her hand frankly and departed, leaving the widow conscious of a certain sympathetic confidence and a little grateful for — she knew not what.

This feeling remained with her most of the afternoon, and even imparted a certain gayety to her spirits, to the extent of causing her to hum softly to herself; the air being oddly enough the Julien Waltz. And when, later in the day, the shadows were closing in with the rain, word was brought to her that a stranger wished to see her in the sitting-room, she carried a less mournful mind to this function of her existence. For Mrs. Wade was accustomed to give audience to traveling agents, tradesmen, working-hands, and servants, as chatelaine of her ranch, and the occasion was not novel. Yet, on entering the room, which she used partly as an office, she found some difficulty in classifying the stranger, who at first glance reminded her of the tramping miner she had seen that night from her window. He was rather incongruously dressed, some articles of his apparel being finer than others; he wore a diamond pin in a scarf folded over a rough "hickory" shirt; his light trousers were tucked in common mining boots that bore stains of travel and a suggestion that he had slept in his clothes. What she could see of his unshaven face in that uncertain light expressed a kind of dogged concentration, overlaid by an assumption of ease. He got up as she came in, and with a slight "How do, ma'am," shut the door behind her, and glanced furtively around the room.

"What I've got to say to ye, Mrs. Wade, — as I reckon you be, — is strictly private and confidential! Why, ye 'll see afore I get through. But I thought I might just as well caution ye agin our being disturbed."

Overcoming a slight instinct of repulsion, Mrs. Wade returned, "You can speak to me here; no one will interrupt you — unless I call them," she added with a little feminine caution.

"And I reckon ye won't do that," he said with a grim smile. "You are the widow o' Pulaski Wade, late o' Heavy Tree Hill, I reckon?"

"I am," said Mrs. Wade.

"And your husband 's buried up thar in the graveyard, with a monument over him setting forth his virtues ez a Christian and a square man and a high-minded citizen? And that he was foully murdered by highwaymen?"

"Yes," said Mrs. Wade, "that is the inscription."

"Well, ma'am, a bigger pack o' lies never was cut on stone!"

Mrs. Wade rose, half in indignation, half in terror.

"Keep your sittin'," said the stranger, with a warning wave of his hand. "Wait till I 'm through, and then you call in the hull State o' Californy, ef ye want."

The stranger's manner was so doggedly confident that Mrs. Wade sank back tremblingly in her chair. The man put his slouch hat on his knee, twirled it round once or twice, and then said with the same stubborn deliberation: —

"The highwayman in that business was your husband — Pulaski Wade — and his gang, and he was killed by one o' the men he was robbin'. Ye see, ma'am, it used to be your husband's little game to rope in three or four strangers in a poker deal at Spanish Jim's saloon — I see you 've heard o' the place," he interpolated as Mrs. Wade drew

back suddenly — "and when he could n't clean 'em out in
that way, or they showed a little more money than they
played, he 'd lay for 'em with his gang in a lone part of
the trail, and go through them like any road agent. That 's
what he did that night — and that 's how he got killed."

"How do you know this?" said Mrs. Wade, with quivering lips.

"I was one o' the men he went through before he was
killed. And I 'd hev got my money back, but the rest o'
the gang came up, and I got away jest in time to save my
life and nothin' else. Ye might remember thar was one
man got away and giv' the alarm, but he was goin' on to
the States by the overland coach that night and could n't
stay to be a witness. *I* was that man. I had paid my
passage through, and I could n't lose *that* too with my
other money, so I went."

Mrs. Wade sat stunned. She remembered the missing
witness, and how she had longed to see the man who was
last with her husband; she remembered Spanish Jim's
saloon — his well-known haunt; his frequent and unaccountable absences, the sudden influx of money which he
always said he had won at cards; the diamond ring he had
given her as the result of "a bet;" the forgotten recurrence
of other robberies by a secret masked gang; a hundred other
things that had worried her, instinctively, vaguely. She
knew now, too, the meaning of the unrest that had driven
her from Heavy Tree Hill — the strange unformulated fears
that had haunted her even here. Yet, with all this she
felt, too, her present weakness — knew that this man had
taken her at a disadvantage, that she ought to indignantly
assert herself, deny everything, demand proof, and brand
him a slanderer!

"How did — you — know it was my husband?" she
stammered.

"His mask fell off in the fight; you know another mask

was found — it was *his*. I saw him as plainly as I see him
there!" he pointed to a daguerreotype of her husband which
stood upon her desk.

Mrs. Wade could only stare vacantly, hopelessly. After
a pause the man continued in a less aggressive manner and
more confidential tone, which, however, only increased her
terror. "I ain't sayin' that *you* knowed anything about
this, ma'am, and whatever other folks might say when *they*
know of it, I 'll allers say that you did n't."

"What, then, did you come here for?" said the widow
desperately.

"What do I come here for?" repeated the man grimly,
looking around the room; "what did I come to this yer
comfortable home — this yer big ranch and to a rich woman
like yourself for? Well, Mrs. Wade, I come to get the
six hundred dollars your husband robbed me of, that 's all!
I ain't askin' more! I ain't askin' interest! I ain't askin'
compensation for havin' to run for my life — and," again
looking grimly round the walls, "I ain't askin' more than
you will give — or is my rights."

"But this house never was his; it was my father's,"
gasped Mrs. Wade; "you have no right" —

"Mebbe 'yes' and mebbe 'no,' Mrs. Wade," interrupted the man, with a wave of his hat; "but how about
them two checks to bearer for two hundred dollars each
found among your husband's effects, and collected by your
lawyer for you — *my checks*, Mrs. Wade?"

A wave of dreadful recollection overwhelmed her. She
remembered the checks found upon her husband's body,
known only to her and her lawyer, believed to be gambling
gains, and collected at once under his legal advice. Yet
she made one more desperate effort in spite of the instinct
that told her he was speaking the truth.

"But you shall have to prove it — before witnesses."

"Do you *want* me to prove it before witnesses?" said

the man, coming nearer her. "Do you want to take my word and keep it between ourselves, or do you want to call in your superintendent and his men, and all Santy Any, to hear me prove your husband was a highwayman, thief, and murderer? Do you want to knock over that monument on Heavy Tree Hill, and upset your standing here among the deacons and elders? Do you want to do all this and be forced, even by your neighbors, to pay me in the end, as you will? Ef you do, call in your witnesses, now, and let's have it over. Mebbe it would look better ef I got the money out of *your friends* than ye — a woman! P'raps you're right!"

He made a step towards the door, but she stopped him.

"No! no! wait! It's a large sum — I have n't it with me," she stammered, thoroughly beaten.

"Ye kin get it."

"Give me time!" she implored. "Look! I'll give you a hundred down now, — all I have here, — the rest another time!" She nervously opened a drawer of her desk and taking out a buckskin bag of gold thrust it in his hand. "There! go away now!" She lifted her thin hands despairingly to her head. "Go! do!"

The man seemed struck by her manner. "I don't want to be hard on a woman," he said slowly. "I'll go now and come back again at nine to-night. You can git the money, or what's as good, a check to bearer, by then. And ef ye'll take my advice, you won't ask no advice from others, ef you want to keep your secret. Just now it's safe with me; I'm a square man, ef I seem to be a hard one." He made a gesture as if to take her hand, but as she drew shrinkingly away, he changed it to an awkward bow, and the next moment was gone.

She started to her feet, but the unwonted strain upon her nerves and frail body had been greater than she knew.

She made a step forward, felt the room whirl round her and then seem to collapse beneath her feet, and, clutching at her chair, sank back into it, fainting.

How long she lay there she never knew. She was at last conscious of some one bending over her, and a voice — the voice of Mr. Brooks — in her ear, saying, "I beg your pardon; you seem ill. Shall I call some one?"

"No!" she gasped, quickly recovering herself with an effort, and staring round her. "Where is — when did you come in?"

"Only this moment. I was leaving to-night, sooner than I expected, and thought I'd say good-by. They told me that you had been engaged with a stranger, but he had just gone. I beg your pardon — I see you are ill. I won't detain you any longer."

"No! no! don't go! I am better — better," she said feverishly. As she glanced at his strong and sympathetic face a wild idea seized her. He was a stranger here, an alien to these people, like herself. The advice that she dare not seek from others, from her half-estranged religious friends, from even her superintendent and his wife, dare she ask from him? Perhaps he saw this frightened doubt, this imploring appeal, in her eyes, for he said gently, "Is it anything I can do for you?"

"Yes," she said, with the sudden desperation of weakness; "I want you to keep a secret."

"Yours? — yes!" he said promptly.

Whereat poor Mrs. Wade instantly burst into tears. Then, amidst her sobs, she told him of the stranger's visit, of his terrible accusations, of his demands, his expected return, and her own utter helplessness. To her terror, as she went on she saw a singular change in his kind face; he was following her with hard, eager intensity. She had half hoped, even through her fateful instincts, that he might have laughed, man-like, at her fears, or pooh-poohed the whole thing. But he did not. "You say he positively recognized your husband?" he repeated quickly.

"Yes, yes!" sobbed the widow, "and knew that daguerreotype!" she pointed to the desk.

Brooks turned quickly in that direction. Luckily his back was towards her, and she could not see his face, and the quick, startled look that came into his eyes. But when they again met hers it was gone, and even their eager intensity had changed to a gentle commiseration. "You have only his word for it, Mrs. Wade," he said gently, "and in telling your secret to another, you have shorn the rascal of half his power over you. And he knew it. Now, dismiss the matter from your mind and leave it all to me. I will be here a few minutes before nine — *and alone in this room.* Let your visitor be shown in here, and don't let us be disturbed. Don't be alarmed," he added with a faint twinkle in his eye, "there will be no fuss and no exposure!"

It lacked a few minutes of nine when Mr. Brooks was ushered into the sitting-room. As soon as he was alone he quietly examined the door and the windows, and having satisfied himself, took his seat in a chair casually placed behind the door. Presently he heard the sound of voices and a heavy footstep in the passage. He lightly felt his waistcoat pocket — it contained a pretty little weapon of power and precision, with a barrel scarcely two inches long.

The door opened, and the person outside entered the room. In an instant Brooks had shut the door and locked it behind him. The man turned fiercely, but was faced by Brooks quietly, with one finger calmly hooked in his waistcoat pocket. The man slightly recoiled from him — not as much from fear as from some vague stupefaction. "What's that for? What's your little game?" he said half contemptuously.

"No game at all," returned Brooks coolly. "You came here to sell a secret. I don't propose to have it given away first to any listener."

"*You* don't — who are *you?*"

"That's a queer question to ask of the man you are trying to personate — but I don't wonder! You're doing it d——d badly."

"Personate — *you?*" said the stranger, with staring eyes.

"Yes, *me*," said Brooks quietly. "I am the only man who escaped from the robbery that night at Heavy Tree Hill and who went home by the Overland Coach."

The stranger stared, but recovered himself with a coarse laugh. "Oh, well! we're on the same lay, it appears! Both after the widow — afore we show up her husband."

"Not exactly," said Brooks, with his eyes fixed intently on the stranger. "You are here to denounce a highwayman who is *dead* and escaped justice. I am here to denounce one who is *living!* — Stop! drop your hand; it's no use. You thought you had to deal only with a woman to-night, and your revolver is n't quite handy enough. There! down! — down! So! That 'll do."

"You can't prove it," said the man hoarsely.

"Fool! In your story to that woman you have given yourself away. There were but two travelers attacked by the highwayman. One was killed — I am the other. Where do *you* come in? What witness can you be — except as the highwayman that you are? Who is left to identify Wade but — his accomplice!"

The man's suddenly whitened face made his unshaven beard seem to bristle over his face like some wild animal's. "Well, ef you kalkilate to blow me, you 've got to blow Wade and his widder, too. Jest you remember that," he said whiningly.

"I 've thought of that," said Brooks coolly, "and I calculate that to prevent it is worth about that hundred dollars you got from that poor woman — and no more! Now, sit down at that table, and write as I dictate."

The man looked at him in wonder, but obeyed.

"Write," said Brooks, "'I hereby certify that my accusations against the late Pulaski Wade of Heavy Tree Hill are erroneous and groundless, and the result of mistaken identity, especially in regard to any complicity of his in the robbery of John Stubbs, deceased, and Henry Brooks, at Heavy Tree Hill, on the night of the 13th August, 1854.'"

The man looked up with a repulsive smile. "Who's the fool now, Cap'n? What's become of your hold on the widder, now?"

"Write!" said Brooks fiercely.

The sound of a pen hurriedly scratching paper followed this first outburst of the quiet Brooks.

"Sign it," said Brooks.

The man signed it.

"Now go," said Brooks, unlocking the door, "but remember, if you should ever be inclined to revisit Santa Ana, you will find *me* living here also."

The man slunk out of the door and into the passage like a wild animal returning to the night and darkness. Brooks took up the paper, rejoined Mrs. Wade in the parlor, and laid it before her.

"But," said the widow, trembling even in her joy, "do you — do you think he was *really* mistaken?"

"Positive," said Brooks coolly. "It's true it's a mistake that has cost you a hundred dollars, but there are some mistakes that are worth that to be kept quiet."

.   .   .   .

They were married a year later; but there is no record that in after years of conjugal relations with a weak, charming, but sometimes trying woman, Henry Brooks was ever tempted to tell her the whole truth of the robbery of Heavy Tree Hill.

THE MERMAID OF LIGHTHOUSE POINT

Some forty years ago, on the northern coast of California, near the Golden Gate, stood a lighthouse. Of a primitive class, since superseded by a building more in keeping with the growing magnitude of the adjacent port, it attracted little attention from the desolate shore, and, it was alleged, still less from the desolate sea beyond. A gray structure of timber, stone, and glass, it was buffeted and harried by the constant trade winds, baked by the unclouded six months' sun, lost for a few hours in the afternoon sea-fog, and laughed over by circling guillemots from the Farallones. It was kept by a recluse — a preoccupied man of scientific tastes, who, in shameless contrast to his fellow immigrants, had applied to the government for this scarcely lucrative position as a means of securing the seclusion he valued more than gold. Some believed that he was the victim of an early disappointment in love — a view charitably taken by those who also believed that the government would not have appointed "a crank" to a position of responsibility. Howbeit, he fulfilled his duties, and, with the assistance of an Indian, even cultivated a small patch of ground beside the lighthouse. His isolation was complete! There was little to attract wanderers here: the nearest mines were fifty miles away; the virgin forest on the mountains inland were penetrated only by sawmills and woodmen from the Bay settlements, equally remote. Although by the shore-line the lights of the great port were sometimes plainly visible, yet the solitude around him was peopled only by Indians, — a branch of the great northern tribe of "root-diggers," —

peaceful and simple in their habits, as yet undisturbed by
the white man, nor stirred into antagonism by aggression.
Civilization only touched him at stated intervals, and then
by the more expeditious sea from the government boat that
brought him supplies. But for his contiguity to the per-
petual turmoil of wind and sea, he might have passed a rest-
ful Arcadian life in his surroundings; for even his solitude
was sometimes haunted by this faint reminder of the great
port hard by that pulsated with an equal unrest. Nevertheless, the sands before his door and the rocks behind him
seemed to have been untrodden by any other white man's
foot since their upheaval from the ocean. It was true that
the little bay beside him was marked on the map as "Sir
Francis Drake's Bay," tradition having located it as the spot
where that ingenious pirate and empire-maker had once
landed his vessels and scraped the barnacles from his adven-
turous keels. But of this Edgar Pomfrey — or "Captain
Pomfrey," as he was called by virtue of his half-nautical
office — had thought little.

For the first six months he had thoroughly enjoyed his
seclusion. In the company of his books, of which he had
brought such a fair store that their shelves lined his snug
corners to the exclusion of more comfortable furniture, he
found his principal recreation. Even his unwonted manual
labor, the trimming of his lamp and cleaning of his reflec-
tors, and his personal housekeeping, in which his Indian
help at times assisted, he found a novel and interesting occupation. For outdoor exercise, a ramble on the sands, a
climb to the rocky upland, or a pull in the lighthouse boat,
amply sufficed him. "Crank" as he was supposed to be,
he was sane enough to guard against any of those early
lapses into barbarism which marked the lives of some solitary gold-miners. His own taste, as well as the duty of
his office, kept his person and habitation sweet and clean,
and his habits regular. Even the little cultivated patch of

ground on the lee side of the tower was symmetrical and
well ordered. Thus the outward light of Captain Pomfrey
shone forth over the wilderness of shore and wave, even
like his beacon, whatever his inward illumination may have
been.

It was a bright summer morning, remarkable even in the
monotonous excellence of the season, with a slight touch of
warmth which the invincible Northwest Trades had not yet
chilled. There was still a faint haze off the coast, as if last
night's fog had been caught in the quick sunshine, and the
shining sands were hot, but without the usual dazzling glare.
A faint perfume from a quaint lilac-colored beach-flower,
whose clustering heads dotted the sand like bits of blown
spume, took the place of that smell of the sea which the
odorless Pacific lacked. A few rocks, half a mile away,
lifted themselves above the ebb tide at varying heights as
they lay on the trough of the swell, were crested with foam
by a striking surge, or cleanly erased in the full sweep of
the sea. Beside, and partly upon one of the higher rocks,
a singular object was moving.

Pomfrey was interested but not startled. He had once
or twice seen seals disporting on these rocks, and on one
occasion a sea-lion, — an estray from the familiar rocks on
the other side of the Golden Gate. But he ceased work in
his garden patch, and coming to his house, exchanged his
hoe for a telescope. When he got the mystery in focus he
suddenly stopped and rubbed the object-glass with his handkerchief. But even when he applied the glass to his eye
for a second time, he could scarcely believe his eyesight.
For the object seemed to be a *woman*, the lower part of
her figure submerged in the sea, her long hair depending
over her shoulders and waist. There was nothing in her
attitude to suggest terror or that she was the victim of some
accident. She moved slowly and complacently with the
sea, and even — a more staggering suggestion —appeared

to be combing out the strands of her long hair with her fingers. With her body half concealed she might have been a mermaid!

He swept the foreshore and horizon with his glass; there was neither boat nor ship — nor anything that moved, except the long swell of the Pacific. She could have come only from the sea; for to reach the rocks by land she would have had to pass before the lighthouse, while the narrow strip of shore which curved northward beyond his range of view he knew was inhabited only by Indians. But the woman was unhesitatingly and appallingly *white*, and her hair light even to a golden gleam in the sunshine.

Pomfrey was a gentleman, and as such was amazed, dismayed, and cruelly embarrassed. If she was a simple bather from some vicinity hitherto unknown and unsuspected by him, it was clearly his business to shut up his glass and go back to his garden patch — although the propinquity of himself and the lighthouse must have been as plainly visible to her as she was to him. On the other hand, if she was the survivor of some wreck and in distress — or, as he even fancied from her reckless manner, bereft of her senses, his duty to rescue her was equally clear. In his dilemma he determined upon a compromise and ran to his boat. He would pull out to sea, pass between the rocks and the curving sand-spit, and examine the sands and sea more closely for signs of wreckage, or some overlooked waiting boat near the shore. He would be within hail if she needed him, or she could escape to her boat if she had one.

In another moment his boat was lifting on the swell towards the rocks. He pulled quickly, occasionally turning to note that the strange figure, whose movements were quite discernible to the naked eye, was still there, but gazing more earnestly towards the nearest shore for any sign of life or occupation. In ten minutes he had reached the curve where the trend opened northward, and the long line of shore stretched before him. He swept it eagerly with a single searching glance. Sea and shore were empty. He turned quickly to the rock, scarcely a hundred yards on his beam. It was empty, too! Forgetting his previous scruples, he pulled directly for it until his keel grated on its submerged base. There was nothing there but the rock, slippery with the yellow-green slime of seaweed and kelp — neither trace nor sign of the figure that had occupied it a moment ago. He pulled around it; there was no cleft or hiding-place. For an instant his heart leaped at the sight of something white, caught in a jagged tooth of the outlying reef, but it was only the bleached fragment of a bamboo orange-crate, cast from the deck of some South Sea trader, such as often strewed the beach. He lay off the rock, keeping way in the swell, and scrutinizing the glittering sea. At last he pulled back to the lighthouse, perplexed and discomfited.

Was it simply a sporting seal, transformed by some trick of his vision? But he had seen it through his glass, and now remembered such details as the face and features framed in their contour of golden hair, and believed he could even have identified them. He examined the rock again with his glass, and was surprised to see how clearly it was outlined now in its barren loneliness. Yet he must have been mistaken. His scientific and accurate mind allowed of no errant fancy, and he had always sneered at the marvelous as the result of hasty or superficial observation. He was a little worried at this lapse of his healthy accuracy, — fearing that it might be the result of his seclusion and loneliness, — akin to the visions of the recluse and solitary. It was strange, too, that it should take the shape of a woman; for Edgar Pomfrey had a story — the usual old and foolish one.

Then his thoughts took a lighter phase, and he turned to the memory of his books, and finally to the books themselves. From a shelf he picked out a volume of old voyages, and turned to a remembered passage: "In other seas doe abound marvells soche as Sea Spyders of the bigness of a pinnace, the wich they have been known to attack and destroy; Sea Vypers which reach to the top of a goodly maste, whereby they are able to draw marinners from the rigging by the suction of their breathes; and Devill Fyshe, which vomit fire by night, which makyth the sea to shine prodigiously, and mermaydes. They are half fyshe and half mayde of grate Beauty, and have been seen of divers godly and creditable witnesses swymming beside rocks, hidden to their waist in the sea, combing of their hayres, to the help of whych they carry a small mirrore of the bigness of their fingers." Pomfrey laid the book aside with a faint smile. To even this credulity he might come!

Nevertheless, he used the telescope again that day. But there was no repetition of the incident, and he was forced to believe that he had been the victim of some extraordinary illusion. The next morning, however, with his calmer judgment doubts began to visit him. There was no one of whom he could make inquiries but his Indian helper, and their conversation had usually been restricted to the language of signs or the use of a few words he had picked up. He contrived, however, to ask if there was a "waugee" (white) woman in the neighborhood. The Indian shook his head in surprise. There was no "waugee" nearer than the remote mountain-ridge to which he pointed. Pomfrey was obliged to be content with this. Even had his vocabulary been larger, he would as soon have thought of revealing the embarrassing secret of this woman, whom he believed to be of his own race, to a mere barbarian as he would of asking him to verify his own impressions by allowing him to look at her that morning. The next day, however, something happened which forced him to resume his inquiries. He was rowing around the curving spot

when he saw a number of black objects on the northern
sands moving in and out of the surf, which he presently
made out as Indians. A nearer approach satisfied him that
they were wading squaws and children gathering seaweed
and shells. He would have pushed his acquaintance still
nearer, but as his boat rounded the point, with one accord
they all scuttled away like frightened sandpipers. Pomfrey,
on his return, asked his Indian retainer if they could swim.
"Oh, yes!" "As far as the rock?" "Yes." Yet Pomfrey was not satisfied. The color of his strange apparition
remained unaccounted for, and it was not that of an Indian
woman.

Trifling events linger long in a monotonous existence,
and it was nearly a week before Pomfrey gave up his daily
telescopic inspection of the rock. Then he fell back upon
his books again, and, oddly enough, upon another volume
of voyages, and so chanced upon the account of Sir Francis
Drake's occupation of the bay before him. He had always
thought it strange that the great adventurer had left no
trace or sign of his sojourn there; still stranger that he
should have overlooked the presence of gold, known even
to the Indians themselves, and have lost a discovery far
beyond his wildest dreams and a treasure to which the car-
goes of those Philippine galleons he had more or less successfully intercepted were trifles. Had the restless explorer
been content to pace those dreary sands during three weeks
of inactivity, with no thought of penetrating the inland for-
ests behind the range, or of even entering the nobler bay
beyond? Or was the location of the spot a mere tradition
as wild and unsupported as the "marvells" of the other
volume? Pomfrey had the skepticism of the scientific,
inquiring mind.

Two weeks had passed and he was returning from a long
climb inland, when he stopped to rest in his descent to the
sea. The panorama of the shore was before him, from its

uttermost limit to the lighthouse on the northern point. The sun was still one hour high, it would take him about that time to reach home. But from this coign of vantage he could see — what he had not before observed — that what he had always believed was a little cove on the northern shore was really the estuary of a small stream which rose near him and eventually descended into the ocean at that point. He could also see that beside it was a long, low erection of some kind, covered with thatched brush, which looked like a "barrow," yet showed signs of habitation in the slight smoke that rose from it and drifted inland. It was not far out of his way, and he resolved to return in that direction. On his way down he once or twice heard the barking of an Indian dog, and knew that he must be in the vicinity of an encampment. A camp-fire, with the ashes yet warm, proved that he was on the trail of one of the nomadic tribes, but the declining sun warned him to hasten home to his duty. When he at last reached the estuary, he found that the building beside it was little else than a long hut, whose thatched and mud-plastered mound-like roof gave it the appearance of a cave. Its single opening and entrance abutted on the water's edge, and the smoke he had noticed rolled through this entrance from a smouldering fire within. Pomfrey had little difficulty in recognizing the purpose of this strange structure from the accounts he had heard from "loggers" of the Indian customs. The cave was a "sweat-house" — a calorific chamber in which the Indians closely shut themselves, naked, with a "smudge" or smouldering fire of leaves, until, perspiring and half suffocated, they rushed from the entrance and threw themselves into the water before it. The still smouldering fire told him that the house had been used that morning, and he made no doubt that the Indians were encamped near by. He would have liked to pursue his researches further, but he found he had already trespassed

upon his remaining time, and he turned somewhat abruptly
away, — so abruptly, in fact, that a figure, which had evidently been cautiously following him at a distance, had not
time to get away. His heart leaped with astonishment.
It was the woman he had seen on the rock.

Although her native dress now only disclosed her head
and hands, there was no doubt about her color, and it was
distinctly white, save for the tanning of exposure and a
slight red ochre marking on her low forehead. And her
hair, long and unkempt as it was, showed that he had not
erred in his first impression of it. It was a tawny flaxen,
with fainter bleachings where the sun had touched it most.
Her eyes were of a clear Northern blue. Her dress, which
was quite distinctive in that it was neither the cast-off
finery of civilization nor the cheap "government" flannels
and calicoes usually worn by the Californian tribes, was
purely native, and of fringed deerskin, and consisted of a
long, loose skirt and leggings worked with bright feathers
and colored shells. A necklace, also of shells and fancy
pebbles, hung round her neck. She seemed to be a fully
developed woman, in spite of the girlishness of her flow-
ing hair, and notwithstanding the shapeless length of her
gaberdine-like garment, taller than the ordinary squaw.

Pomfrey saw all this in a single flash of perception, for
the next instant she was gone, disappearing behind the
sweat-house. He ran after her, catching sight of her again,
half doubled up, in the characteristic Indian trot, dodging
around rocks and low bushes as she fled along the banks of
the stream. But for her distinguishing hair, she looked in
her flight like an ordinary frightened squaw. This, which
gave a sense of unmanliness and ridicule to his own pursuit
of her, with the fact that his hour of duty was drawing
near and he was still far from the lighthouse, checked him
in full career, and he turned regretfully away. He had
called after her at first, and she had not heeded him.

What he would have said to her he did not know. He
hastened home discomfited, even embarrassed — yet excited to a degree he had not deemed possible in himself.

During the morning his thoughts were full of her. Theory after theory for her strange existence there he examined
and dismissed. His first thought, that she was a white
woman — some settler's wife — masquerading in Indian
garb, he abandoned when he saw her moving; no white
woman could imitate that Indian trot, nor would remember
to attempt it if she were frightened. The idea that she
was a captive white, held by the Indians, became ridiculous
when he thought of the nearness of civilization and the
peaceful, timid character of the "digger" tribes. That she
was some unfortunate demented creature who had escaped
from her keeper and wandered into the wilderness, a glance
at her clear, frank, intelligent, curious eyes had contradicted.
There was but one theory left — the most sensible and practical one — that she was the offspring of some white man
and Indian squaw. Yet this he found, oddly enough, the
least palatable to his fancy. And the few half-breeds he
had seen were not at all like her.

The next morning he had recourse to his Indian retainer,
"Jim." With infinite difficulty, protraction, and not a little
embarrassment, he finally made him understand that he had
seen a "white squaw" near the "sweat-house," and that
he wanted to know more about her. With equal difficulty
Jim finally recognized the fact of the existence of such a
person, but immediately afterwards shook his head in an
emphatic negation. With greater difficulty and greater
mortification Pomfrey presently ascertained that Jim's
negative referred to a supposed abduction of the woman
which he understood that his employer seriously contemplated. But he also learned that she was a real Indian,
and that there were three or four others like her, male and
female, in that vicinity; that from a "skeena mowitch"

(little baby) they were all like that, and that their parents were of the same color, but never a white or "waugee" man or woman among them; that they were looked upon as a distinct and superior caste of Indians, and enjoyed certain privileges with the tribe; that they superstitiously avoided white men, of whom they had the greatest fear, and that they were protected in this by the other Indians; that it was marvelous and almost beyond belief that Pomfrey had been able to see one, for no other white man had, or was even aware of their existence.

How much of this he actually understood, how much of it was lying and due to Jim's belief that he wished to abduct the fair stranger, Pomfrey was unable to determine. There was enough, however, to excite his curiosity strongly and occupy his mind to the exclusion of his books — save one. Among his smaller volumes he had found a travel book of the "Chinook Jargon," with a lexicon of many of the words commonly used by the Northern Pacific tribes. An hour or two's trial with the astonished Jim gave him an increased vocabulary and a new occupation. Each day the incongruous pair took a lesson from the lexicon. In a week Pomfrey felt he would be able to accost the mysterious stranger. But he did not again surprise her in any of his rambles, or even in a later visit to the sweat-house. He had learned from Jim that the house was only used by the "bucks," or males, and that her appearance there had been accidental. He recalled that he had had the impression that she had been stealthily following him, and the recollection gave him a pleasure he could not account for. But an incident presently occurred which gave him a new idea of her relations towards him.

The difficulty of making Jim understand had hitherto prevented Pomfrey from intrusting him with the care of the lantern; but with the aid of the lexicon he had been able to make him comprehend its working, and under

Pomfrey's personal guidance the Indian had once or twice lit the lamp and set its machinery in motion. It remained for him only to test Jim's unaided capacity, in case of his own absence or illness. It happened to be a warm, beautiful sunset, when the afternoon fog had for once delayed its invasion of the shore-line, that he left the lighthouse to Jim's undivided care, and reclining on a sand-dune still warm from the sun, lazily watched the result of Jim's first essay. As the twilight deepened, and the first flash of the lantern strove with the dying glories of the sun, Pomfrey presently became aware that he was not the only watcher. A little gray figure creeping on all fours suddenly glided out of the shadow of another sand-dune and then halted, falling back on its knees, gazing fixedly at the growing light. It was the woman he had seen. She was not a dozen yards away, and in her eagerness and utter absorption in the light had evidently overlooked him. He could see her face distinctly, her lips parted half in wonder, half with the breathless absorption of a devotee. A faint sense of disappointment came over him. It was not *he* she was watching, but the light! As it swelled out over the darkening gray sand she turned as if to watch its effect around her, and caught sight of Pomfrey. With a little startled cry — the first she had uttered — she darted away. He did not follow. A moment before, when he first saw her, an Indian salutation which he had learned from Jim had risen to his lips, but in the odd feeling which her fascination of the light had caused him he had not spoken. He watched her bent figure scuttling away like some frightened animal, with a critical consciousness that she was really scarce human, and went back to the lighthouse. He would not run after her again! Yet that evening he continued to think of her, and recalled her voice, which struck him now as having been at once melodious and childlike, and wished he had at least spoken, and perhaps elicited a reply.

He did not, however, haunt the sweat-house near the river again. Yet he still continued his lessons with Jim, and in this way, perhaps, although quite unpremeditatedly, enlisted a humble ally. A week passed in which he had not alluded to her, when one morning, as he was returning from a row, Jim met him mysteriously on the beach.

"S'pose him come slow, slow," said Jim gravely, airing his newly acquired English; "make no noise — plenty catchee Indian maiden." The last epithet was the polite lexicon equivalent of squaw.

Pomfrey, not entirely satisfied in his mind, nevertheless softly followed the noiselessly gliding Jim to the lighthouse. Here Jim cautiously opened the door, motioning Pomfrey to enter.

The base of the tower was composed of two living rooms, a storeroom, and oil-tank. As Pomfrey entered, Jim closed the door softly behind him. The abrupt transition from the glare of the sands and sun to the semi-darkness of the storeroom at first prevented him from seeing anything, but he was instantly distracted by a scurrying flutter and wild beating of the walls, as of a caged bird. In another moment he could make out the fair stranger, quivering with excitement, passionately dashing at the barred window, the walls, the locked door, and circling around the room in her desperate attempt to find an egress, like a captured seagull. Amazed, mystified, indignant with Jim, himself, and even his unfortunate captive, Pomfrey called to her in Chinook to stop, and going to the door, flung it wide open. She darted by him, raising her soft blue eyes for an instant in a swift, sidelong glance of half appeal, half-frightened admiration, and rushed out into the open. But here, to his surprise, she did not run away. On the contrary, she drew herself up with a dignity that seemed to increase her height, and walked majestically towards Jim, who, at her unexpected exit, had suddenly thrown himself upon the sand,

Gazing fixedly at the growing light

in utterly abject terror and supplication. She approached
him slowly, with one small hand uplifted in a menacing
gesture. The man writhed and squirmed before her. Then
she turned, caught sight of Pomfrey standing in the doorway, and walked quietly away. Amazed, yet gratified with
this new assertion of herself, Pomfrey respectfully, but
alas! incautiously, called after her. In an instant, at the
sound of his voice, she dropped again into her slouching
Indian trot and glided away over the sandhills.

Pomfrey did not add any reproof of his own to the discomfiture of his Indian retainer. Neither did he attempt
to inquire the secret of this savage girl's power over him.
It was evident he had spoken truly when he told his master
that she was of a superior caste. Pomfrey recalled her erect
and indignant figure standing over the prostrate Jim, and
was again perplexed and disappointed at her sudden lapse
into the timid savage at the sound of his voice. Would
not this well-meant but miserable trick of Jim's have the
effect of increasing her unreasoning animal-like distrust of
him? A few days later brought an unexpected answer to
his question.

It was the hottest hour of the day. He had been fish-
ing off the reef of rocks where he had first seen her, and
had taken in his line and was leisurely pulling for the lighthouse. Suddenly a little musical cry not unlike a bird's
struck his ear. He lay on his oars and listened. It was
repeated; but this time it was unmistakably recognizable
as the voice of the Indian girl, although he had heard it
but once. He turned eagerly to the rock, but it was
empty; he pulled around it, but saw nothing. He looked
towards the shore, and swung his boat in that direction,
when again the cry was repeated with the faintest quaver of
a laugh, apparently on the level of the sea before him. For
the first time he looked down, and there on the crest of a
wave not a dozen yards ahead danced the yellow hair and

laughing eyes of the girl. The frightened gravity of her
look was gone, lost in the flash of her white teeth and quivering dimples as her dripping face rose above the sea. When
their eyes met she dived again, but quickly reappeared on
the other bow, swimming with lazy, easy strokes, her smiling head thrown back over her white shoulder, as if luring
him to a race. If her smile was a revelation to him, still
more so was this first touch of feminine coquetry in her attitude. He pulled eagerly towards her; with a few long
overhand strokes she kept her distance, or, if he approached
too near, she dived like a loon, coming up astern of him
with the same childlike, mocking cry. In vain he pursued
her, calling her to stop in her own tongue, and laughingly
protested; she easily avoided his boat at every turn. Suddenly, when they were nearly abreast of the river estuary,
she rose in the water, and, waving her little hands with a
gesture of farewell, turned, and curving her back like a dol-
phin, leaped into the surging swell of the estuary bar and
was lost in its foam. It would have been madness for him
to have attempted to follow in his boat, and he saw that
she knew it. He waited until her yellow crest appeared in
the smoother water of the river, and then rowed back. In
his excitement and preoccupation he had quite forgotten his
long exposure to the sun during his active exercise, and
that he was poorly equipped for the cold sea-fog which the
heat had brought in earlier, and which now was quietly
obliterating sea and shore. This made his progress slower
and more difficult, and by the time he had reached the
lighthouse he was chilled to the bone.

The next morning he woke with a dull headache and
great weariness, and it was with considerable difficulty that
he could attend to his duties. At nightfall, feeling worse,
he determined to transfer the care of the light to Jim, but
was amazed to find that he had disappeared, and what was
more ominous, a bottle of spirits which Pomfrey had taken

from his locker the night before had disappeared too. Like
all Indians, Jim's rudimentary knowledge of civilization
included "fire-water;" he evidently had been tempted, had
fallen, and was too ashamed or too drunk to face his master.
Pomfrey, however, managed to get the light in order and
working, and then, he scarcely knew how, betook himself
to bed in a state of high fever. He turned from side to
side racked by pain, with burning lips and pulses. Strange
fancies beset him; he had noticed when he lit his light that
a strange sail was looming off the estuary — a place where
no sail had ever been seen or should be — and was relieved
that the lighting of the tower might show the reckless or
ignorant mariner his real bearings for the "Gate." At
times he had heard voices above the familiar song of the
surf, and tried to rise from his bed, but could not. Sometimes these voices were strange, outlandish, dissonant, in
his own language, yet only partly intelligible; but through
them always rang a single voice, musical, familiar, yet of a
tongue not his own — hers! And then, out of his delirium
— for such it proved afterwards to be — came a strange
vision. He thought that he had just lit the light when,
from some strange and unaccountable reason, it suddenly
became dim and defied all his efforts to revive it. To add
to his discomfiture, he could see quite plainly through the
lantern a strange-looking vessel standing in from the sea.
She was so clearly out of her course for the Gate that he
knew she had not seen the light, and his limbs trembled
with shame and terror as he tried in vain to rekindle the
dying light. Yet to his surprise the strange ship kept
steadily on, passing the dangerous reef of rocks, until she
was actually in the waters of the bay. But stranger than
all, swimming beneath her bows was the golden head and
laughing face of the Indian girl, even as he had seen it the
day before. A strange revulsion of feeling overtook him.
Believing that she was luring the ship to its destruction,

he ran out on the beach and strove to hail the vessel and warn it of its impending doom.   But he could not speak — no sound came from his lips.   And now his attention was absorbed by the ship itself.   High-bowed and pooped, and curved like the crescent moon, it was the strangest craft that he had ever seen.   Even as he gazed it glided on nearer and nearer, and at last beached itself noiselessly on the sands before his own feet.   A score of figures as bizarre and outlandish as the ship itself now thronged its high fore- castle — really a castle in shape and warlike purpose — and leaped from its ports.   The common seamen were nearly naked to the waist; the officers looked more like soldiers than sailors.   What struck him more strangely was that they were one and all seemingly unconscious of the exist- ence of the lighthouse, sauntering up and down carelessly, as if on some uninhabited strand, and even talking — so far as he could understand their old bookish dialect — as if in some hitherto undiscovered land.   Their ignorance of the geography of the whole coast, and even of the sea from which they came, actually aroused his critical indignation; their coarse and stupid allusions to the fair Indian swimmer as the "mermaid" that they had seen upon their bow made him more furious still.   Yet he was helpless to express his contemptuous anger, or even make them conscious of his presence.   Then an interval of incoherency and utter blank- ness followed.   When he again took up the thread of his fancy the ship seemed to be lying on her beam ends on the sand; the strange arrangement of her upper deck and top- hamper, more like a dwelling than any ship he had ever seen, was fully exposed to view, while the seamen seemed to be at work with the rudest contrivances, calking and scraping her barnacled sides.   He saw that phantom crew, when not working, at wassail and festivity; heard the shouts of drunken roisterers; saw the placing of a guard around some of the most uncontrollable, and later detected

the stealthy escape of half a dozen sailors inland, amidst
the fruitless volley fired upon them from obsolete blunder-
busses. Then his strange vision transported him inland,
where he saw these seamen following some Indian women.
Suddenly one of them turned and ran frenziedly towards
him as if seeking succor, closely pursued by one of the sailors. Pomfrey strove to reach her, struggled violently with
the fearful apathy that seemed to hold his limbs, and then,
as she uttered at last a little musical cry, burst his bonds
and — awoke!

As consciousness slowly struggled back to him, he could
see the bare wooden-like walls of his sleeping-room, the
locker, the one window bright with sunlight, the open door
of the tank-room, and the little staircase to the tower.
There was a strange smoky and herb-like smell in the room.
He made an effort to rise, but as he did so a small sunburnt hand was laid gently yet restrainingly upon his
shoulder, and he heard the same musical cry as before, but
this time modulated to a girlish laugh. He raised his head
faintly. Half squatting, half kneeling by his bed, was the
yellow-haired stranger.

With the recollection of his vision still perplexing him,
he said in a weak voice, "Who are you?"

Her blue eyes met his own with quick intelligence and
no trace of her former timidity. A soft, caressing light
had taken its place. Pointing with her finger to her breast
in a childlike gesture, she said, "Me — Olooya."

"Olooya!" He remembered suddenly that Jim had
always used that word in speaking of her, but until then
he had always thought it was some Indian term for her
distinct class.

"Olooya," he repeated. Then, with difficulty attempting to use her own tongue, he asked, "When did you come
here?"

"Last night," she answered in the same tongue. "There

was no witch-fire there," she continued, pointing to the tower; "when it came not, Olooya came! Olooya found white chief sick and alone. White chief could not get up! Olooya lit witch-fire for him."

"You?" he repeated in astonishment. "I lit it myself."

She looked at him pityingly, as if still recognizing his delirium, and shook her head. "White chief was sick — how can know? Olooya made witch-fire."

He cast a hurried glance at his watch hanging on the wall beside him. It had *run down*, although he had wound it the last thing before going to bed. He had evidently been lying there helpless beyond the twenty-four hours!

He groaned and turned to rise, but she gently forced him down again, and gave him some herbal infusion, in which he recognized the taste of the Yerba Buena vine which grew by the river. Then she made him comprehend in her own tongue that Jim had been decoyed, while drunk, aboard a certain schooner lying off the shore at a spot where she had seen some men digging in the sands. She had not gone there, for she was afraid of the bad men, and a slight return of her former terror came into her changeful eyes. She knew how to light the witch-light; she reminded him she had been in the tower before.

"You have saved my light, and perhaps my life," he said weakly, taking her hand.

Possibly she did not understand him, for her only answer was a vague smile. But the next instant she started up, listening intently, and then with a frightened cry drew away her hand and suddenly dashed out of the building. In the midst of his amazement the door was darkened by a figure — a stranger dressed like an ordinary miner. Pausing a moment to look after the flying Olooya, the man turned and glanced around the room, and then with a coarse, familiar smile approached Pomfrey.

"Hope I ain't disturbin' ye, but I allowed I 'd just be neighborly and drop in — seein' as this is gov'nment property, and me and my pardners, as American citizens and tax-payers, helps to support it. We 're coastin' from Trinidad down here and prospectin' along the beach for gold in the sand. Ye seem to hev a mighty soft berth of it here — nothing to do — and lots of purty half-breeds hangin' round!"

The man's effrontery was too much for Pomfrey's self-control, weakened by illness. "It *is* government property," he answered hotly, "and you have no more right to intrude upon it than you have to decoy away my servant, a government employee, during my illness, and jeopardize that property."

The unexpectedness of this attack, and the sudden revelation of the fact of Pomfrey's illness in his flushed face and hollow voice, apparently frightened and confused the stranger. He stammered a surly excuse, backed out of the doorway, and disappeared. An hour later Jim appeared, crestfallen, remorseful, and extravagantly penitent. Pomfrey was too weak for reproaches or inquiry, and he was thinking only of Olooya.

She did not return. His recovery in that keen air, aided, as he sometimes thought, by the herbs she had given him, was almost as rapid as his illness. The miners did not again intrude upon the lighthouse nor trouble his seclusion. When he was able to sun himself on the sands, he could see them in the distance at work on the beach. He reflected that she would not come back while they were there, and was reconciled. But one morning Jim appeared, awkward and embarrassed, leading another Indian, whom he introduced as Olooya's brother. Pomfrey's suspicions were aroused. Except that the stranger had something of the girl's superiority of manner, there was no likeness whatever to his fair-haired acquaintance. But a fury of indignation was added to his suspicions when he learned the amazing purport of their visit.   It was nothing less than an offer from the alleged brother to *sell* his sister to Pomfrey for forty dollars and a jug of whiskey!   Unfortunately, Pomfrey's temper once more got the better of his judgment. With a scathing exposition of the laws under which the Indian and white man equally lived, and the legal punishment of kidnapping, he swept what he believed was the impostor from his presence.   He was scarcely alone again before he remembered that his imprudence might affect the girl's future access to him, but it was too late now.

Still he clung to the belief that he should see her when the prospectors had departed, and he hailed with delight the breaking up of the camp near the "sweat-house" and the disappearance of the schooner.   It seemed that their gold-seeking was unsuccessful; but Pomfrey was struck, on visiting the locality, to find that in their excavations in the sand at the estuary they had uncovered the decaying timbers of a ship's small boat of some ancient and obsolete construction.   This made him think of his strange dream, with a vague sense of warning which he could not shake off, and on his return to the lighthouse he took from his shelves a copy of the old voyages to see how far his fancy had been affected by his reading.   In the account of Drake's visit to the coast he found a footnote which he had overlooked before, and which ran as follows: "The Admiral seems to have lost several of his crew by desertion, who were supposed to have perished miserably by starvation in the inhospitable interior or by the hands of savages.   But later voyagers have suggested that the deserters married Indian wives, and there is a legend that a hundred years later a singular race of half-breeds, bearing unmistakable Anglo-Saxon characteristics, was found in that locality."   Pomfrey fell into a reverie of strange hypotheses and fancies.   He resolved that, when he again saw Olooya, he would question her; her

terror of these men might be simply racial or some heredi-
tary transmission.

But his intention was never fulfilled. For when days
and weeks had elapsed, and he had vainly haunted the river
estuary and the rocky reef before the lighthouse without a
sign of her, he overcame his pride sufficiently to question
Jim. The man looked at him with dull astonishment.

"Olooya gone," he said.

"Gone! — where?"

The Indian made a gesture to seaward which seemed to
encompass the whole Pacific.

"How? With whom?" repeated his angry yet half-
frightened master.

"With white man in ship. You say you no want Olooya
— forty dollars too much. White man give fifty dollars —
takee Olooya all same."

THREE VAGABONDS OF TRINIDAD

"Oh! it 's you, is it?" said the Editor.

The Chinese boy to whom the colloquialism was addressed answered literally, after his habit: —

"Allee same Li Tee; me no changee. Me no ollee China boy."

"That 's so," said the Editor with an air of conviction. "I don't suppose there 's another imp like you in all Trinidad County. Well, next time don't scratch outside there like a gopher, but come in."

"Lass time," suggested Li Tee blandly, "me tap tappee. You no like tap tappee. You say, allee same dam woodpeckel."

It was quite true — the highly sylvan surroundings of the Trinidad "Sentinel" office — a little clearing in a pine forest — and its attendant fauna, made these signals confusing. An accurate imitation of a woodpecker was also one of Li Tee's accomplishments.

The Editor without replying finished the note he was writing; at which Li Tee, as if struck by some coincident recollection, lifted up his long sleeve, which served him as a pocket, and carelessly shook out a letter on the table like a conjuring trick. The Editor, with a reproachful glance at him, opened it. It was only the ordinary request of an agricultural subscriber — one Johnson — that the Editor would "notice" a giant radish grown by the subscriber and sent by the bearer.

"Where 's the radish, Li Tee?" said the Editor suspiciously.

"No hab got. Ask Mellikan boy."

"What?"

Here Li Tee condescended to explain that on passing the schoolhouse he had been set upon by the schoolboys, and that in the struggle the big radish — being, like most such monstrosities of the quick Californian soil, merely a mass of organized water — was "mashed" over the head of some of his assailants. The Editor, painfully aware of these regular persecutions of his errand boy, and perhaps realizing that a radish which could not be used as a bludgeon was not of a sustaining nature, forebore any reproof. "But I cannot notice what I have n't seen, Li Tee," he said good-humoredly.

"S'pose you lie — allee same as Johnson," suggested Li with equal cheerfulness. "He foolee you with lotten stuff — you foolee Mellikan man, allee same."

The Editor preserved a dignified silence until he had addressed his letter. "Take this to Mrs. Martin," he said, handing it to the boy; "and mind you keep clear of the schoolhouse. Don't go by the Flat either if the men are at work, and don't, if you value your skin, pass Flanigan's shanty, where you set off those firecrackers and nearly burnt him out the other day. Look out for Barker's dog at the crossing, and keep off the main road if the tunnel men are coming over the hill." Then remembering that he had virtually closed all the ordinary approaches to Mrs. Martin's house, he added, "Better go round by the woods, where you won't meet *any one.*"

The boy darted off through the open door, and the Editor stood for a moment looking regretfully after him. He liked his little *protégé* ever since that unfortunate child — a waif from a Chinese wash-house — was impounded by some indignant miners for bringing home a highly imperfect and insufficient washing, and kept as hostage for a more proper return of the garments. Unfortunately, another gang

of miners, equally aggrieved, had at the same time looted
the wash-house and driven off the occupants, so that Li
Tee remained unclaimed.   For a few weeks he became a
sporting appendage of the miners' camp; the stolid butt of
good-humored practical jokes, the victim alternately of careless indifference or of extravagant generosity.   He received
kicks and half-dollars intermittently, and pocketed both
with stoical fortitude.   But under this treatment he presently lost the docility and frugality which was part of his
inheritance, and began to put his small wits against his
tormentors, until they grew tired of their own mischief and
his.   But they knew not what to do with him.   His pretty
nankeen-yellow skin debarred him from the white "public
school," while, although as a heathen he might have rea-
sonably claimed attention from the Sabbath-school, the
parents who cheerfully gave their contributions to the
heathen *abroad*, objected to him as a companion of their
children in the church at home.   At this juncture the
Editor offered to take him into his printing office as a
"devil."   For a while he seemed to be endeavoring, in his
old literal way, to act up to that title.   He inked everything
but the press.   He scratched Chinese characters of an abu-
sive import on "leads," printed them, and stuck them
about the office; he put "punk" in the foreman's pipe,
and had been seen to swallow small type merely as a diabolical recreation.   As a messenger he was fleet of foot,
but uncertain of delivery.   Some time previously the Editor had enlisted the sympathies of Mrs. Martin, the good-
natured wife of a farmer, to take him in her household on
trial, but on the third day Li Tee had run away.   Yet the
Editor had not despaired, and it was to urge her to a second
attempt that he dispatched that letter.

He was still gazing abstractedly into the depths of the
wood when he was conscious of a slight movement — but
no sound — in a clump of hazel near him, and a stealthy

figure glided from it. He at once recognized it as "Jim," a well-known drunken Indian vagrant of the settlement — tied to its civilization by the single link of "fire-water," for which he forsook equally the Reservation, where it was forbidden, and his own camps, where it was unknown. Unconscious of his silent observer, he dropped upon all fours, with his ear and nose alternately to the ground like some tracking animal. Then, having satisfied himself, he rose, and bending forward in a dogged trot, made a straight line for the woods. He was followed a few seconds later by his dog — a slinking, rough, wolf-like brute, whose superior instinct, however, made him detect the silent presence of some alien humanity in the person of the Editor, and to recognize it with a yelp of habit, anticipatory of the stone that he knew was always thrown at him.

"That's cute," said a voice, "but it's just what I expected all along."

The Editor turned quickly. His foreman was standing behind him, and had evidently noticed the whole incident.

"It's what I allus said," continued the man. "That boy and that Injin are thick as thieves. Ye can't see one without the other — and they've got their little tricks and signals by which they follow each other. T' other day when you was kalkilatin' Li Tee was doin' your errands I tracked him out on the marsh, just by followin' that ornery, pizenous dog o' Jim's. There was the whole caboodle of 'em — including Jim — campin' out, and eatin' raw fish that Jim had ketched, and green stuff they had both sneaked outer Johnson's garden. Mrs. Martin may *take* him, but she won't keep him long while Jim's round. What makes Li foller that blamed old Injin soaker, and what makes Jim, who, at least, is a 'Merican, take up with a furrin' heathen, just gets me."

The Editor did not reply. He had heard something of

this before. Yet, after all, why should not these equal
outcasts of civilization cling together?

. . . .

Li Tee's stay with Mrs. Martin was brief. His departure was hastened by an untoward event — apparently ushered in, as in the case of other great calamities, by a mysterious portent in the sky. One morning an extraordinary
bird of enormous dimensions was seen approaching from
the horizon, and eventually began to hover over the devoted town. Careful scrutiny of this ominous fowl, however, revealed the fact that it was a monstrous Chinese
kite, in the shape of a flying dragon. The spectacle imparted considerable liveliness to the community, which,
however, presently changed to some concern and indignation. It appeared that the kite was secretly constructed
by Li Tee in a secluded part of Mrs. Martin's clearing, but
when it was first tried by him he found that through some
error of design it required a tail of unusual proportions.
This he hurriedly supplied by the first means he found —
Mrs. Martin's clothes-line, with part of the weekly wash
depending from it. This fact was not at first noticed by
the ordinary sightseer, although the tail seemed peculiar —
yet perhaps not more peculiar than a dragon's tail ought
to be. But when the actual theft was discovered and reported through the town, a vivacious interest was created,
and spy-glasses were used to identify the various articles of
apparel still hanging on that ravished clothes-line. These
garments, in the course of their slow disengagement from
the clothes-pins through the gyrations of the kite, impar-
tially distributed themselves over the town — one of Mrs.
Martin's stockings falling upon the veranda of the Polka
Saloon, and the other being afterwards discovered on the
belfry of the First Methodist Church — to the scandal of
the congregation. It would have been well if the result of
Li Tee's invention had ended here. Alas! the kite-flyer

and his accomplice, "Injin Jim," were tracked by means of the kite's tell-tale cord to a lonely part of the marsh and rudely dispossessed of their charge by Deacon Hornblower and a constable. Unfortunately, the captors overlooked the fact that the kite-flyers had taken the precaution of making a "half-turn" of the stout cord around a log to ease the tremendous pull of the kite — whose power the captors had not reckoned upon — and the Deacon incautiously substituted his own body for the log. A singular spectacle is said to have then presented itself to the on-lookers. The Deacon was seen to be running wildly by leaps and bounds over the marsh after the kite, closely followed by the constable in equally wild efforts to restrain him by tugging at the end of the line. The extraordinary race continued to the town until the constable fell, losing his hold of the line. This seemed to impart a singular specific levity to the Deacon, who, to the astonishment of everybody, incontinently sailed up into a tree! When he was succored and cut down from the demoniac kite, he was found to have sustained a dislocation of the shoulder, and the constable was severely shaken. By that one infelicitous stroke the two outcasts made an enemy of the Law and the Gospel as represented in Trinidad County. It is to be feared also that the ordinary emotional instinct of a frontier community, to which they were now simply abandoned, was as little to be trusted. In this dilemma they disappeared from the town the next day — no one knew where. A pale blue smoke rising from a lonely island in the bay for some days afterwards suggested their possible refuge. But nobody greatly cared. The sympathetic mediation of the Editor was characteristically opposed by Mr. Parkin Skinner, a prominent citizen: —

"It's all very well for you to talk sentiment about niggers, Chinamen, and Injins, and you fellers can laugh about the Deacon being snatched up to heaven like Elijah

in that blamed Chinese chariot of a kite — but I kin tell
you, gentlemen, that this is a white man's country! Yes,
sir, you can't get over it! The nigger of every description
— yeller, brown, or black, call him 'Chinese,' 'Injin,' or
'Kanaka,' or what you like — hez to clar off of God's foot-
stool when the Anglo-Saxon gets started! It stands to
reason that they can't live alongside o' printin' presses,
M'Cormick's reapers, and the Bible! Yes, sir! the Bible;
and Deacon Hornblower kin prove it to you. It 's our
manifest destiny to clar them out — that 's what we was
put here for — and it 's just the work we 've got to do!"

I have ventured to quote Mr. Skinner's stirring remarks
to show that probably Jim and Li Tee ran away only in
anticipation of a possible lynching, and to prove that advanced sentiments of this high and ennobling nature really
obtained forty years ago in an ordinary American frontier
town which did not then dream of Expansion and Empire!

Howbeit, Mr. Skinner did not make allowance for mere
human nature. One morning Master Bob Skinner, his
son, aged twelve, evaded the schoolhouse, and started in an
old Indian "dug-out" to invade the island of the miserable
refugees. His purpose was not clearly defined to himself,
but was to be modified by circumstances. He would either
capture Li Tee and Jim, or join them in their lawless
existence. He had prepared himself for either event by
surreptitiously borrowing his father's gun. He also carried
victuals, having heard that Jim ate grasshoppers and Li
Tee rats, and misdoubting his own capacity for either diet.
He paddled slowly, well in shore, to be secure from observation at home, and then struck out boldly in his leaky
canoe for the island — a tufted, tussocky shred of the
marshy promontory torn off in some tidal storm. It was a
lovely day, the bay being barely ruffled by the afternoon
"trades;" but as he neared the island he came upon the
swell from the bar and the thunders of the distant Pacific,

and grew a little frightened. The canoe, losing way, fell
into the trough of the swell, shipping salt water, still more
alarming to the prairie-bred boy. Forgetting his plan of
a stealthy invasion, he shouted lustily as the helpless and
water-logged boat began to drift past the island; at which
a lithe figure emerged from the reeds, threw off a tattered
blanket, and slipped noiselessly, like some animal, into the
water. It was Jim, who, half wading, half swimming,
brought the canoe and boy ashore. Master Skinner at once
gave up the idea of invasion, and concluded to join the
refugees.

This was easy in his defenseless state, and his manifest
delight in their rude encampment and gypsy life, although
he had been one of Li Tee's oppressors in the past. But
that stolid pagan had a philosophical indifference which
might have passed for Christian forgiveness, and Jim's native reticence seemed like assent. And, possibly, in the
minds of these two vagabonds there might have been a natural sympathy for this other truant from civilization, and
some delicate flattery in the fact that Master Skinner was
not driven out, but came of his own accord. Howbeit,
they fished together, gathered cranberries on the marsh,
shot a wild duck and two plovers, and when Master Skinner
assisted in the cooking of their fish in a conical basket sunk
in the ground, filled with water, heated by rolling red-hot
stones from their drift-wood fire into the buried basket,
the boy's felicity was supreme. And what an afternoon!
To lie, after this feast, on their bellies in the grass, replete
like animals, hidden from everything but the sunshine
above them; so quiet that gray clouds of sandpipers settled
fearlessly around them, and a shining brown muskrat
slipped from the ooze within a few feet of their faces —
was to feel themselves a part of the wild life in earth and
sky. Not that their own predatory instincts were hushed
by this divine peace; that intermitting black spot upon the

water, declared by the Indian to be a seal, the stealthy
glide of a yellow fox in the ambush of a callow brood of
mallards, the momentary straying of an elk from the upland
upon the borders of the marsh, awoke their tingling nerves
to the happy but fruitless chase. And when night came,
too soon, and they pigged together around the warm ashes
of their camp-fire, under the low lodge poles of their wig-
wam of dried mud, reeds, and driftwood, with the combined
odors of fish, wood-smoke, and the warm salt breath of the
marsh in their nostrils, they slept contentedly. The distant lights of the settlement went out one by one, the stars
came out, very large and very silent, to take their places.
The barking of a dog on the nearest point was followed by
another farther inland. But Jim's dog, curled at the feet
of his master, did not reply. What had *he* to do with
civilization?

The morning brought some fear of consequences to Master Skinner, but no abatement of his resolve not to return.
But here he was oddly combated by Li Tee. "S'pose you
go back allee same. You tellee fam'lee canoe go topside
down — you plentee swimee to bush. Allee night in bush.
Housee big way off — how can get? Sabe?"

"And I'll leave the gun, and tell Dad that when the
canoe upset the gun got drowned," said the boy eagerly.

Li Tee nodded.

"And come again Saturday, and bring more powder and
shot and a bottle for Jim," said Master Skinner excitedly.

"Good!" grunted the Indian.

Then they ferried the boy over to the peninsula, and set
him on a trail across the marshes, known only to themselves, which would bring him home. And when the Editor the next morning chronicled among his news, "Adrift
on the Bay — A Schoolboy's Miraculous Escape," he knew
as little what part his missing Chinese errand boy had
taken in it as the rest of his readers.

Meantime the two outcasts returned to their island camp. It may have occurred to them that a little of the sunlight had gone from it with Bob; for they were in a dull, stupid way fascinated by the little white tyrant who had broken bread with them. He had been delightfully selfish and frankly brutal to them, as only a schoolboy could be, with the addition of the consciousness of his superior race. Yet they each longed for his return, although he was seldom mentioned in their scanty conversation — carried on in monosyllables, each in his own language, or with some common English word, or more often restricted solely to signs. By a delicate flattery, when they did speak of him it was in what they considered to be his own language.

"Boston boy, plenty like catchee *him*," Jim would say, pointing to a distant swan. Or Li Tee, hunting a striped water snake from the reeds, would utter stolidly, "Mellikan boy no likee snake." Yet the next two days brought some trouble and physical discomfort to them. Bob had consumed, or wasted, all their provisions — and, still more unfortunately, his righteous visit, his gun, and his superabundant animal spirits had frightened away the game, which their habitual quiet and taciturnity had beguiled into trustfulness. They were half starved, but they did not blame him. It would come all right when he returned. They counted the days, Jim with secret notches on the long pole, Li Tee with a string of copper "cash" he always kept with him. The eventful day came at last, — a warm autumn day, patched with inland fog like blue smoke and smooth, tranquil, open surfaces of wood and sea; but to their waiting, confident eyes the boy came not out of either. They kept a stolid silence all that day until night fell, when Jim said, "Mebbe Boston boy go dead." Li Tee nodded. It did not seem possible to these two heathens that anything else could prevent the Christian child from keeping his word.

After that, by the aid of the canoe, they went much on the marsh, hunting apart, but often meeting on the trail which Bob had taken, with grunts of mutual surprise. These suppressed feelings, never made known by word or gesture, at last must have found vicarious outlet in the taciturn dog, who so far forgot his usual discretion as to once or twice seat himself on the water's edge and indulge in a fit of howling. It had been a custom of Jim's on certain days to retire to some secluded place, where, folded in his blanket, with his back against a tree, he remained motionless for hours. In the settlement this had been usually referred to the after effects of drink, known as the "horrors," but Jim had explained it by saying it was "when his heart was bad." And now it seemed, by these gloomy abstractions, that "his heart was bad" very often. And then the long-withheld rains came one night on the wings of a fierce southwester, beating down their frail lodge and scattering it abroad, quenching their camp-fire, and rolling up the bay until it invaded their reedy island and hissed in their ears. It drove the game from Jim's gun; it tore the net and scattered the bait of Li Tee, the fisherman. Cold and half starved in heart and body, but more dogged and silent than ever, they crept out in their canoe into the storm-tossed bay, barely escaping with their miserable lives to the marshy peninsula. Here, on their enemy's ground, skulking in the rushes, or lying close behind tussocks, they at last reached the fringe of forest below the settlement. Here, too, sorely pressed by hunger, and doggedly reckless of consequences, they forgot their caution, and a flight of teal fell to Jim's gun on the very outskirts of the settlement.

It was a fatal shot, whose echoes awoke the forces of civilization against them. For it was heard by a logger in his hut near the marsh, who, looking out, had seen Jim pass. A careless, good-natured frontiersman, he might have kept the outcasts' mere presence to himself; but there was that damning shot! An Indian with a gun! That weapon, contraband of law, with dire fines and penalties to whoso sold or gave it to him! A thing to be looked into — some one to be punished! An Indian with a weapon that made him the equal of the white! Who was safe? He hurried to town to lay his information before the constable, but, meeting Mr. Skinner, imparted the news to him. The latter pooh-poohed the constable, who he alleged had not yet discovered the whereabouts of Jim, and suggested that a few armed citizens should make the chase themselves. The fact was that Mr. Skinner, never quite satisfied in his mind with his son's account of the loss of the gun, had put two and two together, and was by no means inclined to have his own gun possibly identified by the legal authority. Moreover, he went home and at once attacked Master Bob with such vigor and so highly colored a description of the crime he had committed, and the penalties attached to it, that Bob confessed. More than that, I grieve to say that Bob lied. The Indian had "stoled his gun," and threatened his life if he divulged the theft. He told how he was ruthlessly put ashore, and compelled to take a trail only known to them to reach his home. In two hours it was reported throughout the settlement that the infamous Jim had added robbery with violence to his illegal possession of the weapon. The secret of the island and the trail over the marsh was told only to a few.

Meantime it had fared hard with the fugitives. Their nearness to the settlement prevented them from lighting a fire, which might have revealed their hiding-place, and they crept together, shivering all night in a clump of hazel. Scared thence by passing but unsuspecting wayfarers wandering off the trail, they lay part of the next day and night amid some tussocks of salt grass, blown on by the cold sea-breeze; chilled, but securely hidden from sight. Indeed, thanks to some mysterious power they had of utter immobility, it was wonderful how they could efface themselves, through quiet and the simplest environment. The lee side of a straggling vine in the meadow, or even the thin ridge of cast-up drift on the shore, behind which they would lie for hours motionless, was a sufficient barrier against prying eyes. In this occupation they no longer talked together, but followed each other with the blind instinct of animals — yet always unerringly, as if conscious of each other's plans. Strangely enough, it was the *real* animal alone — their nameless dog — who now betrayed impatience and a certain human infirmity of temper. The concealment they were resigned to, the sufferings they mutely accepted, he alone resented! When certain scents or sounds, imperceptible to their senses, were blown across their path, he would, with bristling back, snarl himself into guttural and strangulated fury. Yet, in their apathy, even this would have passed them unnoticed, but that on the second night he disappeared suddenly, returning after two hours' absence with bloody jaws — replete, but still slinking and snappish. It was only in the morning that, creeping on their hands and knees through the stubble, they came upon the torn and mangled carcass of a sheep. The two men looked at each other without speaking — they knew what this act of rapine meant to themselves. It meant a fresh hue and cry after them, — it meant that their starving companion had helped to draw the net closer round them. The Indian grunted, Li Tee smiled vacantly; but with their knives and fingers they finished what the dog had begun, and became equally culpable. But that they were heathens, they could not have achieved a delicate ethical responsibility in a more Christian-like way.

Yet the rice-fed Li Tee suffered most in their privations. His habitual apathy increased with a certain physical lethargy which Jim could not understand. When they were

apart he sometimes found Li Tee stretched on his back
with an odd stare in his eyes, and once, at a distance, he
thought he saw a vague thin vapor drift from where the
Chinese boy was lying and vanish as he approached.   When
he tried to arouse him there was a weak drawl in his voice
and a drug-like odor in his breath.   Jim dragged him to a
more substantial shelter, a thicket of alder.   It was dangerously near the frequented road, but a vague idea had
sprung up in Jim's now troubled mind that, equal vagabonds though they were, Li Tee had more claims upon civilization, through those of his own race who were permitted
to live among the white men, and were not hunted to "re-
servations" and confined there like Jim's people.   If Li
Tee was "heap sick," other Chinamen might find and nurse
him.   As for Li Tee, he had lately said, in a more lucid
interval: "Me go dead — allee samee Mellikan boy.   You
go dead too — allee samee," and then lay down again with
a glassy stare in his eyes.   Far from being frightened at
this, Jim attributed his condition to some enchantment
that Li Tee had evoked from one of his gods — just as he
himself had seen "medicine-men" of his own tribe fall into
strange trances, and was glad that the boy no longer suffered.   The day advanced, and Li Tee still slept.   Jim
could hear the church bells ringing; he knew it was Sunday — the day on which he was hustled from the main
street by the constable; the day on which the shops were
closed, and the drinking saloons open only at the back
door; the day whereon no man worked — and for that
reason, though he knew it not, the day selected by the ingenious Mr. Skinner and a few friends as especially fitting
and convenient for a chase of the fugitives.   The bell
brought no suggestion of this — though the dog snapped
under his breath and stiffened his spine.   And then he
heard another sound, far off and vague, yet one that brought
a flash into his murky eye, that lit up the heaviness of his

Hebraic face, and even showed a slight color in his high cheek-bones. He lay down on the ground, and listened with suspended breath. He heard it now distinctly. It was the Boston boy calling, and the word he was calling was "Jim."

Then the fire dropped out of his eyes as he turned with his usual stolidity to where Li Tee was lying. Him he shook, saying briefly: "Boston boy come back!" But there was no reply, the dead body rolled over inertly under his hand; the head fell back, and the jaw dropped under the pinched yellow face. The Indian gazed at him slowly, and then gravely turned again in the direction of the voice. Yet his dull mind was perplexed, for, blended with that voice were other sounds like the tread of clumsily stealthy feet. But again the voice called "Jim!" and raising his hands to his lips he gave a low whoop in reply. This was followed by silence, when suddenly he heard the voice — the boy's voice — once again, this time very near him, saying eagerly, —

"There he is!"

Then the Indian knew all. His face, however, did not change as he took up his gun, and a man stepped out of the thicket into the trail: —

"Drop that gun, you d——d Injin!"

The Indian did not move.

"Drop it, I say!"

The Indian remained erect and motionless.

A rifle shot broke from the thicket. At first it seemed to have missed the Indian, and the man who had spoken cocked his own rifle. But the next moment the tall figure of Jim collapsed where he stood into a mere blanketed heap.

The man who had fired the shot walked towards the heap with the easy air of a conqueror. But suddenly there arose before him an awful phantom, the incarnation of savagery

— a creature of blazing eyeballs, flashing tusks, and hot carnivorous breath. He had barely time to cry out "A wolf!" before its jaws met in his throat, and they rolled together on the ground.

But it was no wolf — as a second shot proved — only Jim's slinking dog; the only one of the outcasts who at that supreme moment had gone back to his original nature.

A MERCURY OF THE FOOT-HILLS

IT was high hot noon on the Casket Ridge. Its very
scant shade was restricted to a few dwarf Scotch firs, and
was so perpendicularly cast that Leonidas Boone, seeking
shelter from the heat, was obliged to draw himself up under
one of them, as if it were an umbrella. Occasionally, with
a boy's perversity, he permitted one bared foot to pro-
trude beyond the sharply marked shadow until the burning
sun forced him to draw it in again with a thrill of satisfaction. There was no earthly reason why he had not
sought the larger shadows of the pine trees which reared
themselves against the Ridge on the slope below him, except that he was a boy, and perhaps even more superstitious
and opinionated than most boys. Having got under this
tree with infinite care, he had made up his mind that he
would not move from it until its line of shade reached and
touched a certain stone on the trail near him! *Why* he
did this he did not know, but he clung to his sublime purpose with the courage and tenacity of a youthful Casa-
bianca. He was cramped, tickled by dust and fir sprays;
he was supremely uncomfortable — but he stayed! A
woodpecker was monotonously tapping in an adjacent pine,
with measured intervals of silence, which he always firmly
believed was a certain telegraphy of the bird's own making;
a green-and-gold lizard flashed by his foot to stiffen itself
suddenly with a rigidity equal to his own. Still *he* stirred
not. The shadow gradually crept nearer the mystic stone
— and touched it. He sprang up, shook himself, and prepared to go about his business. This was simply an errand

to the post office at the cross-roads, scarcely a mile from his father's house. He was already halfway there. He had taken only the better part of one hour for this desultory journey!

However, he now proceeded on his way, diverging only to follow a fresh rabbit-track a few hundred yards, to note that the animal had doubled twice against the wind, and then, naturally, he was obliged to look closely for other tracks to determine its pursuers. He paused also, but only for a moment, to rap thrice on the trunk of the pine where the woodpecker was at work, which he knew would make it cease work for a time — as it did. Having thus renewed his relations with nature, he discovered that one of the letters he was taking to the post office had slipped in some mysterious way from the bosom of his shirt, where he carried them, past his waist-band, into his trouser-leg, and was about to make a casual delivery of itself on the trail. This caused him to take out his letters and count them, when he found one missing. He had been given four letters to post — he had only three. There was a big one in his father's handwriting, two indistinctive ones of his mother's, and a smaller one of his sister's — *that* was gone! Not at all disconcerted, he calmly retraced his steps, following his own tracks minutely, with a grim face and a distinct delight in the process, while looking — perfunctorily — for the letter. In the midst of this slow progress a bright idea struck him. He walked back to the fir tree where he had rested, and found the lost missive. It had slipped out of his shirt when he shook himself. He was not particularly pleased. He knew that nobody would give him credit for his trouble in going back for it, or his astuteness in guessing where it was. He heaved the sigh of misunderstood genius, and again started for the post office. This time he carried the letters openly and ostentatiously in his hand.

Presently he heard a voice say, "Hey!" It was a gen-

tle, musical voice, — a stranger's voice, for it evidently did
not know how to call him, and did not say, "Oh, Leonidas!" or "You — look here!" He was abreast of a little
clearing, guarded by a low stockade of bark palings, and
beyond it was a small white dwelling-house. Leonidas
knew the place perfectly well. It belonged to the superintendent of a mining tunnel, who had lately rented it to
some strangers from San Francisco. Thus much he had
heard from his family. He had a mountain boy's contempt
for city folks, and was not himself interested in them. Yet
as he heard the call, he was conscious of a slightly guilty
feeling. He might have been trespassing in following the
rabbit's track; he might have been seen by some one when
he lost the letter and had to go back for it — all grown-up
people had a way of offering themselves as witnesses against
him! He scowled a little as he glanced around him. Then
his eye fell on the caller on the other side of the stockade.

To his surprise it was a woman: a pretty, gentle, fragile
creature, all soft muslin and laces, with her fingers inter-
locked, and leaning both elbows on the top of the stockade
as she stood under the checkered shadow of a buckeye.

"Come here — please — won't you?" she said pleasantly.

It would have been impossible to resist her voice if Leonidas had wanted to, which he didn't. He walked confidently up to the fence. She really was very pretty, with
eyes like his setter's, and as caressing. And there were
little puckers and satiny creases around her delicate nostrils
and mouth when she spoke, which Leonidas knew were
"expression."

"I — I" — she began, with charming hesitation; then
suddenly, "What's your name?"

"Leonidas."

"Leonidas! That's a pretty name!" He thought it
did sound pretty. "Well, Leonidas, I want you to be a

good boy and do a great favor for me, — a very great
favor."

Leonidas's face fell. This kind of prelude and formula
was familiar to him. It was usually followed by, "Promise me that you will never swear again," or, "that you
will go straight home and wash your face," or some other
irrelevant personality. But nobody with that sort of eyes
had ever said it. So he said, a little shyly but sincerely,
"Yes, ma'am."

"You are going to the post office?"

This seemed a very foolish, womanish question, seeing
that he was holding letters in his hand; but he said, "Yes."

"I want you to put a letter of mine among yours and
post them all together," she said, putting one little hand to
her bosom and drawing out a letter. He noticed that she
purposely held the addressed side so that he could not see
it, but he also noticed that her hand was small, thin, and
white, even to a faint tint of blue in it, unlike his sister's,
the baby's, or any other hand he had ever seen. "Can
you read?" she said suddenly, withdrawing the letter.

The boy flushed slightly at the question. "Of course I
can," he said proudly.

"Of course, certainly," she repeated quickly; "but,"
she added, with a mischievous smile, "you must n't *now!*
Promise me! Promise me that you won't read this address, but just post the letter, like one of your own, in the
letter-box with the others."

Leonidas promised readily; it seemed to him a great fuss
about nothing; perhaps it was some kind of game or a bet.
He opened his sunburnt hand, holding his own letters, and
she slipped hers, face downward, between them. Her soft
fingers touched his in the operation, and seemed to leave a
pleasant warmth behind them.

"Promise me another thing," she added; "promise me
you won't say a word of this to any one."

"Of course!" said Leonidas.

"That's a good boy, and I know you will keep your word." She hesitated a moment, smilingly and tentatively, and then held out a bright half-dollar. Leonidas backed from the fence. "I'd rather not," he said shyly.

"But as a present from *me?*"

Leonidas colored — he was really proud; and he was also bright enough to understand that the possession of such unbounded wealth would provoke dangerous inquiry at home. But he didn't like to say it, and only replied, "I can't."

She looked at him curiously. "Then — thank you," she said, offering her white hand, which felt like a bird in his. "Now run on, and don't let me keep you any longer." She drew back from the fence as she spoke, and waved him a pretty farewell. Leonidas, half sorry, half relieved, darted away.

He ran to the post office, which he never had done before. Loyally he never looked at her letter, nor, indeed, at his own again, swinging the hand that held them far from his side. He entered the post office directly, going at once to the letter-box and depositing the precious missive with the others. The post office was also the "country store," and Leonidas was in the habit of still further protracting his errands there by lingering in that stimulating atmosphere of sugar, cheese, and coffee. But to-day his stay was brief, so transitory that the postmaster himself inferred audibly that "old man Boone must have been tanning Lee with a hickory switch." But the simple reason was that Leonidas wished to go back to the stockade fence and the fair stranger, if haply she was still there. His heart sank as, breathless with unwonted haste, he reached the clearing and the empty buckeye shade. He walked slowly and with sad diffidence by the deserted stockade fence. But presently his quick eye discerned a glint of white among the laurels near the house. It was *she*, walking with apparent indifference away from him towards the corner of the clearing and the road. But this he knew would bring her to the end of the stockade fence, where he must pass — and it did. She turned to him with a bright smile of affected surprise. "Why, you're as swift-footed as Mercury!"

Leonidas understood her perfectly. Mercury was the other name for quicksilver — and that was lively, you bet! He had often spilt some on the floor to see it move. She must be awfully cute to have noticed it too — cuter than his sisters. He was quite breathless with pleasure.

"I put your letter in the box all right," he burst out at last.

"Without any one seeing it?" she asked.

"Sure pop! — nary one! The postmaster stuck out his hand to grab it, but I just let on that I didn't see him, and shoved it in myself."

"You're as sharp as you're good," she said smilingly. "Now, there's just *one* thing more I want you to do. Forget all about this — won't you?"

Her voice was very caressing. Perhaps that was why he said boldly, "Yes, ma'am, all except *you*."

"Dear me, what a compliment! How old are you?"

"Goin' on fifteen," said Leonidas confidently.

"And going very fast," said the lady mischievously. "Well, then, you needn't forget *me*. On the contrary," she added, after looking at him curiously, "I would rather you'd remember me. Good-by — or, rather, good-afternoon — if I'm to be remembered, Leon."

"Good-afternoon, ma'am."

She moved away, and presently disappeared among the laurels. But her last words were ringing in his ears. "Leon" — everybody else called him "Lee" for brevity; "Leon" — it was pretty as she said it.

He turned away. But it so chanced that their parting was not to pass unnoticed, for, looking up the hill, Leonidas perceived his elder sister and little brother coming down the road, and knew that they must have seen him from the hilltop. It was like their "snoopin'!" They ran to him eagerly.

"You were talking to the stranger," said his sister breathlessly.

"She spoke to me first," said Leonidas, on the defensive.

"What did she say?"

"Wanted to know the eleckshun news," said Leonidas with cool mendacity, "and I told her."

This improbable fiction nevertheless satisfied them. "What was she like? Oh, do tell us, Lee!" continued his sister.

Nothing would have delighted him more than to expatiate upon her loveliness, the soft white beauty of her hands, the "cunning" little puckers around her lips, her bright tender eyes, the angelic texture of her robes, and the musical tinkle of her voice. But Leonidas had no confidant, and what healthy boy ever trusted his sister in such matter! "*You* saw what she was like," he said, with evasive bluntness.

"But, Lee" —

But Lee was adamant. "Go and ask her," he said.

"Like as not you were sassy to her, and she shut you up," said his sister artfully. But even this cruel suggestion, which he could have so easily flouted, did not draw him, and his ingenious relations flounced disgustedly away.

But Leonidas was not spared any further allusion to the fair stranger; for the fact of her having spoken to him was duly reported at home, and at dinner his reticence was again sorely attacked. "Just like her, in spite of all her airs and graces, to hang out along the fence like any ordi-

nary hired girl, jabberin' with anybody that went along
the road," said his mother incisively. He knew that she
did n't like her new neighbors, so this did not surprise nor
greatly pain him. Neither did the prosaic facts that were
now first made plain to him. His divinity was a Mrs.
Burroughs, whose husband was conducting a series of mining operations, and prospecting with a gang of men on the
Casket Ridge. As his duty required his continual presence
there, Mrs. Burroughs was forced to forego the civilized
pleasures of San Francisco for a frontier life, for which she
was ill fitted and in which she had no interest. All this
was a vague irrelevance to Leonidas, who knew her only as
a goddess in white who had been familiar to him, and kind,
and to whom he was tied by the delicious joy of having a
secret in common, and having done her a special favor.
Healthy youth clings to its own impressions, let reason,
experience, and even facts argue ever to the contrary.

So he kept her secret and his intact, and was rewarded a
few days afterwards by a distant view of her walking in the
garden, with a man whom he recognized as her husband.
It is needless to say that, without any extraneous thought,
the man suffered in Leonidas's estimation by his propinquity to the goddess, and that he deemed him vastly inferior.

It was a still greater reward to his fidelity that she seized
an opportunity when her husband's head was turned to
wave her hand to him. Leonidas did not approach the
fence, partly through shyness and partly through a more
subtle instinct that this man was not in the secret. He
was right, for only the next day, as he passed to the post
office, she called him to the fence.

"Did you see me wave my hand to you yesterday?" she
asked pleasantly.

"Yes, ma'am; but "— he hesitated — "I did n't come
up, for I did n't think you wanted me when any one else
was there."

She laughed merrily, and lifting his straw hat from his head, ran the fingers of the other hand through his damp curls. "You're the brightest, dearest boy I ever knew, Leon," she said, dropping her pretty face to the level of his own, "and I ought to have remembered it. But I don't mind telling you I was dreadfully frightened lest you might misunderstand me and come and ask for another letter — before *him*." As she emphasized the personal pronoun, her whole face seemed to change: the light of her blue eyes became mere glittering points, her nostrils grew white and contracted, and her pretty little mouth seemed to narrow into a straight cruel line, like a cat's. "Not a word ever to *him*, of all men! Do you hear?" she said almost brusquely. Then, seeing the concern in the boy's face, she laughed, and added explanatorily: "He's a bad, bad man, Leon, remember that."

The fact that she was speaking of her husband did not shock the boy's moral sense in the least. The sacredness of those relations, and even of blood kinship, is, I fear, not always so clear to the youthful mind as we fondly imagine. That Mr. Burroughs was a bad man to have excited this change in this lovely woman was Leonidas's only conclusion. He remembered how his sister's soft, pretty little kitten, purring on her lap, used to get its back up and spit at the postmaster's yellow hound.

"I never wished to come unless you called me first," he said frankly.

"What?" she said, in her half-playful, half-reproachful, but wholly caressing way. "You mean to say you would never come to see me unless I sent for you? Oh, Leon! and you'd abandon me in that way?"

But Leonidas was set in his own boyish superstition. "I'd just delight in being sent for by you any time, Mrs. Burroughs, and you kin always find me," he said shyly, but doggedly; "but" — He stopped.

"What an opinionated young gentleman! Well, I see I must do all the courting. So consider that I sent for you this morning. I 've got another letter for you to mail." She put her hand to her breast, and out of the pretty frillings of her frock produced, as before, with the same faint perfume of violets, a letter like the first. But it was unsealed. "Now, listen, Leon; we are going to be great friends — you and I." Leonidas felt his cheeks glowing. "You are going to do me another great favor, and we are going to have a little fun and a great secret all by our own selves. Now, first, have you any correspondent — you know — any one who writes to you — any boy or girl — from San Francisco ? "

Leonidas's cheeks grew redder — alas! from a less happy consciousness. He never received any letters; nobody ever wrote to him. He was obliged to make this shameful admission.

Mrs. Burroughs looked thoughtful. "But you have some friend in San Francisco — some one who *might* write to you ? " she suggested pleasantly.

"I knew a boy once who went to San Francisco," said Leonidas doubtfully. "At least, he allowed he was goin' there."

"That will do," said Mrs. Burroughs. "I suppose your parents know him or of him ? "

"Why," said Leonidas, "he used to live here."

"Better still. For, you see, it would n't be strange if he *did* write. What was the gentleman's name ? "

"Jim Belcher," returned Leonidas hesitatingly, by no means sure that the absent Belcher knew how to write. Mrs. Burroughs took a tiny pencil from her belt, opened the letter she was holding in her hand, and apparently wrote the name in it. Then she folded it and sealed it, smiling charmingly at Leonidas's puzzled face.

"Now, Leon, listen; for here is the favor I am asking.

Mr. Jim Belcher " — she pronounced the name with great gravity — "will write to you in a few days. But inside of *your* letter will be a little note to me, which you will bring me. You can show your letter to your family, if they want to know who it is from; but no one must see *mine.* Can you manage that ? "

"Yes," said Leonidas. Then, as the whole idea flashed upon his quick intelligence, he smiled until he showed his dimples. Mrs. Burroughs leaned forward over the fence, lifted his torn straw hat, and dropped a fluttering little kiss on his forehead. It seemed to the boy, flushed and rosy as a maid, as if she had left a shining star there for every one to see.

"Don't smile like that, Leon, you 're positively irresistible! It will be a nice little game, won't it ? Nobody in it but you and me — and Belcher! We 'll outwit them yet. And, you see, you 'll be obliged to come to me, after all, without my asking."

They both laughed; indeed, quite a dimpled, bright-eyed, rosy, innocent pair, though I think Leonidas was the more maidenly.

"And," added Leonidas, with breathless eagerness, "I can sometimes write to — to — Jim, and inclose your letter."

"Angel of wisdom! certainly. Well, now, let 's see — have you got any letters for the post to-day ? " He colored again, for in anticipation of meeting her he had hurried up the family post that morning. He held out his letters: she thrust her own among them. "Now," she said, laying her cool, soft hand against his hot cheek, "run along, dear; you must not be seen loitering here."

Leonidas ran off, buoyed up on ambient air. It seemed just like a fairy-book. Here he was, the confidant of the most beautiful creature he had seen, and there was a mysterious letter coming to him — Leonidas — and no one to

know why. And now he had a "call" to see her often;
she would not forget him — he need n't loiter by the fence-
post to see if she wanted him — and his boyish pride and
shyness were appeased. There was no question of moral
ethics raised in Leonidas's mind; he knew that it would
not be the real Jim Belcher who would write to him,
but that made the prospect the more attractive. Nor did
another circumstance trouble his conscience. When he
reached the post office, he was surprised to see the man
whom he knew to be Mr. Burroughs talking with the postmaster. Leonidas brushed by him and deposited his letters
in the box in discreet triumph. The postmaster was evidently officially resenting some imputation of carelessness,
and, concluding his defense, "No, sir," he said, "you kin
bet your boots that ef any letter hez gone astray for you
or your wife — Ye said your wife, did n't ye?"

"Yes," said Burroughs hastily, with a glance around the
shop.

"Well, for you or anybody at your house — it ain't here
that's the fault. You hear me! I know every letter that
comes in and goes outer this office, I reckon, and handle
'em all," — Leonidas pricked up his ears, — "and if anybody oughter know, it's me. Ye kin paste that in your
hat, Mr. Burroughs." Burroughs, apparently disconcerted
by the intrusion of a third party — Leonidas — upon what
was evidently a private inquiry, murmured something sur-
lily, and passed out.

Leonidas was puzzled. That big man seemed to be
"snoopin'" around for something! He knew that he dared
not touch the letter-bag, — Leonidas had heard somewhere
that it was a deadly crime to touch any letters after the
Government had got hold of them once, and he had no
fears for the safety of hers. But ought he not go back at
once and tell her about her husband's visit, and the alarming fact that the postmaster was personally acquainted with

all the letters? He instantly saw, too, the wisdom of her inclosing her letter hereafter in another address. Yet he finally resolved not to tell her to-day, — it would look like "hanging round" again; and — another secret reason — he was afraid that any allusion to her husband's interference would bring back that change in her beautiful face which he did not like. The better to resist temptation, he went back another way.

It must not be supposed that, while Leonidas indulged in this secret passion for the beautiful stranger, it was to the exclusion of his boyish habits. It merely took the place of his intellectual visions and his romantic reading. He no longer carried books in his pocket on his lazy rambles. What were mediæval legends of high-born ladies and their pages to this real romance of himself and Mrs. Burroughs? What were the exploits of boy captains and juvenile trappers and the Indian maidens and Spanish señoritas to what was now possible to himself and his divinity here — upon Casket Ridge! The very ground around her was now consecrated to romance and adventure. Consequently, he visited a few traps on his way back which he had set for "jackass-rabbits" and wildcats, — the latter a vindictive reprisal for aggression upon an orphan brood of mountain quail which he had taken under his protection. For, while he nourished a keen love of sport, it was controlled by a boy's larger understanding of nature: a pantheistic sympathy with man and beast and plant, which made him keenly alive to the strange cruelties of creation, revealed to him some queer animal feuds, and made him a chivalrous partisan of the weaker. He had even gone out of his way to defend, by ingenious contrivances of his own, the hoard of a golden squirrel and the treasures of some wild bees from a predatory bear, although it did not prevent him later from capturing the squirrel by an equally ingenious contrivance, and from eventually eating some of the honey.

He was late home that evening. But this was "vacation," — the district school was closed, and but for the household "chores," which occupied his early mornings, each long summer day was a holiday. So two or three passed; and then one morning, on his going to the post office, the postmaster threw down upon the counter a real and rather bulky letter, duly stamped, and addressed to Mr. Leonidas Boone! Leonidas was too discreet to open it before witnesses, but in the solitude of the trail home broke the seal. It contained another letter with no address — clearly the one *she* expected — and, more marvelous still, a sheaf of trout-hooks, with delicate gut-snells such as Leonidas had only dared to dream of. The letter to himself was written in a clear, distinct hand, and ran as follows: —

DEAR LEE, — How are you getting on on old Casket Ridge? It seems a coon's age since you and me was together, and times I get to think I must just run up and see you! We're having bully times in 'Frisco, you bet! though there ain't anything wild worth shucks to go to see — 'cept the sea lions at the Cliff House. They're just stunning — big as a grizzly, and bigger — climbing over a big rock or swimming in the sea like an otter or muskrat. I'm sending you some snells and hooks, such as you can't get at Casket. Use the fine ones for pot-holes and the bigger ones for running water or falls. Let me know when you've got 'em. Write to Lock Box No. 1290. That's where dad's letters come. So no more at present.

From yours truly
JIM BELCHER.

Not only did Leonidas know that this was not from the real Jim, but he felt the vague contact of a new, charming, and original personality that fascinated him. Of course, it was only natural that one of *her* friends — as he must be — should be equally delightful.   There was no jealousy in Leonidas's devotion; he knew only a joy in this fellowship of admiration for her which he was satisfied that the other boy must feel.   And only the right kind of boy could know the importance of his ravishing gift, and this Jim was evidently "no slouch"!   Yet, in Leonidas's new joy he did not forget *her!*   He ran back to the stockade fence and lounged upon the road in view of the house, but she did not appear.

Leonidas lingered on the top of the hill, ostentatiously examining a young hickory for a green switch, but to no effect.   Then it suddenly occurred to him that she might be staying in purposely, and, perhaps a little piqued by her indifference, he ran off.   There was a mountain stream hard by, now dwindled in the summer drouth to a mere trickling thread among the boulders, and there was a certain "pothole" that he had long known.   It was the lurking-place of a phenomenal trout, — an almost historic fish in the district, which had long resisted the attempt of such rude sportsmen as miners, or even experts like himself.   Few had seen it, except as a vague, shadowy bulk in the four feet of depth and gloom in which it hid; only once had Leonidas's quick eye feasted on its fair proportions.   On that memorable occasion Leonidas, having exhausted every kind of lure of painted fly and living bait, was rising from his knees behind the bank, when a pink five-cent stamp dislodged from his pocket fluttered in the air, and descended slowly upon the still pool.   Horrified at his loss, Leonidas leaned over to recover it, when there was a flash like lightning in the black depths, a dozen changes of light and shadow on the surface, a little whirling wave splashing against the side of the rock, and the postage stamp was gone.   More than that — for one instant the trout remained visible, stationary, and expectant!   Whether it was the instinct of sport, or whether the fish had detected a new, subtle, and original flavor in the gum and paper, Leonidas never knew. Alas! he had not another stamp; he was obliged to leave the fish, but carried a brilliant idea away with him. Ever since then he had cherished it — and another extra stamp in his pocket. And now, with this strong but gossamer-like snell, this new hook, and this freshly cut hickory rod, he would make the trial!

But fate was against him! He had scarcely descended the narrow trail to the pine-fringed margin of the stream before his quick ear detected an unusual rustling through the adjacent underbrush, and then a voice that startled him! It was *hers!* In an instant all thought of sport had fled. With a beating heart, half-opened lips, and uplifted lashes, Leonidas awaited the coming of his divinity like a timorous virgin at her first tryst.

But Mrs. Burroughs was clearly not in an equally responsive mood. With her fair face reddened by the sun, the damp tendrils of her unwound hair clinging to her forehead, and her smart little slippers red with dust, there was also a querulous light in her eyes, and a still more querulous pinch in her nostrils, as she stood panting before him.

"You tiresome boy!" she gasped, holding one little hand to her side as she gripped her brambled skirt around her ankles with the other. "Why did n't you wait? Why did you make me run all this distance after you?"

Leonidas timidly and poignantly protested. He had waited before the house and on the hill; he thought she did n't want him.

"Could n't you see that *that man* kept me in?" she went on peevishly. "Have n't you sense enough to know that he suspects something, and follows me everywhere, dogging my footsteps every time the post comes in, and even going to the post office himself, to make sure that he

sees all my letters? Well," she added impatiently, "have
you anything for me? Why don't you speak?"

Crushed and remorseful, Leonidas produced her letter.
She almost snatched it from his hand, opened it, read a few
lines, and her face changed. A smile strayed from her eyes
to her lips, and back again. Leonidas's heart was lifted;
she was so forgiving and so beautiful!

"Is he a boy, Mrs. Burroughs?" asked Leonidas shyly.

"Well — not exactly," she said, her charming face all
radiant again. "He's older than you. What has he written to you?"

Leonidas put his letter in her hand for reply.

"I wish I could see him, you know," he said shyly.
"That letter's bully — it's just rats! I like him pow'ful."

Mrs. Burroughs had skimmed through the letter, but not
interestedly.

"You mustn't like him more than you like me," she
said laughingly, caressing him with her voice and eyes, and
even her straying hand.

"I couldn't do that! I never could like anybody as I
like you," said Leonidas gravely. There was such appalling truthfulness in the boy's voice and frankly opened eyes
that the woman could not evade it, and was slightly disconcerted. But she presently started up with a vexatious cry.
"There's that wretch following me again, I do believe,"
she said, staring at the hilltop. "Yes! Look, Leon, he's
turning to come down this trail. What's to be done? He
mustn't see me here!"

Leonidas looked. It was indeed Mr. Burroughs; but
he was evidently only taking a short cut towards the Ridge,
where his men were working. Leonidas had seen him take
it before. But it was the principal trail on the steep hillside, and they must eventually meet. A man might evade
it by scrambling through the brush to a lower and rougher
trail; but a woman, never! But an idea had seized Leon-

idas. "I can stop him," he said confidently to her. "You just lie low here behind that rock till I come back. He has n't seen you yet."

She had barely time to draw back before Leonidas darted down the trail towards her husband. Yet, in her intense curiosity, she leaned out the next moment to watch him. He paused at last, not far from the approaching figure, and seemed to kneel down on the trail. What was he doing? Her husband was still slowly advancing. Suddenly he stopped. At the same moment she heard their two voices in excited parley, and then, to her amazement, she saw her husband scramble hurriedly down the trail to the lower level, and with an occasional backward glance, hasten away until he had passed beyond her view.

She could scarcely realize her narrow escape when Leonidas stood by her side. "How did you do it?" she said eagerly.

"With a rattler!" said the boy gravely.

"With a what?"

"A rattlesnake — pizen snake, you know."

"A rattlesnake?" she said, staring at Leonidas with a quick snatching away of her skirts.

The boy, who seemed to have forgotten her in his other abstraction of adventure, now turned quickly, with devoted eyes and a reassuring smile.

"Yes; but I would n't let him hurt you," he said gently.

"But what did you *do?*"

He looked at her curiously. "You won't be frightened if I show you?" he said doubtfully. "There 's nothin' to be afeerd of s' long as you 're with me," he added proudly.

"Yes — that is" — she stammered, and then, her curiosity getting the better of her fear, she added in a whisper, "Show me quick!"

He led the way up the narrow trail until he stopped

where he had knelt before.   It was a narrow, sunny ledge
of rock, scarcely wide enough for a single person to pass.
He silently pointed to a cleft in the rock, and kneeling
down again, began to whistle in a soft, fluttering way.
There was a moment of suspense, and then she was conscious of an awful gliding something, — a movement so measured yet so exquisitely graceful that she stood enthralled.
A narrow, flattened, expressionless head was followed by
a foot-long strip of yellow-barred scales; then there was a
pause, and the head turned, in a beautifully symmetrical
half-circle, towards the whistler.   The whistling ceased;
the snake, with half its body out of the cleft, remained
poised in air as if stiffened to stone.

"There," said Leonidas quietly, "that's what Mr. Burroughs saw and that's *why* he scooted off the trail. I just
called out William Henry, — I call him William Henry,
and he knows his name, — and then I sang out to Mr.
Burroughs what was up; and it was lucky I did, for the
next moment he'd have been on top of him and have been
struck, for rattlers don't give way to any one."

"Oh, why didn't you let" — She stopped herself
quickly, but could not stop the fierce glint in her eye nor
the sharp curve in her nostril.   Luckily, Leonidas did not
see this, being preoccupied with his other graceful charmer,
William Henry.

"But how did you know it was here?" said Mrs. Burroughs, recovering herself.

"Fetched him here," said Leonidas briefly.

"What — in your hands?" she said, drawing back.

"No! made him follow! I *have* handled him, but it
was after I'd first made him strike his pizen out upon a
stick. Ye know, after he strikes four times he ain't got
any pizen left.   Then ye kin do anythin' with him, and
he knows it. He knows me, you bet! I've been three
months trainin' him. Look! Don't be frightened," he

said, as Mrs. Burroughs drew hurriedly back; "see him mind me. Now scoot home, William Henry."

He accompanied the command with a slow, dominant movement of the hickory rod he was carrying. The snake dropped its head, and slid noiselessly out of the cleft across the trail and down the hill.

"Thinks my rod is witch-hazel, which rattlers can't abide," continued Leonidas, dropping into a boy's breathless abbreviated speech. "Lives down your way — just back of your farm. Show ye some day. Suns himself on a flat stone every day — always cold — never can get warm. Eh?"

She had not spoken, but was gazing into space with a breathless rigidity of attitude and a fixed look in her eye, not unlike the motionless orbs of the reptile that had glided away.

"Does anybody else know you keep him?" she asked.

"Nary one. I never showed him to anybody but you," replied the boy.

"Don't! You must show me where he hides to-morrow," she said, in her old laughing way. "And now, Leon, I must go back to the house."

"May I write to him — to Jim Belcher, Mrs. Burroughs?" said the boy timidly.

"Certainly. And come to me to-morrow with your letter — I will have mine ready. Good-by." She stopped and glanced at the trail. "And you say that if that man had kept on, the snake would have bitten him?"

"Sure pop! — if he'd trod on him — as he was sure to. The snake wouldn't have known he didn't mean it. It's only natural," continued Leonidas, with glowing partisanship for the gentle and absent William Henry. " *You* wouldn't like to be trodden upon, Mrs. Burroughs!"

"No! I'd strike out!" she said quickly. She made a rapid motion forward with her low forehead and level head, leaving it rigid the next moment, so that it reminded him of the snake, and he laughed. At which she laughed too, and tripped away.

Leonidas went back and caught his trout. But even this triumph did not remove a vague sense of disappointment which had come over him. He had often pictured to himself a Heaven-sent meeting with her in the woods, a walk with her, alone, where he could pick her the rarest flowers and herbs and show her his woodland friends; and it had only ended in this, and an exhibition of William Henry! He ought to have saved *her* from something, and not her husband. Yet he had no ill-feeling for Burroughs, only a desire to circumvent him, on behalf of the unprotected, as he would have baffled a hawk or a wildcat. He went home in dismal spirits, but later that evening constructed a boyish letter of thanks to the apocryphal Belcher and told him all about — the trout!

He brought her his letter the next day, and received hers to inclose. She was pleasant, her own charming self again, but she seemed more interested in other things than himself, as, for instance, the docile William Henry, whose hiding-place he showed, and whose few tricks she made him exhibit to her, and which the gratified Leonidas accepted as a delicate form of flattery to himself. But his yearning, innocent spirit detected a something lacking, which he was too proud to admit even to himself. It was his own fault; he ought to have waited for her, and not gone for the trout!

So a fortnight passed with an interchange of the vicarious letters, and brief, hopeful, and disappointing meetings to Leonidas. To add to his unhappiness, he was obliged to listen to sneering disparagement of his goddess from his family, and criticisms which, happily, his innocence did not comprehend. It was his own mother who accused her of shamefully "making up" to the good-looking express-

man at church last Sunday, and declared that Burroughs
ought to "look after that wife of his," — two statements
which the simple Leonidas could not reconcile. He had
seen the incident, and only thought her more lovely than
ever. Why should not the expressman think so too?
And yet the boy was not happy; something intruded upon
his sports, upon his books, making them dull and vapid,
and yet that something was she! He grew pale and preoccupied. If he had only some one in whom to confide —
some one who could explain his hopes and fears. That one
was nearer than he thought!

It was quite three weeks since the rattlesnake incident,
and he was wandering moodily over Casket Ridge. He
was near the Casket, that abrupt upheaval of quartz and
gneiss, shaped like a coffer, from which the mountain took
its name. It was a favorite haunt of Leonidas, one of
whose boyish superstitions was that it contained a treasure
of gold, and one of whose brightest dreams had been that
he should yet discover it. This he did not do to-day, but
looking up from the rocks that he was listlessly examining,
he made the almost as thrilling discovery that near him on
the trail was a distinguished-looking stranger.

He was bestriding a shapely mustang, which well became
his handsome face and slight, elegant figure, and he was
looking at Leonidas with an amused curiosity and a certain
easy assurance that were difficult to withstand. It was
with the same fascinating self-confidence of smile, voice,
and manner that he rode up to the boy, and leaning lightly
over his saddle, said with exaggerated politeness: "I believe I have the pleasure of addressing Mr. Leonidas Boone?"

The rising color in Leonidas's face was apparently a sufficient answer to the stranger, for he continued smilingly,
"Then permit me to introduce myself as Mr. James Belcher.
As you perceive, I have grown considerably since you last
saw me. In fact, I 've done nothing else. It 's surprising

what a fellow can do when he sets his mind on one thing. And then, you know, they 're always telling you that San Francisco is a 'growing place.' That accounts for it!"

Leonidas, dazed, dazzled, but delighted, showed all his white teeth in a shy laugh. At which the enchanting stranger leaped from his horse like a very boy, drew his arm through the rein, and going up to Leonidas, lifted the boy's straw hat from his head and ran his fingers through his curls. There was nothing original in that — everybody did that to him as a preliminary to conversation. But when this ingenuous fine gentleman put his own Panama hat on Leonidas's head, and clapped Leonidas's torn straw on his own, and, passing his arm through the boy's, began to walk on with him, Leonidas's simple heart went out to him at once.

"And now, Leon," said the delightful stranger, "let 's you and me have a talk. There 's a nice cool spot under these laurels; I 'll stake out Pepita, and we 'll just lie off there and gab, and not care if school keeps or not."

"But you know you ain't really Jim Belcher," said the boy shyly.

"I 'm as good a man as he is any day, whoever *I* am," said the stranger, with humorous defiance, "and can lick him out of his boots, whoever *he* is. That ought to satisfy you. But if you want my certificate, here 's your own letter, old man," he said, producing Leonidas's last scrawl from his pocket.

"And *hers?* " said the boy cautiously.

The stranger's face changed a little. "And *hers,*" he repeated gravely, showing a little pink note which Leonidas recognized as one of Mrs. Burroughs's inclosures. The boy was silent until they reached the laurels, where the stranger tethered his horse and then threw himself in an easy attitude beneath the tree, with the back of his head upon his clasped hands. Leonidas could see his curved brown mustaches and silky lashes that were almost as long, and thought him the handsomest man he had ever beheld.

"Well, Leon," said the stranger, stretching himself out comfortably and pulling the boy down beside him, "how are things going on the Casket? All serene, eh?"

The inquiry so dismally recalled Leonidas's late feelings that his face clouded, and he involuntarily sighed. The stranger instantly shifted his head and gazed curiously at him. Then he took the boy's sunburnt hand in his own, and held it a moment. "Well, go on," he said.

"Well, Mr. — Mr. — I can't go on — I won't!" said Leonidas, with a sudden fit of obstinacy. "I don't know what to call you."

"Call me ' Jack ' — ' Jack Hamlin ' when you're not in a hurry. Ever heard of me before?" he added, suddenly turning his head towards Leonidas.

The boy shook his head. "No."

Mr. Jack Hamlin lifted his lashes in affected expostulation to the skies. "And this is Fame!" he murmured audibly.

But this Leonidas did not comprehend. Nor could he understand why the stranger, who clearly must have come to see *her*, should not ask about her, should not rush to seek her, but should lie back there all the while so contentedly on the grass. *He* would n't. He half resented it, and then it occurred to him that this fine gentleman was like himself — shy. Who could help being so before such an angel? *He* would help him on.

And so, shyly at first, but bit by bit emboldened by a word or two from Jack, he began to talk of her — of her beauty — of her kindness — of his own unworthiness — of what she had said and done — until, finding in this gracious stranger the vent his pent-up feelings so long had sought, he sang then and there the little idyl of his boyish life. He told of his decline in her affections after his unpardonable sin in keeping her waiting while he went for the trout, and added the miserable mistake of the rattlesnake episode. "For it was a mistake, Mr. Hamlin. I ought n't to have let a lady like that know anything about snakes — just because *I* happen to know them."

"It *was* an awful slump, Lee," said Hamlin gravely. "Get a woman and a snake together — and where are you? Think of Adam and Eve and the serpent, you know."

"But it was n't that way," said the boy earnestly. "And I want to tell you something else that 's just makin' me sick, Mr. Hamlin. You know I told you William Henry lives down at the bottom of Burroughs's garden, and how I showed Mrs. Burroughs his tricks! Well, only two days ago I was down there looking for him, and could n't find him anywhere. There 's a sort of narrow trail from the garden to the hill, a short cut up to the Ridge, instead o' going by their gate. It 's just the trail any one would take in a hurry, or if they did n't want to be seen from the road. Well! I was looking this way and that for William Henry, and whistlin' for him, when I slipped on to the trail. There, in the middle of it, was an old bucket turned upside down — just the thing a man would kick away or a woman lift up. Well, Mr. Hamlin, I kicked it away, and " — the boy stopped, with rounded eyes and bated breath, and added — "I just had time to give one jump and save myself! For under that pail, cramped down so he could n't get out, and just bilin' over with rage, and chockful of pizen, was William Henry! If it had been anybody else less spry, they 'd have got bitten, — and that 's just what the sneak who put it there knew."

Mr. Hamlin uttered an exclamation under his breath, and rose to his feet.

"What did you say?" asked the boy quickly.

"Nothing," said Mr. Hamlin.

But it had sounded to Leonidas like an oath.

Mr. Hamlin walked a few steps, as if stretching his limbs, and then said: "And you think Burroughs would have been bitten?"

"Why, no!" said Leonidas in astonished indignation; "of course not — not *Burroughs.* It would have been poor *Mrs.* Burroughs. For of course *he* set that trap for her — don't you see? Who else would do it?"

"Of course, of course! Certainly," said Mr. Hamlin coolly. "Of course, as you say, *he* set the trap — yes — you just hang on to that idea."

But something in Mr. Hamlin's manner, and a peculiar look in his eye, did not satisfy Leonidas. "Are you going to see her now?" he said eagerly. "I can show you the house, and then run in and tell her you're outside in the laurels."

"Not just yet," said Mr. Hamlin, laying his hand on the boy's head after having restored his own hat. "You see, I thought of giving her a surprise. A big surprise!" he added slowly. After a pause, he went on, "Did you tell her what you had seen?"

"Of course I did," said Leonidas reproachfully. "Did you think I was going to let her get bit? It might have killed her."

"And it might not have been an unmixed pleasure for William Henry. I mean," said Mr. Hamlin gravely, correcting himself, "*you* would never have forgiven him. But what did she say?"

The boy's face clouded. "She thanked me and said it was very thoughtful — and kind — though it might have been only an accident" — he stammered — "and then she said perhaps I was hanging round and coming there a little too much lately, and that as Burroughs was very watchful, I'd better quit for two or three days." The tears were rising to his eyes, but by putting his two clinched fists into his pockets, he managed to hold them down. Perhaps Mr.

Hamlin's soft hand on his head assisted him. Mr. Hamlin took from his pocket a note-book, and tearing out a leaf, sat down again and began to write on his knee. After a pause, Leonidas said, —

"Was you ever in love, Mr. Hamlin?"

"Never," said Mr. Hamlin, quietly continuing to write. "But, now you speak of it, it's a long-felt want in my nature that I intend to supply some day. But not until I've made my pile. And don't *you* either." He continued writing, for it was this gentleman's peculiarity to talk without apparently the slightest concern whether anybody else spoke, whether he was listened to, or whether his remarks were at all relevant to the case. Yet he was always listened to for that reason. When he had finished writing, he folded up the paper, put it in an envelope, and addressed it.

"Shall I take it to her?" said Leonidas eagerly.

"It's not for *her*; it's for him — Mr. Burroughs," said Mr. Hamlin quietly.

The boy drew back. "To get him out of the way," added Hamlin explanatorily. "When he gets it, lightning wouldn't keep him here. Now, how to send it," he said thoughtfully.

"You might leave it at the post office," said Leonidas timidly. "He always goes there to watch his wife's letters."

For the first time in their interview Mr. Hamlin distinctly laughed.

"Your head is level, Leo, and I'll do it. Now the best thing you can do is to follow Mrs. Burroughs's advice. Quit going to the house for a day or two." He walked towards his horse. The boy's face sank, but he kept up bravely. "And will I see you again?" he said wistfully.

Mr. Hamlin lowered his face so near the boy's that Leonidas could see himself in the brown depths of Mr.

Hamlin's eyes. "I hope you will," he said gravely. He mounted, shook the boy's hand, and rode away in the lengthening shadows. Then Leonidas walked sadly home.

There was no need for him to keep his promise; for the next morning the family were stirred by the announcement that Mr. and Mrs. Burroughs had left Casket Ridge that night by the down stage for Sacramento, and that the house was closed. There were various rumors concerning the reason of this sudden departure, but only one was persistent, and borne out by the postmaster. It was that Mr. Burroughs had received that afternoon an anonymous note that his wife was about to elope with the notorious San Francisco gambler, Jack Hamlin.

But Leonidas Boone, albeit half understanding, kept his miserable secret with a still hopeful and trustful heart. It grieved him a little that William Henry was found a few days later dead, with his head crushed. Yet it was not until years later, when he had made a successful "prospect" on Casket Ridge, that he met Mr. Hamlin in San Francisco, and knew how he had played the part of Mercury upon that "heaven-kissing hill."

COLONEL STARBOTTLE FOR THE PLAINTIFF

It had been a day of triumph for Colonel Starbottle.
First, for his personality, as it would have been difficult to
separate the Colonel's achievements from his individuality;
second, for his oratorical abilities as a sympathetic pleader;
and third, for his functions as the leading legal counsel for
the Eureka Ditch Company *versus* the State of California.
On his strictly legal performances in this issue I prefer not
to speak; there were those who denied them, although the
jury had accepted them in the face of the ruling of the half-
amused, half-cynical Judge himself. For an hour they had
laughed with the Colonel, wept with him, been stirred to
personal indignation or patriotic exaltation by his passionate and lofty periods, — what else could they do than give
him their verdict? If it was alleged by some that the
American eagle, Thomas Jefferson, and the Resolutions of
'98 had nothing whatever to do with the contest of a ditch
company over a doubtfully worded legislative document;
that wholesale abuse of the State Attorney and his political
motives had not the slightest connection with the legal
question raised — it was, nevertheless, generally accepted
that the losing party would have been only too glad to have
the Colonel on their side. And Colonel Starbottle knew
this, as, perspiring, florid, and panting, he rebuttoned the
lower buttons of his blue frock-coat, which had become
loosed in an oratorical spasm, and readjusted his old-fashioned, spotless shirt frill above it as he strutted from the
court-room amidst the handshakings and acclamations of his
friends.

And here an unprecedented thing occurred. The Colonel absolutely declined spirituous refreshment at the neighboring Palmetto Saloon, and declared his intention of proceeding directly to his office in the adjoining square. Nevertheless, the Colonel quitted the building alone, and apparently unarmed, except for his faithful gold-headed stick, which hung as usual from his forearm. The crowd gazed after him with undisguised admiration of this new evidence of his pluck. It was remembered also that a mysterious note had been handed to him at the conclusion of his speech, — evidently a challenge from the State Attorney. It was quite plain that the Colonel — a practiced duelist — was hastening home to answer it.

But herein they were wrong. The note was in a female hand, and simply requested the Colonel to accord an interview with the writer at the Colonel's office as soon as he left the court. But it was an engagement that the Colonel — as devoted to the fair sex as he was to the "code" — was no less prompt in accepting. He flicked away the dust from his spotless white trousers and varnished boots with his handkerchief, and settled his black cravat under his Byron collar as he neared his office. He was surprised, however, on opening the door of his private office, to find his visitor already there; he was still more startled to find her somewhat past middle age and plainly attired. But the Colonel was brought up in a school of Southern politeness, already antique in the republic, and his bow of courtesy belonged to the epoch of his shirt frill and strapped trousers. No one could have detected his disappointment in his manner, albeit his sentences were short and incomplete. But the Colonel's colloquial speech was apt to be fragmentary incoherencies of his larger oratorical utterances.

"A thousand pardons — for — er — having kept a lady waiting — er! But — er — congratulations of friends — and — er — courtesy due to them — er — interfered with

— though perhaps only heightened — by procrastination —
the pleasure of — ha!" And the Colonel completed his
sentence with a gallant wave of his fat but white and well-
kept hand.

"Yes! I came to see you along o' that speech of yours.
I was in court. When I heard you gettin' it off on that
jury, I says to myself, 'That's the kind o' lawyer *I* want.
A man that's flowery and convincin'! Just the man to
take up our case.'"

"Ah! It's a matter of business, I see," said the Colonel, inwardly relieved, but externally careless. "And — er
— may I ask the nature of the case?"

"Well! it's a breach-o'-promise suit," said the visitor
calmly.

If the Colonel had been surprised before, he was now
really startled, and with an added horror that required all
his politeness to conceal. Breach-of-promise cases were
his peculiar aversion. He had always held them to be a
kind of litigation which could have been obviated by the
prompt killing of the masculine offender — in which case
he would have gladly defended the killer. But a suit for
damages, — *damages !* — with the reading of love-letters
before a hilarious jury and court, was against all his instincts. His chivalry was outraged; his sense of humor
was small, and in the course of his career he had lost one
or two important cases through an unexpected development
of this quality in a jury.

The woman had evidently noticed his hesitation, but
mistook its cause. "It ain't me — but my darter."

The Colonel recovered his politeness. "Ah! I am relieved, my dear madam! I could hardly conceive a man
ignorant enough to — er — er — throw away such evident
good fortune — or base enough to deceive the trustfulness
of womanhood — matured and experienced only in the
chivalry of our sex, ha!"

The woman smiled grimly. "Yes! — it's my darter, Zaidee Hooker — so ye might spare some of them pretty speeches for *her* — before the jury."

The Colonel winced slightly before this doubtful prospect, but smiled. "Ha! Yes! — certainly — the jury. But — er — my dear lady, need we go as far as that? Cannot this affair be settled — er — out of court? Could not this — er — individual — be admonished — told that he must give satisfaction — personal satisfaction — for his dastardly conduct — to — er — near relative — or even valued personal friend? The — er — arrangements necessary for that purpose I myself would undertake."

He was quite sincere; indeed, his small black eyes shone with that fire which a pretty woman or an "affair of honor" could alone kindle. The visitor stared vacantly at him, and said slowly, "And what good is that goin' to do *us?*"

"Compel him to — er — perform his promise," said the Colonel, leaning back in his chair.

"Ketch him doin' it!" she exclaimed scornfully. "No — that ain't wot we're after. We must make him *pay!* Damages — and nothin' short o' *that.*"

The Colonel bit his lip. "I suppose," he said gloomily, "you have documentary evidence — written promises and protestations — er — er — love-letters, in fact?"

"No — nary a letter! Ye see, that's jest it — and that's where *you* come in. You've got to convince that jury yourself. You've got to show what it is — tell the whole story your own way. Lord! to a man like you that's nothin'."

Startling as this admission might have been to any other lawyer, Starbottle was absolutely relieved by it. The absence of any mirth-provoking correspondence, and the appeal solely to his own powers of persuasion, actually struck his fancy. He lightly put aside the compliment with a wave of his white hand.

"Of course," he said confidently, "there is strongly presumptive and corroborative evidence? Perhaps you can give me — er — a brief outline of the affair?"

"Zaidee kin do that straight enough, I reckon," said the woman; "what I want to know first is, kin you take the case?"

The Colonel did not hesitate; his curiosity was piqued. "I certainly can. I have no doubt your daughter will put me in possession of sufficient facts and details — to constitute what we call — er — a brief."

"She kin be brief enough — or long enough — for the matter of that," said the woman, rising. The Colonel accepted this implied witticism with a smile.

"And when may I have the pleasure of seeing her?" he asked politely.

"Well, I reckon as soon as I can trot out and call her. She's just outside, meanderin' in the road — kinder shy, ye know, at first."

She walked to the door. The astounded Colonel nevertheless gallantly accompanied her as she stepped out into the street and called shrilly, "You Zaidee!"

A young girl here apparently detached herself from a tree and the ostentatious perusal of an old election poster, and sauntered down towards the office door. Like her mother, she was plainly dressed; unlike her, she had a pale, rather refined face, with a demure mouth and downcast eyes. This was all the Colonel saw as he bowed profoundly and led the way into his office, for she accepted his salutations without lifting her head. He helped her gallantly to a chair, on which she seated herself sideways, somewhat ceremoniously, with her eyes following the point of her parasol as she traced a pattern on the carpet. A second chair offered to the mother, that lady, however, declined. "I reckon to leave you and Zaidee together to talk it out," she said; turning to her daughter, she added,

"Jest you tell him all, Zaidee," and before the Colonel could rise again, disappeared from the room. In spite of his professional experience, Starbottle was for a moment embarrassed. The young girl, however, broke the silence without looking up.

"Adoniram K. Hotchkiss," she began, in a monotonous voice, as if it were a recitation addressed to the public, "first began to take notice of me a year ago. Arter that — off and on " —

"One moment," interrupted the astounded Colonel; "do you mean Hotchkiss the President of the Ditch Company ? " He had recognized the name of a prominent citizen — a rigid, ascetic, taciturn, middle-aged man — a deacon — and more than that, the head of the company he had just defended. It seemed inconceivable.

"That's him," she continued, with eyes still fixed on the parasol and without changing her monotonous tone — "off and on ever since. Most of the time at the Free-Will Baptist Church — at morning service, prayer-meetings, and such. And at home — outside — er — in the road."

"Is it this gentleman — Mr. Adoniram K. Hotchkiss — who — er — promised marriage ? " stammered the Colonel.

"Yes."

The Colonel shifted uneasily in his chair. "Most extraordinary! for — you see — my dear young lady — this becomes — a — er — most delicate affair."

"That's what maw said," returned the young woman simply, yet with the faintest smile playing around her demure lips and downcast cheek.

"I mean," said the Colonel, with a pained yet courteous smile, "that this — er — gentleman — is in fact — er — one of my clients."

"That's what maw said too, and of course your knowing him will make it all the easier for you."

A slight flush crossed the Colonel's cheek as he returned

quickly and a little stiffly, "On the contrary — er — it may make it impossible for me to — er — act in this matter."

The girl lifted her eyes. The Colonel held his breath as the long lashes were raised to his level. Even to an ordinary observer that sudden revelation of her eyes seemed to transform her face with subtle witchery. They were large, brown, and soft, yet filled with an extraordinary penetration and prescience. They were the eyes of an experienced woman of thirty fixed in the face of a child. What else the Colonel saw there Heaven only knows! He felt his inmost secrets plucked from him — his whole soul laid bare — his vanity, belligerency, gallantry — even his mediæval chivalry, penetrated, and yet illuminated, in that single glance. And when the eyelids fell again, he felt that a greater part of himself had been swallowed up in them.

"I beg your pardon," he said hurriedly. "I mean — this matter may be arranged — er — amicably. My interest with — and as you wisely say — my — er — knowledge of my client — er — Mr. Hotchkiss — may effect — a compromise."

"And *damages*," said the young girl, readdressing her parasol, as if she had never looked up.

The Colonel winced. "And — er — undoubtedly *compensation* — if you do not press a fulfillment of the promise. Unless," he said, with an attempted return to his former easy gallantry, which, however, the recollection of her eyes made difficult, "it is a question of — er — the affections."

"Which?" asked his fair client softly.

"If you still love him?" explained the Colonel, actually blushing.

Zaidee again looked up; again taking the Colonel's breath away with eyes that expressed not only the fullest perception of what he had *said*, but of what he thought and had not said, and with an added subtle suggestion of what he might have thought.   "That 's tellin'," she said, dropping her long lashes again.

The Colonel laughed vacantly.   Then feeling himself growing imbecile, he forced an equally weak gravity. "Pardon me — I understand there are no letters; may I know the way in which he formulated his declaration and promises ? "

"Hymn-books."

"I beg your pardon," said the mystified lawyer.

"Hymn-books — marked words in them with pencil — and passed 'em on to me," repeated Zaidee.   "Like ' love,' ' dear,' ' precious,' ' sweet,' and ' blessed,' " she added, accenting each word with a push of her parasol on the carpet. "Sometimes a whole line outer Tate and Brady — and Solomon's Song, you know, and sich."

"I believe," said the Colonel loftily, "that the — er — phrases of sacred psalmody lend themselves to the language of the affections.   But in regard to the distinct promise of marriage — was there — er — no *other* expression ? "

"Marriage Service in the prayer-book — lines and words outer that — all marked," Zaidee replied.

The Colonel nodded naturally and approvingly.   "Very good.   Were others cognizant of this ?   Were there any witnesses ? "

"Of course not," said the girl.   "Only me and him.   It was generally at church-time — or prayer-meeting.   Once, in passing the plate, he slipped one o' them peppermint lozenges with the letters stamped on it ' I love you ' for me to take."

The Colonel coughed slightly.   "And you have the lozenge ? "

"I ate it."

"Ah," said the Colonel.   After a pause he added delicately, "But were these attentions — er — confined to — er — sacred precincts ?   Did he meet you elsewhere ? "

"Useter pass our house on the road," returned the girl, dropping into her monotonous recital, "and useter signal."

"Ah, signal?" repeated the Colonel approvingly.

"Yes! He'd say 'Keerow,' and I'd say 'Keeree.' Suthing like a bird, you know."

Indeed, as she lifted her voice in imitation of the call, the Colonel thought it certainly very sweet and birdlike. At least as *she* gave it.   With his remembrance of the grim deacon he had doubts as to the melodiousness of *his* utterance.   He gravely made her repeat it.

"And after that signal?" he added suggestively.

"He'd pass on."

The Colonel again coughed slightly, and tapped his desk with his penholder.

"Were there any endearments — er — caresses — er — such as taking your hand — er — clasping your waist?" he suggested, with a gallant yet respectful sweep of his white hand and bowing of his head; "er — slight pressure of your fingers in the changes of a dance — I mean," he corrected himself, with an apologetic cough — "in the passing of the plate?"

"No; he was not what you'd call 'fond,'" returned the girl.

"Ah! Adoniram K. Hotchkiss was not 'fond' in the ordinary acceptance of the word," noted the Colonel, with professional gravity.

She lifted her disturbing eyes, and again absorbed his in her own.   She also said "Yes," although her eyes in their mysterious prescience of all he was thinking disclaimed the necessity of any answer at all.   He smiled vacantly.   There was a long pause; on which she slowly disengaged her parasol from the carpet pattern, and stood up.

"I reckon that's about all," she said.

"Er — yes — but one moment," began the Colonel vaguely.   He would have liked to keep her longer, but

with her strange premonition of him he felt powerless to
detain her, or explain his reason for doing so. He instinctively knew she had told him all; his professional judgment told him that a more hopeless case had never come to
his knowledge. Yet he was not daunted, only embarrassed.
"No matter," he said. "Of course I shall have to consult
with you again."

Her eyes again answered that she expected he would,
and she added simply, "When?"

"In the course of a day or two," he replied quickly.
"I will send you word."

She turned to go. In his eagerness to open the door for
her, he upset his chair, and with some confusion, that was
actually youthful, he almost impeded her movements in the
hall, and knocked his broad-brimmed Panama hat from his
bowing hand in a final gallant sweep. Yet as her small,
trim, youthful figure, with its simple Leghorn straw hat
confined by a blue bow under her round chin, passed away
before him, she looked more like a child than ever.

The Colonel spent that afternoon in making diplomatic
inquiries. He found his youthful client was the daughter
of a widow who had a small ranch on the cross-roads, near
the new Free-Will Baptist Church — the evident theatre
of this pastoral. They led a secluded life, the girl being
little known in the town, and her beauty and fascination
apparently not yet being a recognized fact. The Colonel
felt a pleasurable relief at this, and a general satisfaction he
could not account for. His few inquiries concerning Mr.
Hotchkiss only confirmed his own impressions of the alleged lover, — a serious-minded, practically abstracted man,
abstentive of youthful society, and the last man apparently
capable of levity of the affections or serious flirtation. The
Colonel was mystified, but determined of purpose, whatever
that purpose might have been.

The next day he was at his office at the same hour. He

was alone — as usual — the Colonel's office being really his private lodgings, disposed in connecting rooms, a single apartment reserved for consultation. He had no clerk, his papers and briefs being taken by his faithful body-servant and ex-slave "Jim" to another firm who did his office work since the death of Major Stryker, the Colonel's only law partner, who fell in a duel some years previous. With a fine constancy the Colonel still retained his partner's name on his doorplate, and, it was alleged by the superstitious, kept a certain invincibility also through the *manes* of that lamented and somewhat feared man.

The Colonel consulted his watch, whose heavy gold case still showed the marks of a providential interference with a bullet destined for its owner, and replaced it with some difficulty and shortness of breath in his fob. At the same moment he heard a step in the passage, and the door opened to Adoniram K. Hotchkiss. The Colonel was impressed; he had a duelist's respect for punctuality.

The man entered with a nod and the expectant inquiring look of a busy man. As his feet crossed that sacred threshold the Colonel became all courtesy; he placed a chair for his visitor, and took his hat from his half-reluctant hand. He then opened a cupboard and brought out a bottle of whiskey and two glasses.

"A — er — slight refreshment, Mr. Hotchkiss," he suggested politely.

"I never drink," replied Hotchkiss, with the severe attitude of a total abstainer.

"Ah — er — not the finest Bourbon whiskey, selected by a Kentucky friend? No? Pardon me! A cigar, then — the mildest Havana."

"I do not use tobacco nor alcohol in any form," repeated Hotchkiss ascetically. "I have no foolish weaknesses."

The Colonel's moist, beady eyes swept silently over his client's sallow face. He leaned back comfortably in his chair, and half closing his eyes as in dreamy reminiscence, said slowly: "Your reply, Mr. Hotchkiss, reminds me of — er — sing'lar circumstance that — er — occurred, in point of fact — at the St. Charles Hotel, New Orleans.   Pinkey Hornblower — personal friend — invited Senator Doolittle to join him in social glass.   Received, sing'larly enough, reply similar to yours.   'Don't drink nor smoke?' said Pinkey.   'Gad, sir, you must be mighty sweet on the ladies.'   Ha!"   The Colonel paused long enough to allow the faint flush to pass from Hotchkiss's cheek, and went on, half closing his eyes: "'I allow no man, sir, to discuss my personal habits,' declared Doolittle, over his shirt collar.   'Then I reckon shootin' must be one of those habits,' said Pinkey coolly.   Both men drove out on the Shell Road back of cemetery next morning.   Pinkey put bullet at twelve paces through Doolittle's temple.   Poor Doo never spoke again.   Left three wives and seven children, they say — two of 'em black."

"I got a note from you this morning," said Hotchkiss, with badly concealed impatience.   "I suppose in reference to our case.   You have taken judgment, I believe."

The Colonel, without replying, slowly filled a glass of whiskey and water.   For a moment he held it dreamily before him, as if still engaged in gentle reminiscences called up by the act.   Then tossing it off, he wiped his lips with a large white handkerchief, and leaning back comfortably in his chair, said, with a wave of his hand, "The interview I requested, Mr. Hotchkiss, concerns a subject — which I may say is — er — er — at present *not* of a public or business nature — although *later* it might become — er — er — both.   It is an affair of some — er — delicacy."

The Colonel paused, and Mr. Hotchkiss regarded him with increased impatience.   The Colonel, however, continued, with unchanged deliberation: "It concerns — er — er — a young lady — a beautiful, high-souled creature, sir,

who, apart from her personal loveliness — er — er — I may
say is of one of the first families of Missouri, and — er —
not remotely connected by marriage with one of — er — er
— my boyhood's dearest friends." The latter, I grieve to
say, was a pure invention of the Colonel's — an oratorical
addition to the scanty information he had obtained the
previous day. "The young lady," he continued blandly,
"enjoys the further distinction of being the object of such
attention from you as would make this interview — really
— a confidential matter — er — er — among friends and —
er — er — relations in present and future. I need not say
that the lady I refer to is Miss Zaidee Juno Hooker, only
daughter of Almira Ann Hooker, relict of Jefferson Brown
Hooker, formerly of Boone County, Kentucky, and latterly
of — er — Pike County, Missouri."

The sallow, ascetic hue of Mr. Hotchkiss's face had
passed through a livid and then a greenish shade, and finally
settled into a sullen red. "What's all this about?" he
demanded roughly.

The least touch of belligerent fire came into Starbottle's
eye, but his bland courtesy did not change. "I believe,"
he said politely, "I have made myself clear as between —
er — gentlemen, though perhaps not as clear as I should to
— er — er — jury."

Mr. Hotchkiss was apparently struck with some significance in the lawyer's reply. "I don't know," he said, in
a lower and more cautious voice, "what you mean by what
you call 'my attentions' to — any one — or how it concerns you. I have not exchanged half a dozen words with
— the person you name — have never written her a line —
nor even called at her house."

He rose with an assumption of ease, pulled down his
waistcoat, buttoned his coat, and took up his hat. The
Colonel did not move.

"I believe I have already indicated my meaning in what

I have called 'your attentions,' " said the Colonel blandly, "and given you my ' concern ' for speaking as — er — er — mutual friend. As to *your* statement of your relations with Miss Hooker, I may state that it is fully corroborated by the statement of the young lady herself in this very office yesterday."

"Then what does this impertinent nonsense mean? Why am I summoned here?" demanded Hotchkiss furiously.

"Because," said the Colonel deliberately, "that statement is infamously — yes, damnably to your discredit, sir!"

Mr. Hotchkiss was here seized by one of those impotent and inconsistent rages which occasionally betray the habitually cautious and timid man. He caught up the Colonel's stick, which was lying on the table. At the same moment the Colonel, without any apparent effort, grasped it by the handle. To Mr. Hotchkiss's astonishment, the stick separated in two pieces, leaving the handle and about two feet of narrow glittering steel in the Colonel's hand. The man recoiled, dropping the useless fragment. The Colonel picked it up, fitted the shining blade in it, clicked the spring, and then rising with a face of courtesy yet of unmistakably genuine pain, and with even a slight tremor in his voice, said gravely, —

"Mr. Hotchkiss, I owe you a thousand apologies, sir, that — er — a weapon should be drawn by me — even through your own inadvertence — under the sacred protection of my roof, and upon an unarmed man. I beg your pardon, sir, and I even withdraw the expressions which provoked that inadvertence. Nor does this apology prevent you from holding me responsible — personally responsible — *elsewhere* for an indiscretion committed in behalf of a lady — my — er — client."

"Your client? Do you mean you have taken her case?

You, the counsel for the Ditch Company?" asked Mr. Hotchkiss, in trembling indignation.

"Having won *your* case, sir," replied the Colonel coolly, "the — er — usages of advocacy do not prevent me from espousing the cause of the weak and unprotected."

"We shall see, sir," said Hotchkiss, grasping the handle of the door and backing into the passage. "There are other lawyers who" —

"Permit me to see you out," interrupted the Colonel, rising politely.

— "will be ready to resist the attacks of blackmail," continued Hotchkiss, retreating along the passage.

"And then you will be able to repeat your remarks to me *in the street*," continued the Colonel, bowing, as he persisted in following his visitor to the door.

But here Mr. Hotchkiss quickly slammed it behind him, and hurried away. The Colonel returned to his office, and sitting down, took a sheet of letter-paper bearing the inscription "Starbottle and Stryker, Attorneys and Counselors," and wrote the following lines: —

HOOKER *versus* HOTCHKISS.

DEAR MADAM, — Having had a visit from the defendant in above, we should be pleased to have an interview with you at two P. M. to-morrow.

Your obedient servants,
STARBOTTLE AND STRYKER.

This he sealed and dispatched by his trusted servant Jim, and then devoted a few moments to reflection. It was the custom of the Colonel to act first, and justify the action by reason afterwards.

He knew that Hotchkiss would at once lay the matter before rival counsel. He knew that they would advise

him that Miss Hooker had "no case" — that she would be
nonsuited on her own evidence, and he ought not to compromise, but be ready to stand trial. He believed, however, that Hotchkiss feared such exposure, and although
his own instincts had been at first against this remedy, he
was now instinctively in favor of it. He remembered his
own power with a jury; his vanity and his chivalry alike
approved of this heroic method; he was bound by no prosaic facts — he had his own theory of the case, which no
mere evidence could gainsay. In fact, Mrs. Hooker's admission that he was to "tell the story in his own way"
actually appeared to him an inspiration and a prophecy.

Perhaps there was something else, due possibly to the
lady's wonderful eyes, of which he had thought much.
Yet it was not her simplicity that affected him solely; on
the contrary, it was her apparent intelligent reading of the
character of her recreant lover — and of his own! Of all
the Colonel's previous "light" or "serious" loves, none
had ever before flattered him in that way. And it was
this, combined with the respect which he had held for their
professional relations, that precluded his having a more
familiar knowledge of his client, through serious questioning or playful gallantry. I am not sure it was not part of
the charm to have a rustic *femme incomprise* as a client.

Nothing could exceed the respect with which he greeted
her as she entered his office the next day. He even affected not to notice that she had put on her best clothes,
and, he made no doubt, appeared as when she had first attracted the mature yet faithless attentions of Deacon Hotchkiss at church. A white virginal muslin was belted around
her slim figure by a blue ribbon, and her Leghorn hat was
drawn around her oval cheek by a bow of the same color.
She had a Southern girl's narrow feet, encased in white
stockings and kid slippers, which were crossed primly before her as she sat in a chair, supporting her arm by her

faithful parasol planted firmly on the floor. A faint odor of southernwood exhaled from her, and, oddly enough, stirred the Colonel with a far-off recollection of a pine-shaded Sunday-school on a Georgia hillside, and of his first love, aged ten, in a short starched frock. Possibly it was the same recollection that revived something of the awkwardness he had felt then.

He, however, smiled vaguely, and sitting down, coughed slightly, and placed his finger-tips together. "I have had an — er — interview with Mr. Hotchkiss, but — I — er — regret to say there seems to be no prospect of — er — compromise."

He paused, and to his surprise her listless "company" face lit up with an adorable smile. "Of course! — ketch him!" she said. "Was he mad when you told him?" She put her knees comfortably together and leaned forward for a reply.

For all that, wild horses could not have torn from the Colonel a word about Hotchkiss's anger. "He expressed his intention of employing counsel — and defending a suit," returned the Colonel, affably basking in her smile.

She dragged her chair nearer his desk. "Then you'll fight him tooth and nail?" she asked eagerly; "you'll show him up? You'll tell the whole story your own way? You'll give him fits? — and you'll make him pay? Sure?" she went on breathlessly.

"I — er — will," said the Colonel almost as breathlessly.

She caught his fat white hand, which was lying on the table, between her own and lifted it to her lips. He felt her soft young fingers even through the lisle-thread gloves that encased them, and the warm moisture of her lips upon his skin. He felt himself flushing — but was unable to break the silence or change his position. The next moment she had scuttled back with her chair to her old position.

"I — er — certainly shall do my best," stammered the Colonel, in an attempt to recover his dignity and composure.

"That's enough! You'll *do* it," said she enthusiastically. "Lordy! Just you talk for *me* as ye did for *his* old Ditch Company, and you'll fetch it — every time! Why, when you made that jury sit up the other day — when you got that off about the Merrikan flag waving equally over the rights of honest citizens banded together in peaceful commercial pursuits, as well as over the fortress of official proflig — "

"Oligarchy," murmured the Colonel courteously.

— "oligarchy," repeated the girl quickly, "my breath was just took away. I said to maw, 'Ain't he too sweet for anything!' I did, honest Injin! And when you rolled it all off at the end — never missing a word (you didn't need to mark 'em in a lesson-book, but had 'em all ready on your tongue) — and walked out — Well! I did n't know you nor the Ditch Company from Adam, but I could have just run over and kissed you there before the whole court!"

She laughed, with her face glowing, although her strange eyes were cast down. Alack! the Colonel's face was equally flushed, and his own beady eyes were on his desk. To any other woman he would have voiced the banal gallantry that he should now, himself, look forward to that reward, but the words never reached his lips. He laughed, coughed slightly, and when he looked up again she had fallen into the same attitude as on her first visit, with her parasol point on the floor.

"I must ask you to — er — direct your memory to — er — another point: the breaking off of the — er — er — er — engagement. Did he — er — give any reason for it? Or show any cause?"

"No; he never said anything," returned the girl.

"Not in his usual way? — er — no reproaches out of the hymn-book? — or the sacred writings?"

"No; he just *quit*."

"Er — ceased his attentions," said the Colonel gravely. "And naturally you — er — were not conscious of any cause for his doing so."

The girl raised her wonderful eyes so suddenly and so penetratingly without replying in any other way that the Colonel could only hurriedly say: "I see! None, of course!"

At which she rose, the Colonel rising also. "We — shall begin proceedings at once. I must, however, caution you to answer no questions, nor say anything about this case to any one until you are in court."

She answered his request with another intelligent look and a nod. He accompanied her to the door. As he took her proffered hand, he raised the lisle-thread fingers to his lips with old-fashioned gallantry. As if that act had condoned for his first omissions and awkwardness, he became his old-fashioned self again, buttoned his coat, pulled out his shirt frill, and strutted back to his desk.

A day or two later it was known throughout the town that Zaidee Hooker had sued Adoniram Hotchkiss for breach of promise, and that the damages were laid at five thousand dollars. As in those bucolic days the Western press was under the secure censorship of a revolver, a cautious tone of criticism prevailed, and any gossip was confined to personal expression, and even then at the risk of the gossiper. Nevertheless, the situation provoked the intensest curiosity. The Colonel was approached — until his statement that he should consider any attempt to overcome his professional secrecy a personal reflection withheld further advances. The community were left to the more ostentatious information of the defendant's counsel, Messrs. Kitcham and Bilser, that the case was "ridiculous" and "rotten," that the plaintiff would be nonsuited, and the fire-eating Starbottle would be taught a lesson that he could not "bully" the law, and there were some dark hints of a conspiracy. It was even hinted that the "case" was the revengeful and preposterous outcome of the refusal of Hotchkiss to pay Starbottle an extravagant fee for his late services to the Ditch Company. It is unnecessary to say that these words were not reported to the Colonel. It was, however, an unfortunate circumstance for the calmer, ethical consideration of the subject that the Church sided with Hotchkiss, as this provoked an equal adherence to the plaintiff and Starbottle on the part of the larger body of non-church-goers, who were delighted at a possible exposure of the weakness of religious rectitude. "I've allus had my suspicions o' them early candle-light meetings down at that gospel shop," said one critic, "and I reckon Deacon Hotchkiss didn't rope in the gals to attend jest for psalm-singing." "Then for him to get up and leave the board afore the game's finished and try to sneak out of it," said another, — "I suppose that's what they call *religious*."

It was therefore not remarkable that the court-house three weeks later was crowded with an excited multitude of the curious and sympathizing. The fair plaintiff, with her mother, was early in attendance, and under the Colonel's advice appeared in the same modest garb in which she had first visited his office. This and her downcast, modest demeanor were perhaps at first disappointing to the crowd, who had evidently expected a paragon of loveliness in this Circe of that grim, ascetic defendant, who sat beside his counsel. But presently all eyes were fixed on the Colonel, who certainly made up in *his* appearance any deficiency of his fair client. His portly figure was clothed in a blue dress coat with brass buttons, a buff waistcoat which permitted his frilled shirt-front to become erectile above it, a black satin stock which confined a boyish turned-down collar around his full neck, and immaculate drill trousers, strapped over varnished boots. A murmur ran round the court. "Old 'Personally Responsible' has got his war-paint on;" "The Old War-Horse is smelling powder," were whispered comments. Yet for all that, the most ir-reverent among them recognized vaguely, in this bizarre figure, something of an honored past in their country's his-tory, and possibly felt the spell of old deeds and old names that had once thrilled their boyish pulses. The new Dis-trict Judge returned Colonel Starbottle's profoundly punc-tilious bow. The Colonel was followed by his negro ser-vant, carrying a parcel of hymn-books and Bibles, who, with a courtesy evidently imitated from his master, placed one before the opposite counsel. This, after a first curious glance, the lawyer somewhat superciliously tossed aside. But when Jim, proceeding to the jury-box, placed with equal politeness the remaining copies before the jury, the opposite counsel sprang to his feet.

"I want to direct the attention of the Court to this un-precedented tampering with the jury, by this gratuitous exhibition of matter impertinent and irrelevent to the issue."

The Judge cast an inquiring look at Colonel Starbottle.

"May it please the Court," returned Colonel Starbottle with dignity, ignoring the counsel, "the defendant's coun-sel will observe that he is already furnished with the mat-ter — which I regret to say he has treated — in the pre-sence of the Court — and of his client, a deacon of the church — with — er — great superciliousness. When I state to your Honor that the books in question are hymn-books and copies of the Holy Scriptures, and that they are for the instruction of the jury, to whom I shall have to refer them in the course of my opening, I believe I am within my rights."

"The act is certainly unprecedented," said the Judge dryly, "but unless the counsel for the plaintiff expects the jury to *sing* from these hymn-books, their introduction is not improper, and I cannot admit the objection. As defendant's counsel are furnished with copies also, they cannot plead 'surprise,' as in the introduction of new matter, and as plaintiff's counsel relies evidently upon the jury's attention to his opening, he would not be the first person to distract it." After a pause he added, addressing the Colonel, who remained standing, "The Court is with you, sir; proceed."

But the Colonel remained motionless and statuesque, with folded arms.

"I have overruled the objection," repeated the Judge; "you may go on."

"I am waiting, your Honor, for the — er — withdrawal by the defendant's counsel of the word 'tampering,' as refers to myself, and of 'impertinent,' as refers to the sacred volumes."

"The request is a proper one, and I have no doubt will be acceded to," returned the Judge quietly. The defendant's counsel rose and mumbled a few words of apology, and the incident closed. There was, however, a general feeling that the Colonel had in some way "scored," and if his object had been to excite the greatest curiosity about the books, he had made his point.

But impassive of his victory, he inflated his chest, with his right hand in the breast of his buttoned coat, and began. His usual high color had paled slightly, but the small pupils of his prominent eyes glittered like steel. The young girl leaned forward in her chair with an attention so breathless, a sympathy so quick, and an admiration so artless and unconscious that in an instant she divided with the speaker the attention of the whole assemblage. It was very hot; the court was crowded to suffocation; even the open windows revealed a crowd of faces outside the building, eagerly following the Colonel's words.

He would remind the jury that only a few weeks ago he stood there as the advocate of a powerful Company, then represented by the present defendant. He spoke then as the champion of strict justice against legal oppression; no less should he to-day champion the cause of the unprotected and the comparatively defenseless — save for that paramount power which surrounds beauty and innocence — even though the plaintiff of yesterday was the defendant of to-day. As he approached the court a moment ago he had raised his eyes and beheld the starry flag flying from its dome, and he knew that glorious banner was a symbol of the perfect equality, under the Constitution, of the rich and the poor, the strong and the weak — an equality which made the simple citizen taken from the plough in the field, the pick in the gulch, or from behind the counter in the mining town, who served on that jury, the equal arbiters of justice with that highest legal luminary whom they were proud to welcome on the bench to-day. The Colonel paused, with a stately bow to the impassive Judge. It was this, he continued, which lifted his heart as he approached the building. And yet — he had entered it with an uncertain — he might almost say — a timid step. And why? He knew, gentlemen, he was about to confront a profound — ay! a sacred responsibility! Those hymnbooks and holy writings handed to the jury were *not*, as his Honor had surmised, for the purpose of enabling the jury to indulge in — er — preliminary choral exercise! He might, indeed, say, "Alas, not!" They were the damning, incontrovertible proofs of the perfidy of the defendant. And they would prove as terrible a warning to him as the fatal characters upon Belshazzar's wall. There was a strong sensation. Hotchkiss turned a sallow green. His lawyers assumed a careless smile.

It was his duty to tell them that this was not one of those ordinary "breach-of-promise" cases which were too often the occasion of ruthless mirth and indecent levity in the court-room. The jury would find nothing of that here. There were no love-letters with the epithets of endearment, nor those mystic crosses and ciphers which, he had been credibly informed, chastely hid the exchange of those mutual caresses known as "kisses." There was no cruel tearing of the veil from those sacred privacies of the human affection; there was no forensic shouting out of those fond confidences meant only for *one*. But there was, he was shocked to say, a new sacrilegious intrusion. The weak pipings of Cupid were mingled with the chorus of the saints, — the sanctity of the temple known as the "meeting-house" was desecrated by proceedings more in keeping with the shrine of Venus; and the inspired writings themselves were used as the medium of amatory and wanton flirtation by the defendant in his sacred capacity as deacon.

The Colonel artistically paused after this thunderous denunciation. The jury turned eagerly to the leaves of the hymn-books, but the larger gaze of the audience remained fixed upon the speaker and the girl, who sat in rapt admiration of his periods. After the hush, the Colonel continued in a lower and sadder voice: "There are, perhaps, few of us here, gentlemen, — with the exception of the defendant, — who can arrogate to themselves the title of regular church-goers, or to whom these humbler functions of the prayer-meeting, the Sunday-school, and the Bible-class are habitually familiar. Yet" — more solemnly — "down in our hearts is the deep conviction of our shortcomings and failings, and a laudable desire that others, at least, should profit by the teachings we neglect. Perhaps," he continued, closing his eyes dreamily, "there is not a man here who does not recall the happy days of his boyhood, the rustic village spire, the lessons shared with some artless village maiden, with whom he later sauntered, hand in hand, through the woods, as the simple rhyme rose upon their lips, —

> 'Always make it a point to have it a rule,
> Never to be late at the Sabbath-school.'

He would recall the strawberry feasts, the welcome annual picnic, redolent with hunks of gingerbread and sarsaparilla. How would they feel to know that these sacred recollections were now forever profaned in their memory by the knowledge that the defendant was capable of using such occasions to make love to the larger girls and teachers, whilst his artless companions were innocently — the Court will pardon me for introducing what I am credibly informed is the local expression — 'doing gooseberry'?" The tremulous flicker of a smile passed over the faces of the listening crowd, and the Colonel slightly winced. But he recovered himself instantly, and continued, —

"My client, the only daughter of a widowed mother — who has for years stemmed the varying tides of adversity, in the western precincts of this town — stands before you to-day invested only in her own innocence. She wears no — er — rich gifts of her faithless admirer — is panoplied in no jewels, rings, nor mementos of affection such as lovers delight to hang upon the shrine of their affections; hers is not the glory with which Solomon decorated the Queen of Sheba, though the defendant, as I shall show later, clothed her in the less expensive flowers of the king's poetry. No, gentlemen! The defendant exhibited in this affair a certain frugality of — er — pecuniary investment, which I am willing to admit may be commendable in his class. His only gift was characteristic alike of his methods and his economy. There is, I understand, a certain not unimportant feature of religious exercise known as 'taking a collection.' The defendant, on this occasion, by the mute presentation of a tin plate covered with baize, solicited the

pecuniary contributions of the faithful. On approaching
the plaintiff, however, he himself slipped a love-token upon
the plate and pushed it towards her. That love-token was
a lozenge — a small disk, I have reason to believe, concocted of peppermint and sugar, bearing upon its reverse
surface the simple words, ' I love you! ' I have since ascertained that these disks may be bought for five cents a
dozen — or at considerably less than one half cent for the
single lozenge. Yes, gentlemen, the words ' I love you! '
— the oldest legend of all; the refrain ' when the morning
stars sang together ' — were presented to the plaintiff by a
medium so insignificant that there is, happily, no coin in
the republic low enough to represent its value.

"I shall prove to you, gentlemen of the jury," said the
Colonel solemnly, drawing a Bible from his coat-tail pocket,
"that the defendant for the last twelve months conducted
an amatory correspondence with the plaintiff by means of
underlined words of Sacred Writ and church psalmody,
such as ' beloved,' ' precious,' and ' dearest,' occasionally
appropriating whole passages which seemed apposite to his
tender passion. I shall call your attention to one of them.
The defendant, while professing to be a total abstainer, —
a man who, in my own knowledge, has refused spirituous
refreshment as an inordinate weakness of the flesh, — with
shameless hypocrisy underscores with his pencil the following passage, and presents it to the plaintiff. The gentlemen of the jury will find it in the Song of Solomon, page
548, chapter ii., verse 5." After a pause, in which the
rapid rustling of leaves was heard in the jury-box, Colonel
Starbottle declaimed in a pleading, stentorian voice, "'Stay
me with — er — *flagons*, comfort me with — er — apples —
for I am — er — sick of love.' Yes, gentlemen! — yes,
you may well turn from those accusing pages and look at
the double-faced defendant. He desires — to — er — be —
' stayed with flagons '! I am not aware at present what

kind of liquor is habitually dispensed at these meetings, and for which the defendant so urgently clamored; but it will be my duty, before this trial is over, to discover it, if I have to summon every barkeeper in this district. For the moment I will simply call your attention to the *quantity*. It is not a single drink that the defendant asks for — not a glass of light and generous wine, to be shared with his inamorata, but a number of flagons or vessels, each possibly holding a pint measure — *for himself!* "

The smile of the audience had become a laugh. The Judge looked up warningly, when his eye caught the fact that the Colonel had again winced at this mirth. He regarded him seriously. Mr. Hotchkiss's counsel had joined in the laugh affectedly, but Hotchkiss himself sat ashy pale. There was also a commotion in the jury-box, a hurried turning over of leaves, and an excited discussion.

"The gentlemen of the jury," said the Judge, with official gravity, "will please keep order and attend only to the speeches of counsel. Any discussion *here* is irregular and premature, and must be reserved for the jury-room after they have retired."

The foreman of the jury struggled to his feet. He was a powerful man, with a good-humored face, and, in spite of his unfelicitous nickname of "The Bone-Breaker," had a kindly, simple, but somewhat emotional nature. Nevertheless, it appeared as if he were laboring under some powerful indignation.

"Can we ask a question, Judge?" he said respectfully, although his voice had the unmistakable Western American ring in it, as of one who was unconscious that he could be addressing any but his peers.

"Yes," said the Judge good-humoredly.

"We're finding in this yere piece, out o' which the Kernel hes just bin a-quotin', some language that me and my pardners allow hadn't orter be read out afore a young lady in court, and we want to know of you — ez a fa'r-minded and impartial man — ef this is the reg'lar kind o' book given to gals and babies down at the meetin'-house."

"The jury will please follow the counsel's speech without comment," said the Judge briefly, fully aware that the defendant's counsel would spring to his feet, as he did promptly.

"The Court will allow us to explain to the gentlemen that the language they seem to object to has been accepted by the best theologians for the last thousand years as being purely mystic. As I will explain later, those are merely symbols of the Church " —

"Of wot?" interrupted the foreman, in deep scorn.

"Of the Church!"

"We ain't askin' any questions o' *you*, and we ain't takin any answers," said the foreman, sitting down abruptly.

"I must insist," said the Judge sternly, "that the plaintiff's counsel be allowed to continue his opening without interruption. You" (to defendant's counsel) "will have your opportunity to reply later."

The counsel sank down in his seat with the bitter conviction that the jury was manifestly against him, and the case as good as lost. But his face was scarcely as disturbed as his client's, who, in great agitation, had begun to argue with him wildly, and was apparently pressing some point against the lawyer's vehement opposal. The Colonel's murky eyes brightened as he still stood erect, with his hand thrust in his breast.

"It will be put to you, gentlemen, when the counsel on the other side refrains from mere interruption and confines himself to reply, that my unfortunate client has no action — no remedy at law — because there were no spoken words of endearment. But, gentlemen, it will depend upon *you* to say what are and what are not articulate expressions of love. We all know that among the lower animals, with whom you may possibly be called upon to classify the defendant, there are certain signals more or less harmonious, as the case may be. The ass brays, the horse neighs, the sheep bleats — the feathered denizens of the grove call to their mates in more musical roundelays. These are recognized facts, gentlemen, which you yourselves, as dwellers among nature in this beautiful land, are all cognizant of. They are facts that no one would deny — and we should have a poor opinion of the ass who, at — er — such a supreme moment, would attempt to suggest that his call was unthinking and without significance. But, gentlemen, I shall prove to you that such was the foolish, self-convicting custom of the defendant. With the greatest reluctance, and the — er — greatest pain, I succeeded in wresting from the maidenly modesty of my fair client the innocent confession that the defendant had induced her to correspond with him in these methods. Picture to yourself, gentlemen, the lonely moonlight road beside the widow's humble cottage. It is a beautiful night, sanctified to the affections, and the innocent girl is leaning from her casement. Presently there appears upon the road a slinking, stealthy figure, the defendant on his way to church. True to the instruction she has received from him, her lips part in the musical utterance " (the Colonel lowered his voice in a faint falsetto, presumably in fond imitation of his fair client), " ' Keeree ! ' Instantly the night becomes resonant with the impassioned reply " (the Colonel here lifted his voice in stentorian tones), " ' Keerow.' Again, as he passes, rises the soft ' Keeree ; ' again, as his form is lost in the distance, comes back the deep ' Keerow.' "

A burst of laughter, long, loud, and irrepressible, struck the whole court-room, and before the Judge could lift his half-composed face and take his handkerchief from his mouth, a faint "Keeree " from some unrecognized obscurity of the court-room was followed by a loud "Keerow" from some opposite locality. "The Sheriff will clear the court," said the Judge sternly; but, alas! as the embarrassed and choking officials rushed hither and thither, a soft "Keeree" from the spectators at the window, outside the court house, was answered by a loud chorus of "Keerows" from the opposite windows, filled with onlookers. Again the laughter arose everywhere, — even the fair plaintiff herself sat convulsed behind her handkerchief.

The figure of Colonel Starbottle alone remained erect — white and rigid. And then the Judge, looking up, saw — what no one else in the court had seen — that the Colonel was sincere and in earnest; that what he had conceived to be the pleader's most perfect acting and most elaborate irony were the deep, serious, mirthless *convictions* of a man without the least sense of humor. There was the respect of this conviction in the Judge's voice as he said to him gently, "You may proceed, Colonel Starbottle."

"I thank your Honor," said the Colonel slowly, "for recognizing and doing all in your power to prevent an interruption that, during my thirty years' experience at the bar, I have never been subjected to without the privilege of holding the instigators thereof responsible — *personally* responsible. It is possibly my fault that I have failed, oratorically, to convey to the gentlemen of the jury the full force and significance of the defendant's signals. I am aware that my voice is singularly deficient in producing either the dulcet tones of my fair client or the impassioned vehemence of the defendant's response. I will," continued the Colonel, with a fatigued but blind fatuity that ignored the hurriedly knit brows and warning eyes of the Judge, "try again. The note uttered by my client" (lowering his voice to the faintest of falsettos) "was 'Keeree;' the response was 'Keerow-ow.'" And the Colonel's voice fairly shook the dome above him.

Another uproar of laughter followed this apparently audacious repetition, but was interrupted by an unlooked-for incident. The defendant rose abruptly, and tearing himself away from the withholding hand and pleading protestations of his counsel, absolutely fled from the court-room, his appearance outside being recognized by a prolonged "Keerow" from the bystanders, which again and again followed him in the distance.

In the momentary silence which followed, the Colonel's voice was heard saying, "We rest here, your Honor," and he sat down. No less white, but more agitated, was the face of the defendant's counsel, who instantly rose.

"For some unexplained reason, your Honor, my client desires to suspend further proceedings, with a view to effect a peaceable compromise with the plaintiff. As he is a man of wealth and position, he is able and willing to pay liberally for that privilege. While I, as his counsel, am still convinced of his legal irresponsibility, as he has chosen publicly to abandon his rights here, I can only ask your Honor's permission to suspend further proceedings until I can confer with Colonel Starbottle."

"As far as I can follow the pleadings," said the Judge gravely, "the case seems to be hardly one for litigation, and I approve of the defendant's course, while I strongly urge the plaintiff to accept it."

Colonel Starbottle bent over his fair client. Presently he rose, unchanged in look or demeanor. "I yield, your Honor, to the wishes of my client, and — er — lady. We accept."

Before the court adjourned that day it was known throughout the town that Adoniram K. Hotchkiss had compromised the suit for four thousand dollars and costs.

Colonel Starbottle had so far recovered his equanimity as to strut jauntily towards his office, where he was to meet his fair client. He was surprised, however, to find her already there, and in company with a somewhat sheep-ish-looking young man — a stranger. If the Colonel had any disappointment in meeting a third party to the inter-view, his old-fashioned courtesy did not permit him to show it. He bowed graciously, and politely motioned them each to a seat.

"I reckoned I'd bring Hiram round with me," said the young lady, lifting her searching eyes, after a pause, to the Colonel's, "though he *was* awful shy, and allowed that you did n't know him from Adam, or even suspect his ex-istence. But I said, 'That's just where you slip up, Hi-ram; a pow'ful man like the Colonel knows everything — and I've seen it in his eye.' Lordy!" she continued, with a laugh, leaning forward over her parasol, as her eyes again sought the Colonel's, "don't you remember when you asked me if I loved that old Hotchkiss, and I told you, 'That's tellin',' and you looked at me — Lordy! I knew *then* you suspected there was a Hiram *somewhere*, as good as if I'd told you. Now you jest get up, Hiram, and give the Colonel a good handshake. For if it was n't for *him* and *his* searchin' ways, and *his* awful power of language, I would n't hev got that four thousand dollars out o' that flirty fool Hotchkiss — enough to buy a farm, so as you and me could get married! That's what you owe to *him*. Don't stand there like a stuck fool starin' at him. He won't eat you — though he's killed many a better man. Come, have *I* got to do *all* the kissin'?"

It is of record that the Colonel bowed so courteously and so profoundly that he managed not merely to evade the prof-fered hand of the shy Hiram, but to only lightly touch the franker and more impulsive finger-tips of the gentle Zaidee. "I — er — offer my sincerest congratulations — though I think you — er — overestimate — my — er — powers of pene-tration. Unfortunately, a pressing engagement, which may oblige me also to leave town to-night, forbids my saying more. I have — er — left the — er — business settlement of this — er — case in the hands of the lawyers who do my office work, and who will show you every attention. And now let me wish you a very good afternoon."

Nevertheless, the Colonel returned to his private room, and it was nearly twilight when the faithful Jim entered, to find him sitting meditatively before his desk. "'Fo' God! Kernel, I hope dey ain't nuffin de matter, but you 's lookin' mighty solemn! I ain't seen you look dat way, Kernel, since de day pooh Massa Stryker was fetched home shot froo de head."

"Hand me down the whiskey, Jim," said the Colonel, rising slowly.

The negro flew to the closet joyfully, and brought out the bottle. The Colonel poured out a glass of the spirit and drank it with his old deliberation.

"You're quite right, Jim," he said, putting down his glass, "but I 'm — er — getting old — and — somehow — I am missing poor Stryker damnably!"

THE LANDLORD OF THE BIG FLUME HOTEL

THE Big Flume stage-coach had just drawn up at the Big Flume Hotel simultaneously with the ringing of a large dinner bell in the two hands of a negro waiter, who, by certain gyrations of the bell was trying to impart to his performance that picturesque elegance and harmony which the instrument and its purpose lacked. For the refreshment thus proclaimed was only the ordinary station dinner, protracted at Big Flume for three quarters of an hour, to allow for the arrival of the connecting mail from Sacramento, although the repast was of a nature that seldom prevailed upon the traveler to linger the full period over its details. The ordinary cravings of hunger were generally satisfied in half an hour, and the remaining minutes were employed by the passengers in drowning the memory of their meal in "drinks at the bar," in smoking, and even in a hurried game of "old sledge," or dominoes. Yet to-day the deserted table was still occupied by a belated traveler, and a lady — separated by a wilderness of empty dishes — who had arrived after the stage-coach. Observing which, the landlord, perhaps touched by this unwonted appreciation of his fare, moved forward to give them his personal attention.

He was a man, however, who seemed to be singularly deficient in those supreme qualities which in the West have exalted the ability to "keep a hotel" into a proverbial synonym for superexcellence. He had little or no innovating genius, no trade devices, no assumption, no faculty for advertisement, no progressiveness, and no "racket." He had the tolerant good-humor of the Southwestern pioneer, to whom cyclones, famine, drought, floods, pestilence, and savages were things to be accepted, and whom disaster, if it did not stimulate, certainly did not appall. He received the insults, complaints, and criticisms of hurried and hungry passengers, the comments and threats of the Stage Company as he had submitted to the aggressions of a stupid, unjust, but overruling Nature — with unshaken calm. Perhaps herein lay his strength. People were obliged to submit to him and his hotel as part of the unfinished civilization, and they even saw something humorous in his impassiveness. Those who preferred to remonstrate with him emerged from the discussion with the general feeling of having been played with by a large-hearted and paternally disposed bear. Tall and long-limbed, with much strength in his lazy muscles, there was also a prevailing impression that this feeling might be intensified if the discussion were ever carried to physical contention. Of his personal history it was known only that he had emigrated from Wisconsin in 1855, that he had calmly unyoked his ox teams at Big Flume, then a trackless wilderness, and on the opening of a wagon road to the new mines had built a wayside station which eventually developed into the present hotel. He had been divorced in a Western State by his wife "Rosalie," locally known as "The Prairie Flower of Elkham Creek," for incompatibility of temper! Her temper was not stated.

Such was Abner Langworthy, the proprietor, as he moved leisurely down towards the lady guest, who was nearest, and who was sitting with her back to the passage between the tables. Stopping, occasionally, to professionally adjust the tablecloths and glasses, he at last reached her side.

"Ef there's anythin' more ye want that ye ain't seein', ma'am," he began — and stopped suddenly. For the lady had looked up at the sound of his voice.   It was his divorced wife, whom he had not seen since their separation. The recognition was instantaneous, mutual, and characterized by perfect equanimity on both sides.

"Well! I wanter know!" said the lady, although the exclamation point was purely conventional. "Abner Langworthy! though perhaps I've no call to say 'Abner.'"

"Same to you, Rosalie — though I say it too," returned the landlord. "But hol' on just a minit." He moved forward to the other guest, put the same perfunctory question regarding his needs, received a negative answer, and then returned to the lady and dropped into a chair opposite to her.

"You're looking peart and — fleshy," he said resignedly, as if he were tolerating his own conventional politeness with his other difficulties; "unless," he added cautiously, "you're takin' on some new disease."

"No! I'm fairly comf'ble," responded the lady calmly, "and you're gettin' on in the vale, ez is natural — though you still kind o' run to bone, as you used."

There was not a trace of malevolence in either of their comments, only a resigned recognition of certain unpleasant truths which seemed to have been habitual to both of them. Mr. Langworthy paused to flick away some flies from the butter with his professional napkin, and resumed, —

"It must be a matter o' five years sens I last saw ye, isn't it? — in court arter you got the decree — you remember?"

"Yes — the 28th o' July, '51. I paid Lawyer Hoskins's bill that very day — that's how I remember," returned the lady. "You've got a big business here," she continued, glancing round the room; "I reckon you're makin' it pay. Don't seem to be in your line, though; but then, thar was n't many things that was."

"No, — that's so," responded Mr. Langworthy, nodding

his head, as assenting to an undeniable proposition, "and you — I suppose you 're gettin' on too. I reckon you 're — er — married — eh ? " — with a slight suggestion of putting the question delicately.

The lady nodded, ignoring the hesitation. "Yes, let me see, it 's just three years and three days. Constantine Byers — I don't reckon you know him — from Milwaukee. Timber merchant. Standin' timber 's his specialty."

"And I reckon he 's — satisfactory ? "

"Yes! Mr. Byers is a good provider — and handy. And you ? I should say you 'd want a wife in this business ? "

Mr. Langworthy's serious half-perfunctory manner here took on an appearance of interest. "Yes — I 've been thinkin' that way. Thar 's a young woman helpin' in the kitchen ez might do, though I 'm not certain, and I ain't lettin' on anything as yet. You might take a look at her, Rosalie, — I orter say Mrs. Byers ez is, — and kinder size her up, and gimme the result. It 's still wantin' seven minutes o' schedule time afore the stage goes, and — if you ain't wantin' more food " — delicately, as became a landlord — "and ain't got anythin' else to do, it might pass the time."

Strange as it may seem, Mrs. Byers here displayed an equal animation in her fresh face as she rose promptly to her feet and began to rearrange her dust cloak around her buxom figure. "I don't mind, Abner," she said, "and I don't think that Mr. Byers would mind either; " then seeing Langworthy hesitating at the latter unexpected suggestion, she added confidently, "and I would n't mind even if he did, for I 'm sure if I don't know the kind o' woman you 'd be likely to need, I don't know who would. Only last week I was sayin' like that to Mr. Byers " —

"To Mr. Byers ? " said Abner, with some surprise.

"Yes — to him. I said, 'We 've been married three years, Constantine, and ef I don't know by this time what

kind o' woman you need now — and might need in future
— why, thar ain't much use in matrimony.'"

"You was always wise, Rosalie," said Abner, with reminiscent appreciation.

"I was always there, Abner," returned Mrs. Byers, with
a complacent show of dimples, which she, however, chas-
tened into that resignation which seemed characteristic of
the pair. "Let 's see your ' intended ' — as might be."

Thus supported, Mr. Langworthy led Mrs. Byers into
the hall through a crowd of loungers, into a smaller hall,
and there opened the door of the kitchen. It was a large
room, whose windows were half darkened by the encom-
passing pines which still pressed around the house on the
scantily cleared site. A number of men and women, among
them a Chinaman and a negro, were engaged in washing
dishes and other culinary duties; and beside the window
stood a young blonde girl, who was wiping a tin pan which
she was also using to hide a burst of laughter evidently
caused by the abrupt entrance of her employer. A quantity of fluffy hair and part of a white, bared arm were nevertheless visible outside the disk, and Mrs. Byers gathered
from the direction of Mr. Langworthy's eyes, assisted by
a slight nudge from his elbow, that this was the selected
fair one. His feeble explanatory introduction, addressed
to the occupants generally, "Just showing the house to
Mrs. — er — Dusenberry," convinced her that the circumstances of his having been divorced he had not yet confided
to the young woman. As he turned almost immediately
away, Mrs. Byers in following him managed to get a better
look at the girl, as she was exchanging some facetious remark to a neighbor. Mr. Langworthy did not speak until
they had reached the deserted dining-room again.

"Well?" he said briefly, glancing at the clock, "what
did ye think o' Mary Ellen?"

To any ordinary observer the girl in question would

have seemed the least fitted in age, sobriety of deportment, and administrative capacity to fill the situation thus proposed for her, but Mrs. Byers was not an ordinary observer, and her auditor was not an ordinary listener.

"She's older than she gives herself out to be," said Mrs. Byers tentatively, "and them kitten ways don't amount to much."

Mr. Langworthy nodded. Had Mrs. Byers discovered a homicidal tendency in Mary Ellen he would have been equally unmoved.

"She don't handsome much," continued Mrs. Byers musingly, "but" —

"I never was keen on good looks in a woman, Rosalie. You know that!"

Mrs. Byers received the equivocal remark unemotionally, and returned to the subject.

"Well!" she said contemplatively, "I should think you could make her suit."

Mr. Langworthy nodded with resigned toleration of all that might have influenced her judgment and his own. "I was wantin' a fa'r-minded opinion, Rosalie, and you happened along jest in time. Kin I put up anythin' in the way of food for ye?" he added, as a stir outside and the words "All aboard!" proclaimed the departing of the stage-coach, — "an orange or a hunk o' gingerbread, freshly baked?"

"Thank ye kindly, Abner, but I shan't be usin' anythin' afore supper," responded Mrs. Byers, as they passed out into the veranda beside the waiting coach.

Mr. Langworthy helped her to her seat. "Ef you're passin' this way ag'in" — he hesitated delicately.

"I'll drop in, or I reckon Mr. Byers might, he havin' business along the road," returned Mrs. Byers with a cheerful nod, as the coach rolled away and the landlord of the Big Flume Hotel reëntered his house.

For the next three weeks, however, it did not appear that Mr. Langworthy was in any hurry to act upon the advice of his former wife. His relations to Mary Ellen Budd were characterized by his usual tolerance to his employees' failings, — which in Mary Ellen's case included many "breakages," — but were not marked by the invasion of any warmer feeling, or a desire for confidences. The only perceptible divergence from his regular habits was a disposition to be on the veranda at the arrival of the stage-coach, and when his duties permitted this, a cautious survey of his female guests at the beginning of dinner. This probably led to his more or less ignoring any peculiarities in his masculine patrons or their claims to his personal attention. Particularly so, in the case of a red-bearded man, in a long linen duster, both heavily freighted with the red dust of the stage road, which seemed to have invaded his very eyes as he watched the landlord closely. Towards the close of the dinner, when Abner, accompanied by a negro waiter after his usual custom, passed down each side of the long table, collecting payment for the meal, the stranger looked up. "You air the landlord of this hotel, I reckon?"

"I am," said Abner tolerantly.

"I'd like a word or two with ye."

But Abner had been obliged to have a formula for such occasions. "Ye'll pay for yer dinner first," he said submissively but firmly, "and make yer remarks agin the food arter."

The stranger flushed quickly, and his eye took an additional shade of red, but meeting Abner's serious gray ones, he contented himself with ostentatiously taking out a handful of gold and silver and paying his bill. Abner passed on, but after dinner was over he found the stranger in the hall.

"Ye pulled me up rather short in thar," said the man gloomily, "but it's just as well, as the talk I was wantin' with ye was kinder betwixt and between ourselves, and not hotel business. My name's Byers, and my wife let on she met ye down here."

For the first time it struck Abner as incongruous that another man should call Rosalie "his wife," although the fact of her remarriage had been made sufficiently plain to him. He accepted it as he would an earthquake, or any other dislocation, with his usual tolerant smile, and held out his hand.

Mr. Byers took it, seemingly mollified, and yet inwardly disturbed, — more even than was customary in Abner's guests after dinner.

"Have a drink with me," he suggested, although it had struck him that Mr. Byers had been drinking before dinner.

"I'm agreeable," responded Byers promptly; "but," with a glance at the crowded bar-room, "couldn't we go somewhere, jest you and me, and have a quiet confab?"

"I reckon. But ye must wait till we get her off."

Mr. Byers started slightly, but it appeared that the impedimental sex in this case was the coach, which, after a slight feminine hesitation, was at last started. Whereupon Mr. Langworthy, followed by a negro with a tray bearing a decanter and glasses, grasped Mr. Byers's arm, and walked along a small side veranda the depth of the house, stepped off, and apparently plunged with his guest into the primeval wilderness.

It has already been indicated that the site of the Big Flume Hotel had been scantily cleared; but Mr. Byers, backwoodsman though he was, was quite unprepared for so abrupt a change. The hotel, with its noisy crowd and garish newness, although scarcely a dozen yards away, seemed lost completely to sight and sound. A slight fringe of old tin cans, broken china, shavings, and even of the long-dried chips of the felled trees, once crossed, the two men were alone! From the tray, deposited at the foot of an enormous pine, they took the decanter, filled their glasses, and then disposed of themselves comfortably against a spreading root. The curling tail of a squirrel disappeared behind them; the far-off tap of a woodpecker accented the loneliness. And then, almost magically as it seemed, the thin veneering of civilization on the two men seemed to be cast off like the bark of the trees around them, and they lounged before each other in aboriginal freedom. Mr. Byers removed his restraining duster and undercoat. Mr. Langworthy resigned his dirty white jacket, his collar, and unloosed a suspender, with which he played.

"Would it be a fair question between two fa'r-minded men, ez hez lived alone," said Mr. Byers, with a gravity so supernatural that it could be referred only to liquor, "to ask ye in what sort o' way did Mrs. Byers show her temper?"

"Show her temper?" echoed Abner vacantly.

"Yes — in course, I mean when you and Mrs. Byers was — was — one? You know the di-vorce was for in-com-pat-ibility of temper."

"But she got the divorce from me, so I reckon I had the temper," said Langworthy, with great simplicity.

"Wha-at?" said Mr. Byers, putting down his glass and gazing with drunken gravity at the sad-eyed yet good-humoredly tolerant man before him. "You? — you had the temper?"

"I reckon that's what the court allowed," said Abner simply.

Mr. Byers stared. Then after a moment's pause he nodded with a significant yet relieved face. "Yes, I see, in course. Times when you'd h'isted too much o' this corn juice," lifting up his glass, "inside ye — ye sorter bu'st out ravin'?"

But Abner shook his head. "I wuz a total abstainer in them days," he said quietly.

Mr. Byers got unsteadily on his legs and looked around him. "Wot might hev been the general gait o' your temper, pardner?" he said in a hoarse whisper.

"Don't know. I reckon that's jest whar the incompatibility kem in."

"And when she hove plates at your head, wot did you do?"

"She didn't hove no plates," said Abner gravely; "did she say she did?"

"No, no!" returned Byers hastily, in crimson confusion. "I kinder got it mixed with suthin' else." He waved his hand in a lordly way, as if dismissing the subject. "Howsumever, you and her is 'off' anyway," he added with badly concealed anxiety.

"I reckon: there's the decree," returned Abner, with his usual resigned acceptance of the fact.

"Mrs. Byers wuz allowin' ye wuz thinkin' of a second. How's that comin' on?"

"Jest whar it was," returned Abner. "I ain't doin' anything yet. Ye see I've got to tell the gal, naterally, that I'm di-vorced. And as that isn't known hereabouts, I don't keer to do so till I'm pretty certain. And then, in course, I've got to."

"Why hev ye 'got to'?" asked Byers abruptly.

"Because it wouldn't be on the square with the girl," said Abner. "How would you like it if Mrs. Byers had never told you she'd been married to me? And s'pose you'd happen to hev been a di-vorced man and hadn't told her, eh? Well," he continued, sinking back resignedly against the tree, "I ain't sayin' anythin' but she'd hev got another di-vorce, and *from* you on the spot — you bet!"

"Well! all I kin say is," said Mr. Byers, lifting his voice excitedly, "that" — but he stopped short, and was about to fill his glass again from the decanter when the hand of Abner stopped him.

"Ye've got ez much ez ye kin carry now, Byers," he said slowly, "and that's about ez much ez I allow a man to take in at the Big Flume Hotel. Treatin' is treatin', hospitality is hospitality; ef you and me was squattin' out on the prairie I'd let you fill your skin with that pizen and wrap ye up in yer blankets afterwards. But here at Big Flume, the Stage Kempenny and the wimen and children passengers hez their rights." He paused a moment, and added, "And so I reckon hez Mrs. Byers, and I ain't goin' to send you home to her outer my house blind drunk. It's mighty rough on you and me, I know, but there's a lot o' roughness in this world ez hez to be got over, and life, ez far ez I kin see, ain't all a clearin'."

Perhaps it was his good-humored yet firm determination, perhaps it was his resigned philosophy, but something in the speaker's manner affected Mr. Byers's alcoholic susceptibility, and hastened his descent from the passionate heights of intoxication to the maudlin stage whither he was drifting. The fire of his red eyes became filmed and dim, an equal moisture gathered in his throat as he pressed Abner's hand with drunken fervor. "Thash so! your thinking o' me an' Mish Byersh is like troo fr'en'," he said thickly. "I wosh only goin' to shay that wotever Mish Byersh wosh — even if she wosh wife o' yours — she wosh — noble woman! Such a woman," continued Mr. Byers, dreamily regarding space, "can't have too many husbands."

"You jest sit back here a minit, and have a quiet smoke till I come back," said Abner, handing him his tobacco plug. "I've got to give the butcher his order — but I won't be a minit." He secured the decanter as he spoke, and evading an apparent disposition of his companion to fall upon his neck, made his way with long strides to the hotel, as Mr. Byers, sinking back against the tree, began certain futile efforts to light his unfilled pipe.

Whether Abner's attendance on the butcher was merely

an excuse to withdraw with the decanter, I cannot say.
He, however, dispatched his business quickly, and returned
to the tree. But to his surprise Mr. Byers was no longer
there. He explored the adjacent woodland with non-suc-
cess, and no reply to his shouting. Annoyed but not
alarmed, as it seemed probable that the missing man had
fallen in a drunken sleep in some hidden shadows, he returned to the house, when it occurred to him that Byers
might have sought the bar-room for some liquor. But he
was still more surprised when the barkeeper volunteered the
information that he had seen Mr. Byers hurriedly pass down
the side veranda into the high-road. An hour later this
was corroborated by an arriving teamster, who had passed
a man answering to the description of Byers, "mor' 'n half
full," staggeringly but hurriedly walking along the road
"two miles back." There seemed to be no doubt that the
missing man had taken himself off in a fit of indignation or
of extreme thirst. Either hypothesis was disagreeable to
Abner, in his queer sense of responsibility to Mrs. Byers,
but he accepted it with his usual good-humored resignation.

Yet it was difficult to conceive what connection this episode had in his mind with his suspended attention to Mary
Ellen, or why it should determine his purpose. But he had
a logic of his own, and it seemed to have demonstrated to
him that he must propose to the girl at once. This was no
easy matter, however; he had never shown her any previous attention, and her particular functions in the hotel —
the charge of the few bedrooms for transient guests — seldom brought him in contact with her. His interview would
have to appear to be a business one — which, however, he
wished to avoid from a delicate consciousness of its truth.
While making up his mind, for a few days he contented
himself with gravely regarding her in his usual resigned,
tolerant way, whenever he passed her. Unfortunately the
first effect of this was an audible giggle from Mary Ellen,

later some confusion and anxiety in her manner, and finally
a demeanor of resentment and defiance.

This was so different from what he had expected that
he was obliged to precipitate matters. The next day was
Sunday, — a day on which his employees, in turns, were
allowed the recreation of being driven to Big Flume City,
eight miles distant, to church, or for the day's holiday. In
the morning Mary Ellen was astonished by Abner's informing her that he designed giving her a separate holiday with
himself. It must be admitted that the girl, who was already
"prinked up" for the enthrallment of the youth of Big
Flume City, did not appear as delighted with the change of
plan as a more exacting lover would have liked. Howbeit,
as soon as the wagon had left with its occupants, Abner, in
the unwonted disguise of a full suit of black clothes, turned
to the girl, and offering her his arm, gravely proceeded along
the side veranda across the mound of débris already de-
scribed, to the adjacent wilderness and the very trees under
which he and Byers had sat.

"It 's about ez good a place for a little talk, Miss Budd,"
he said, pointing to a tree root, "ez ef we went a spell further, and it 's handy to the house. And ef you 'll jest say
what you 'd like outer the cupboard or the bar — no matter
which — I 'll fetch it to you."

But Mary Ellen Budd seated herself sideways on the
root, with her furled white parasol in her lap, her skirts
fastidiously tucked about her feet, and glancing at the
fatuous Abner from under her stack of fluffy hair and
light eyelashes, simply shook her head and said that "she
reckoned she was n't hankering much for anything" that
morning.

"I 've been calkilatin' to myself, Miss Budd," said Abner resignedly, "that when two folks — like ez you and me
— meet together to kinder discuss things that might go so
far ez to keep them together, if they hez had anything of

that sort in their lives afore, they ought to speak of it confidentially like together."

"Ef any one o' them sneakin', soulless critters in the kitchen hez been slingin' lies to ye about me — or carryin' tales," broke in Mary Ellen Budd, setting every one of her thirty-two strong, white teeth together with a snap, "well — ye might hev told me so to oncet without spilin' my Sunday! But ez fer yer keepin' me a minit longer, ye 've only got to pay me my salary to-day and " — but here she stopped, for the astonishment in Abner's face was too plain to be misunderstood.

"Nobody 's been slinging any lies about ye, Miss Budd," he said slowly, recovering himself resignedly from this last back-handed stroke of fate. "I warn't talkin' o' you, but myself. I was only allowin' to say that I was a di-vorced man."

As a sudden flush came over Mary Ellen's brownish-white face while she stared at him, Abner hastened to delicately explain. "It was n't no onfaithfulness, Miss Budd — no philanderin' o' mine, but only 'incompatibility o' temper.'"

"Temper — your temper!" gasped Mary Ellen.

"Yes," said Abner.

And here a sudden change came over Mary Ellen's face, and she burst into a shriek of laughter. She laughed with her hands slapping the sides of her skirt, she laughed with her hands clasping her narrow, hollow waist, laughed with her head down on her knees and her fluffy hair tumbling over it. Abner was relieved, and yet it seemed strange to him that this revelation of his temper should provoke such manifest incredulity in both Byers and Mary Ellen. But perhaps these things would be made plain to him hereafter; at present they must be accepted "in the day's work " and tolerated.

"Your temper," gurgled Mary Ellen. "Saints alive! What kind o' temper?"

"Well, I reckon," returned Abner submissively, and selecting a word to give his meaning more comprehension, — "I reckon it was kinder — aggeravokin'."

Mary Ellen sniffed the air for a moment in speechless incredulity, and then, locking her hands around her knees and bending forward, said, "Look here! Ef that old woman o' yours ever knew what temper was in a man; ef she 's ever been tied to a brute that treated her like a nigger till she dare n't say her soul was her own; who struck her with his eyes and tongue when he had n't anythin' else handy; who made her life miserable when he was sober, and a terror when he was drunk; who at last drove her away, and then divorced her for desertion — then — then she might talk. But ' incompatibility o' temper ' with you! Oh, go away — it makes me sick!"

How far Abner was impressed with the truth of this, how far it prompted his next question, nobody but Abner knew. For he said deliberately, "I was only goin' to ask ye, if, knowin' I was a di-vorced man, ye would mind marryin' me!"

Mary Ellen's face changed; the evasive instincts of her sex rose up. "Did n't I hear ye sayin' suthin' about refreshments?" she said archly. "Mebbe you would n't mind gettin' me a bottle o' lemming sody outer the bar!"

Abner got up at once, perhaps not dismayed by this diversion, and departed for the refreshment. As he passed along the side veranda the recollection of Mr. Byers and his mysterious flight occurred to him. For a wild moment he thought of imitating him. But it was too late now — he had spoken. Besides, he had no wife to fly to, and the thirsty or indignant Byers had — his wife! Fate was indeed hard. He returned with the bottle of lemon soda on a tray and a resigned spirit equal to her decrees. Mary Ellen, remarking that he had brought nothing for himself, archly insisted upon his sharing with her the bottle of soda, and even coquettishly touched his lips with her glass. Abner smiled patiently.

But here, as if playfully exhilarated by the naughty foaming soda, she regarded him with her head — and a good deal of her blonde hair — very much on one side, as she said, "Do you know that all along o' you bein' so free with me in tellin' your affairs I kinder feel like just telling you mine ? "

"Don't," said Abner promptly.

"Don't ? " echoed Miss Budd.

"Don't," repeated Abner. "It 's nothing to me. What I said about myself is different, for it might make some difference to you. But nothing you could say of yourself would make any change in me. I stick to what I said just now."

"But," said Miss Budd, — in half-real, half-simulated threatening, — "what if it had suthin' to do with my answer to what you said just now ? "

"It could n't. So, if it 's all the same to you, Miss Budd, I 'd rather ye would n't."

"That," said the lady still more archly, lifting a playful finger, "is your temper."

"Mebbe it is," said Abner suddenly, with a wondering sense of relief.

It was, however, settled that Miss Budd should go to Sacramento to visit her friends, that Abner would join her later, when their engagement would be announced, and that she should not return to the hotel until they were married. The compact was sealed by the interchange of a friendly kiss from Miss Budd with a patient, tolerating one from Abner, and then it suddenly occurred to them both that they might as well return to their duties in the hotel, which they did. Miss Budd's entire outing that Sunday lasted only half an hour.

A week elapsed. Miss Budd was in Sacramento, and the

landlord of the Big Flume Hotel was standing at his usual post in the doorway during dinner, when a waiter handed him a note. It contained a single line scrawled in pencil: —

"Come out and see me behind the house as before. I dussent come in on account of her.

C. BYERS."

"On account of 'her'!" Abner cast a hurried glance around the tables. Certainly Mrs. Byers was not there! He walked in the hall and the veranda — she was not there. He hastened to the rendezvous evidently meant by the writer, the wilderness behind the house. Sure enough, Byers, drunk and maudlin, supporting himself by the tree root, staggered forward, clasped him in his arms, and murmured hoarsely, —

"She's gone!"

"Gone?" echoed Abner, with a whitening face. "Mrs. Byers? Where?"

"Run away! Never come back no more! Gone!"

A vague idea that had been in Abner's mind since Byers's last visit now took awful shape. Before the unfortunate Byers could collect his senses he felt himself seized in a giant's grasp and forced against the tree.

"You coward!" said all that was left of the tolerant Abner — his even voice — "you hound! Did you dare to abuse her? to lay your vile hands on her — to strike her? Answer me."

The shock — the grasp — perhaps Abner's words, momentarily silenced Byers. "Did I strike her?" he said dazedly; "did I abuse her? Oh, yes!" with deep irony. "Certainly! In course! Look yer, pardner!" — he suddenly dragged up his sleeve from his red, hairy arm, exposing a blue cicatrix in its centre — "that's a jab from her scissors about three months ago; look yer!" — he bent his

head and showed a scar along the scalp — "that 's her play-
fulness with a fire shovel! Look yer!" — he quickly
opened his collar, where his neck and cheek were striped
and crossed with adhesive plaster — "that 's all that was
left o' a glass jar o' preserves — the preserves got away,
but some of the glass got stuck! That 's when she heard
I was a di-vorced man and had n't told her."

"Were you a di-vorced man?" gasped Abner.

"You know that; in course I was," said Byers scornfully; "d' ye meanter say she did n't tell ye?"

"She?" echoed Abner vaguely. "Your wife — you said
just now she did n't know it before."

"My wife ez oncet was, I mean! Mary Ellen — your
wife ez is to be," said Byers with deep irony. "Oh, come
now. Pretend ye don't know! Hi there! Hands off!
Don't strike a man when he 's down, like I am."

But Abner's clutch of Byers's shoulder relaxed, and he
sank down to a sitting posture on the root. In the mean
time Byers, overcome by a sense of this new misery added
to his manifold grievances, gave way to maudlin silent
tears.

"Mary Ellen — your first wife?" repeated Abner vacantly.

"Yesh!" said Byers thickly, "my first wife — shelected
and picked out fer your shecond wife — by your first —
like d——d conundrum. How wash I t' know?" he said,
with a sudden shriek of public expostulation — "thash
what I wanter know. Here I come to talk with fr'en',
like man to man, unshuspecting, innoshent as chile, about
my shecond wife! Fr'en' drops out, carryin' off the whiskey. Then I hear all o' suddent voice o' Mary Ellen
talkin' in kitchen; then I come round softly and see Mary
Ellen — my wife as useter be — standin' at fr'en's kitchen
winder. Then I lights out quicker 'n lightnin' and scoots!
And when I gets back home, I ups and tells my wife. And

whosh fault ish't! Who shaid a man oughter tell hish wife? You! Who keepsh other mensh' first wivesh at kishen winder to frighten 'em to tell? You!"

But a change had already come over the face of Abner Langworthy. The anger, anxiety, astonishment, and vacuity that was there had vanished, and he looked up with his usual resigned acceptance of the inevitable as he said, "I reckon that's so! And seein' it's so," with good-natured tolerance, he added, "I reckon I'll break rules for oncet and stand ye another drink."

He stood another drink and yet another, and eventually put the doubly widowed Byers to bed in his own room. These were but details of a larger tribulation, — and yet he knew instinctively that his cup was not yet full. The further drop of bitterness came a few days later in a line from Mary Ellen: "I needn't tell you that all betwixt you and me is off, and you kin tell your old woman that her selection for a second wife for you wuz about as bad as your own first selection. Ye kin tell Mr. Byers — yer great friend whom ye never let on ye knew — that when I want another husband I shan't take the trouble to ask him to fish one out for me. It would be kind — but confusin'."

He never heard from her again. Mr. Byers was duly notified that Mrs. Byers had commenced action for divorce in another State in which concealment of a previous divorce invalidated the marriage, but he did not respond. The two men became great friends — and assured celibates. Yet they always spoke reverently of their "wife," with the touching prefix of "our."

"She was a good woman, pardner," said Byers.

"And she understood us," said Abner resignedly.

Perhaps she had.

THE REINCARNATION OF SMITH

THE extravagant supper party by which Mr. James Farendell celebrated the last day of his bachelorhood was protracted so far into the night, that the last guest who parted from him at the door of the principal Sacramento restaurant was for a moment impressed with the belief that a certain ruddy glow in the sky was already the dawn. But Mr. Farendell had kept his head clear enough to recognize it as the light of some burning building in a remote business district, a not infrequent occurrence in the dry season. When he had dismissed his guest he turned away in that direction for further information. His own counting-house was not in that immediate neighborhood, but Sacramento had been once before visited by a rapid and far-sweeping conflagration, and it behooved him to be on the alert even on this night of festivity.

Perhaps also a certain anxiety arose out of the occasion. He was to be married to-morrow to the widow of his late partner, and the marriage, besides being an attractive one, would settle many business difficulties. He had been a fortunate man, but, like many more fortunate men, was not blind to the possibilities of a change of luck. The death of his partner in a successful business had at first seemed to betoken that change, but his successful though hasty courtship of the inexperienced widow had restored his chances without greatly shocking the decorum of a pioneer community. Nevertheless, he was not a contented man, and hardly a determined — although an energetic one.

A walk of a few moments brought him to the levee of

the river, — a favored district, where his counting-house, with many others, was conveniently situated. In these early days only a few of these buildings could be said to be permanent, — fire and flood perpetually threatened them. They were merely temporary structures of wood, or in the case of Mr. Farendell's office, a shell of corrugated iron, sheathing a one-storied wooden frame, more or less elaborate in its interior decorations. By the time he had reached it, the distant fire had increased. On his way he had met and recognized many of his business acquaintances hurrying thither, — some to save their own property, or to assist the imperfectly equipped volunteer fire department in their unselfish labors. It was probably Mr. Farendell's peculiar preoccupation on that particular night which had prevented his joining in their brotherly zeal.

He unlocked the iron door, and lit the hanging lamp that was used in all-night sittings on steamer days. It revealed a smartly furnished office, with a high desk for his clerks, and a smaller one for himself in one corner. In the centre of the wall stood a large safe. This he also unlocked and took out a few important books, as well as a small drawer containing gold coin and dust to the amount of about five hundred dollars, the large balance having been deposited in bank on the previous day. The act was only precautionary, as he did not exhibit any haste in removing them to a place of safety, and remained meditatively absorbed in looking over a packet of papers taken from the same drawer. The closely shuttered building, almost hermetically sealed against light, and perhaps sound, prevented his observing the steadily increasing light of the conflagration, or hearing the nearer tumult of the firemen, and the invasion of his quiet district by other equally solicitous tenants. The papers seemed also to possess some importance, for the stillness being suddenly broken by the turning of the handle of the heavy door he had just closed, and its opening with difficulty, his first act was to hurriedly conceal them, without apparently paying a thought to the exposed gold before him. And his expression and attitude in facing round towards the door was quite as much of nervous secretiveness as of indignation at the interruption.

Yet the intruder appeared, though singular, by no means formidable. He was a man slightly past the middle age, with a thin face, hollowed at the cheeks and temples as if by illness or asceticism, and a grayish beard that encircled his throat like a soiled worsted "comforter" below his clean-shaven chin and mouth. His manner was slow and methodical, and even when he shot the bolt of the door behind him, the act did not seem aggressive. Nevertheless Mr. Farendell half rose with his hand on his pistol-pocket, but the stranger merely lifted his own hand with a gesture of indifferent warning, and, drawing a chair towards him, dropped into it deliberately.

Mr. Farendell's angry stare changed suddenly to one of surprised recognition. "Josh Scranton," he said hesitatingly.

"I reckon," responded the stranger slowly. "That's the name I allus bore, and *you* called yourself Farendell. Well, we ain't seen each other sens the spring o' '50, when ye left me lying nigh petered out with chills and fever on the Stanislaus River, and sold the claim that me and Duffy worked under our very feet, and skedaddled for 'Frisco!"

"I only exercised my right as principal owner, and to secure my advances," began the late Mr. Farendell sharply.

But again the thin hand was raised, this time with a slow, scornful waiving of any explanations. "It ain't that in partickler that I've kem to see ye for to-night," said the stranger slowly, "nor it ain't about your takin' the name o' 'Farendell,' that friend o' yours who died on the passage here with ye, and whose papers ye borrowed! Nor it ain't on account o' that wife of yours ye left behind in Missouri, and whose letters you never answered.   It's them things all together — and suthin' else!"

"What the d——l do you want, then?" said Farendell, with a desperate directness that was, however, a tacit confession of the truth of these accusations.

"Yer allowin' that ye'll get married to-morrow?" said Scranton slowly.

"Yes, and be d——d to you," said Farendell fiercely.

"Yer *not*," returned Scranton. "Not if *I* knows it. Yer goin' to climb down. Yer goin' to get up and get! Yer goin' to step down and out! Yer goin' to shut up your desk and your books and this hull consarn inside of an hour, and vamose the ranch. Arter an hour from now thar won't be any Mr. Farendell, and no weddin' to-morrow."

"If that's your game — perhaps you'd like to murder me at once?" said Farendell with a shifting eye, as his hand again moved towards his revolver.

But again the thin hand of the stranger was also lifted. "We ain't in the business o' murderin' or bein' murdered, or we might hev kem here together, me and Duffy. Now if anything happens to me Duffy will be left, and *he*'s got the proofs."

Farendell seemed to recognize the fact with the same directness. "That's it, is it?" he said bluntly. "Well, how much do you want? Only, I warn you that I haven't much to give."

"Wotever you've got, if it was millions, it ain't enough to buy us up, and ye ought to know that by this time," responded Scranton, with a momentary flash in his eyes. But the next moment his previous passionless deliberation returned, and leaning his arm on the desk of the man before him he picked up a paperweight carelessly and turned it over as he said slowly, "The fact is, Mr. Farendell, you've been making us, me and Duffy, tired. We've been watchin' you and your doin's, lyin' low and sayin' nothin', till we concluded that it was about time you handed in your checks and left the board.   We ain't wanted nothin' of ye, we ain't begrudged ye nothin', but we 've allowed that this yer thing must stop."

"And what if I refuse ? " said Farendell.

"Thar 'll be some cussin' and a big row from *you*, I kalkilate — and maybe some fightin' all round," said Scranton dispassionately.   "But .it will be all the same in the end. The hull thing will come out, and you 'll hev to slide just the same.   T' otherwise, ef ye slide out *now*, it 's without a row."

"And do you suppose a business man like me can disappear without a fuss over it ? " said Farendell angrily.   "Are you mad ? "

"I reckon the hole *you* 'll make kin be filled up," said Scranton dryly.   "But ef ye go *now*, you won't be bothered by the fuss, while if you stay you 'll have to face the music, and go too! "

Farendell was silent.   Possibly the truth of this had long since been borne upon him.   No one but himself knew the incessant strain of these years of evasion and concealment, and how he often had been near to some such desperate culmination.   The sacrifice offered to him was not, therefore, so great as it might have seemed.   The knowledge of this might have given him a momentary superiority over his antagonist had Scranton's motive been a purely selfish or malignant one, but as it was not, and as he may have had some instinctive idea of Farendell's feeling also, it made his ultimatum appear the more passionless and fateful. And it was this quality which perhaps caused Farendell to burst out with desperate abruptness, —

"What in h——ll ever put you up to this! "

Scranton folded his arms upon Farendell's desk, and slowly wiping his clean jaw with one hand, repeated delib-

erately, "Wall — I reckon I told ye that before! You 've
been making us — me and Duffy — tired!" He paused for
a moment, and then, rising abruptly, with a careless gesture
towards the uncovered tray of gold, said, "Come! ye kin
take enuff o' that to get away with; the less ye take,
though, the less likely you 'll be to be followed!"

He went to the door, unlocked and opened it. A strange
light, as of a lurid storm interspersed by sheet-like lightning, filled the outer darkness, and the silence was now
broken by dull crashes and nearer cries and shouting. A
few figures were also dimly flitting around the neighboring
empty offices, some of which, like Farendell's, had been
entered by their now alarmed owners.

"You 've got a good chance now," continued Scranton;
"ye could n't hev a better. It 's a big fire — a scorcher
— and jest the time for a man to wipe himself out and
not be missed. Make tracks where the crowd is thickest
and whar ye 're likely to be seen, ez ef ye were helpin'!
Ther' 'll be other men missed to-morrow beside you," he
added with grim significance; "but nobody 'll know that
you was one who really got away."

Where the imperturbable logic of the strange man might
have failed, the noise, the tumult, the suggestion of swift-
coming disaster, and the necessity for some immediate action of any kind, was convincing. Farendell hastily stuffed
his pockets with gold and the papers he had found, and
moved to the door. Already he fancied he felt the hot
breath of the leaping conflagration beyond. "And you?"
he said, turning suspiciously to Scranton.

"When you 're shut of this and clean off, I 'll fix things
and leave too — but not before. I reckon," he added
grimly, with a glance at the sky, now streaming with sparks
like a meteoric shower, "thar won't be much left here in
the morning."

A few dull embers pattered on the iron roof of the low

building and bounded off in ashes. Farendell cast a final
glance around him, and then darted from the building.
The iron door clanged behind him — he was gone.

Evidently not too soon, for the other buildings were already deserted by their would-be salvors, who had filled the
streets with piles of books and valuables waiting to be carried away. Then occurred a terrible phenomenon, which
had once before in such disasters paralyzed the efforts of
the firemen. A large wooden warehouse in the centre
of the block of offices, many hundred feet from the scene of
active conflagration — which had hitherto remained intact
— suddenly became enveloped in clouds of smoke, and without warning burst as suddenly from roof and upper story
into vivid flame. There were eye-witnesses who declared
that a stream of living fire seemed to leap upon it from the
burning district, and connected the space between them
with an arch of luminous heat. In another instant the
whole district was involved in a whirlwind of smoke and
flame, out of whose seething vortex the corrugated iron
buildings occasionally showed their shriveling or glowing
outlines. And then the fire swept on and away.

When the sun again arose over the panic-stricken and
devastated city, all personal incident and disaster was forgotten in the larger calamity. It was two or three days before
the full particulars could be gathered — even while the
dominant and resistless energy of the people was erecting
new buildings upon the still-smoking ruins. It was only
on the third day afterwards that James Farendell, on the
deck of a coasting steamer, creeping out through the fogs
of the Golden Gate, read the latest news in a San Francisco
paper brought by the pilot. As he hurriedly comprehended
the magnitude of the loss, which was far beyond his previous conception, he experienced a certain satisfaction in
finding his position no worse materially than that of many
of his fellow workers. *They* were ruined like himself;

they must begin their life afresh — but then! Ah! there
was still that terrible difference. He drew his breath
quickly, and read on. Suddenly he stopped, transfixed by
a later paragraph. For an instant he failed to grasp its full
significance. Then he read it again, the words imprinting
themselves on his senses with a slow deliberation that
seemed to him as passionless as Scranton's utterances on
that fateful night.

"The loss of life, it is now feared, is much greater than at
first imagined. To the list that has been already published
we must add the name of James Farendell, the energetic
contractor so well known to our citizens, who was missing
the morning after the fire. His calcined remains were
found this afternoon in the warped and twisted iron shell of
his counting-house, the wooden frame having been reduced
to charcoal in the intense heat. The unfortunate man
seems to have gone there to remove his books and papers,
— as was evidenced by the iron safe being found open, —
but to have been caught and imprisoned in the building
through the heat causing the metal sheathing to hermetically
seal the doors and windows. He was seen by some neighbors to enter the building while the fire was still distant, and
his remains were identified by his keys, which were found
beneath him. A poignant interest is added to his untimely
fate by the circumstance that he was to have been married
on the following day to the widow of his late partner, and
that he had, at the call of duty, that very evening left a
dinner party given to celebrate the last day of his bachelorhood — or, as it has indeed proved, of his earthly existence. Two families are thus placed in mourning, and it is
a singular sequel that by this untoward calamity the well-
known firm of Farendell & Cutler may be said to have
ceased to exist."

Mr. Farendell started to his feet. But a lurch of the
schooner as she rose on the long swell of the Pacific sent

him staggering dizzily back to his seat, and checked his first wild impulse to return. He saw it all now, — the fire had avenged him by wiping out his persecutor, Scranton, but in the eyes of his contemporaries it had only erased *him !* He might return to refute the story in his own person, but the dead man's partner still lived with his secret, and his own rehabilitation could only revive his former peril.

.   .   .   .

Four years elapsed before the late Mr. Farendell again set foot on the levee of Sacramento. The steamboat that brought him from San Francisco was a marvel to him in size, elegance, and comfort; so different from the little, crowded, tri-weekly packet he remembered; and it might, in a manner, have prepared him for the greater change in the city. But he was astounded to find nothing to remind him of the past, — no landmark, nor even ruin, of the place he had known. Blocks of brick buildings, with thorough-fares having strange titles, occupied the district where his counting-house had stood, and even obliterated its site; equally strange names were upon the shops and warehouses. In his four years' wanderings he had scarcely found a place as unfamiliar. He had trusted to the great change in his own appearance — the full beard that he wore and the tan-ning of a tropical sun — to prevent recognition, but the precaution was unnecessary; there were none to recognize him in the new faces which were the only ones he saw in the transformed city. A cautious allusion to the past which he had made on the boat to a fellow passenger had brought only the surprised rejoinder, "Oh, that must have been before the big fire," as if it was an historic epoch. There was something of pain even in this assured security of his loneliness. His obliteration was complete.

For the late Mr. Farendell had suffered some change of mind with his other mutations. He had been singularly lucky. The schooner in which he had escaped brought him to Acapulco, where, as a returning Californian, and a presumably successful one, his services and experience were eagerly sought by an English party engaged in developing certain disused Mexican mines. As the post, however, was perilously near the route of regular emigration, as soon as he had gained a sufficient sum he embarked with some goods to Callao, where he presently established himself in business, resuming his *real* name — the unambitious but indistinctive one of "Smith." It is highly probable that this prudential act was also his first step towards rectitude. For whether the change was a question of moral ethics, or merely a superstitious essay in luck, he was thereafter strictly honest in business. He became prosperous. He had been sustained in his flight by the intention that, if he were successful elsewhere, he would endeavor to communicate with his abandoned *fiancée*, and ask her to join him, and share not his name but fortune in exile. But as he grew rich, the difficulties of carrying out this intention became more apparent; he was by no means certain of her loyalty surviving the deceit he had practiced and the revelation he would have to make; he was doubtful of the success of any story which at other times he would have glibly invented to take the place of truth. Already several months had elapsed since his supposed death; could he expect her to be less accessible to premature advances now than when she had been a widow? Perhaps this made him think of the wife he had deserted so long ago. He had been quite content to live without regret or affection, forgetting and forgotten; but in his present prosperity he felt there was some need of putting his domestic affairs into a more secure and legitimate shape, to avert any catastrophe like the last. *Here* at least would be no difficulty; husbands had deserted their wives before this in Californian emigration, and had been heard of only after they had made their fortune. Any plausible story would be accepted by

her in the joy of his reappearance; or if, indeed, as he reflected with equal complacency, she was dead or divorced
from him through his desertion — a sufficient cause in her
own State — and re-married, he would at least be more secure. He began, without committing himself, by inquiry
and anonymous correspondence. His wife, he learnt, had
left Missouri for Sacramento only a month or two after his
own disappearance from that place, and her address was
unknown!

A complication so unlooked for disquieted him, and yet
whetted his curiosity. The only person she might meet in
California who could possibly identify him with the late
Mr. Farendell was Duffy; he had often wondered if that
mysterious partner of Scranton's had been deceived with
the others, or had ever suspected that the body discovered
in the counting-house was Scranton's. If not, he must
have accepted the strange coincidence that Scranton had
disappeared also the same night. In the first six months
of his exile he had searched the Californian papers thoroughly, but had found no record of any doubt having been
thrown on the accepted belief. It was these circumstances,
and perhaps a vague fascination not unlike that which im-
pels the malefactor to haunt the scene of his crime, that, at
the end of four years, had brought him, a man of middle
age and assured occupation and fortune, back to the city
he had fled from.

A few days at one of the new hotels convinced him thoroughly that he was in no danger of recognition, and gave
him the assurance to take rooms more in keeping with his
circumstances and his own frankly avowed position as the
head of a South American house. A cautious acquaintance
— through the agency of his banker — with a few business
men gave him some occupation, and the fact of his South
American letters being addressed to Don Diego Smith gave
a foreign flavor to his individuality, which his tanned face

and dark beard had materially helped. A stronger test convinced him how complete was the obliteration of his former identity. One day at the bank he was startled at being introduced by the manager to a man whom he at once recognized as a former business acquaintance. But the shock was his alone; the formal approach and unfamiliar manner of the man showed that he had failed to recognize even a resemblance. But would he equally escape detection by his wife if he met her as accidentally, — an encounter not to be thought of until he knew something more of her? He became more cautious in going to public places, but luckily for him the proportion of women to men was still small in California, and they were more observed than observing.

A month elapsed; in that time he had thoroughly exhausted the local Directories in his cautious researches among the "Smiths," for in his fear of precipitating a premature disclosure he had given up his former anonymous advertising. And there was a certain occupation in this personal quest that filled his business time. He was in no hurry. He had a singular faith that he would eventually discover her whereabouts, be able to make all necessary inquiries into her conduct and habits, and perhaps even enjoy a brief season of unsuspected personal observation before revealing himself. And this faith was as singularly rewarded.

Having occasion to get his watch repaired one day, he entered a large jeweler's shop, and while waiting its examination his attention was attracted by an ordinary old-fashioned daguerreotype case in the form of a heart-shaped locket lying on the counter with other articles left for repairs. Something in its appearance touched a chord in his memory; he lifted the half-opened case and saw a much faded daguerreotype portrait of himself taken in Missouri before he left in the Californian emigration. He recognized it at once as one he had given to his wife; the faded likeness was so little like his present self that he boldly examined it and asked the jeweler one or two questions. The man was communicative. Yes, it was an old-fashioned affair which had been left for repairs a few days ago by a lady whose name and address, written by herself, were on the card tied to it.

Mr. James Smith had by this time fully controlled the emotion he felt as he recognized his wife's name and handwriting, and knew that at last the clue was found! He laid down the case carelessly, gave the final directions for the repairs of his watch, and left the shop. The address, of which he had taken a mental note, was, to his surprise, very near his own lodgings; but he went straight home. Here a few inquiries of his janitor elicited the information that the building indicated in the address was a large one of furnished apartments and offices like his own, and that the "Mrs. Smith" must be simply the housekeeper of the landlord, whose name appeared in the Directory, but not her own. Yet he waited until evening before he ventured to reconnoitre the premises; with the possession of his clue came a slight cooling of his ardor and extreme caution in his further proceedings. The house — a reconstructed wooden building — offered no external indication of the rooms she occupied in the uniformly curtained windows that fronted the street. Yet he felt an odd and pleasurable excitement in passing once or twice before those walls that hid the goal of his quest. As yet he had not seen her, and there was naturally the added zest of expectation. He noticed that there was a new building opposite, with vacant offices to let. A project suddenly occurred to him, which by morning he had fully matured. He hired a front room on the first floor of the new building, had it hurriedly furnished as a private office, and on the second morning of his discovery was installed behind his desk at the window commanding a full view of the opposite house. There was nothing strange in the South American capitalist selecting a private office in so popular a locality.

Two or three days elapsed without any result from his espionage.   He came to know by sight the various tenants, the two Chinese servants, and the solitary Irish housemaid, but as yet had no glimpse of the housekeeper.   She evidently led a secluded life among her duties; it occurred to him that perhaps she went out, possibly to market, earlier than he came, or later, after he had left the office.   In this belief he arrived one morning after an early walk in a smart spring shower, the lingering straggler of the winter rains. There were few people astir, yet he had been preceded for two or three blocks by a tall woman whose umbrella partly concealed her head and shoulders from view.   He had noticed, however, even in his abstraction, that she walked well, and managed the lifting of her skirt over her trim ankles and well-booted feet with some grace and cleverness. Yet it was only on her unexpectedly turning the corner of his own street that he became interested.   She continued on until within a few doors of his office, when she stopped to give an order to a tradesman, who was just taking down his shutters.   He heard her voice distinctly; in the quick emotion it gave him he brushed hurriedly past her without lifting his eyes.   Gaining his own doorway he rushed upstairs to his office, hastily unlocked it, and ran to the window.   The lady was already crossing the street.   He saw her pause before the door of the opposite house, open it with a latchkey, and caught a full view of her profile in the single moment that she turned to furl her umbrella and enter.   It was his wife's voice he had heard; it was his wife's face that he had seen in profile.

Yet she was changed from the lanky young schoolgirl he had wedded ten years ago, or, at least, compared to what his recollection of her had been.   Had he ever seen her as she really was?   Surely somewhere in that timid, freckled, half-grown bride he had known in the first year of their marriage the germ of this self-possessed, matured woman was hidden. There was the tone of her voice; he had never recalled it before as a lover might, yet now it touched him; her profile he certainly remembered, but not with the feeling it now produced in him. Would he have ever abandoned her had she been like that? Or had *he* changed, and was this no longer his old self? — perhaps even a self *she* would never recognize again? James Smith had the superstitions of a gambler, and that vague idea of fate that comes to weak men; a sudden fright seized him, and he half withdrew from the window lest she should observe him, recognize him, and by some act precipitate that fate.

By lingering beyond the usual hour for his departure he saw her again, and had even a full view of her face as she crossed the street. The years had certainly improved her; he wondered with a certain nervousness if she would think they had done the same for him. The complacency with which he had at first contemplated her probable joy at recovering him had become seriously shaken since he had seen her; a woman as well preserved and good-looking as that, holding a certain responsible and, no doubt, lucrative position, must have many admirers and be independent. He longed to tell her now of his fortune, and yet shrank from the test its exposure implied. He waited for her return until darkness had gathered, and then went back to his lodgings a little chagrined and ill at ease. It was rather late for her to be out alone. After all, what did he know of her habits or associations? He recalled the freedom of Californian life, and the old scandals relating to the lapses of many women who had previously led blameless lives in the Atlantic States. Clearly it behooved him to be cautious. Yet he walked late that night before the house again, eager to see if she had returned, and with *whom?* He was restricted in his eagerness by the fear of detection, but he gathered very little knowledge of her habits; singularly enough nobody seemed to care. A little piqued at this, he began to wonder if he were not thinking too much of this woman to whom he still hesitated to reveal himself. Nevertheless, he found himself that night again wandering around the house, and even watching with some anxiety the shadow which he believed to be hers on the window-blind of the room where he had by discreet inquiry located her. Whether his memory was stimulated by his quest he never knew, but presently he was able to recall step by step and incident by incident his early courtship of her and the brief days of their married life. He even remembered the day she accepted him, and even dwelt upon it with a sentimental thrill that he probably never felt at the time, and it was a distinct feature of his extraordinary state of mind and its concentration upon this particular subject that he presently began to look upon *himself* as the abandoned and deserted conjugal partner, and to nurse a feeling of deep injury at her hands. The fact that he was thinking of her, and she, probably, contented with her lot, was undisturbed by any memory of him, seemed to him a logical deduction of his superior affection.

It was, therefore, quite as much in the attitude of a reproachful and avenging husband as of a merely curious one that, one afternoon, seeing her issue from her house at an early hour, he slipped down the stairs and began to follow her at a secure distance. She turned into the principal thoroughfare, and presently made one of the crowd who were entering a popular place of amusement where there was an afternoon performance. So complete was his selfish hallucination, that he smiled bitterly at this proof of heartless indifference, and even so far overcame his previous caution as to actually brush by her somewhat rudely as he entered the building at the same moment. He was conscious that she lifted her eyes a little impatiently to the face of the awkward stranger; he was equally, but more bitterly, conscious that she had not recognized him. He dropped into a seat behind her; she did not look at him again with even a sense of disturbance; the momentary contact had evidently left no impression upon her. She glanced casually at her neighbors on either side, and presently became absorbed in the performance. When it was over she rose, and on her way out recognized and exchanged a few words with one or two acquaintances. Again he heard her familiar voice, almost at his elbow, raised with no more consciousness of her contiguity to him than if he were a mere ghost. The thought struck him for the first time with a hideous and appalling significance. What was he but a ghost to her — to every one! A man dead, buried, and forgotten! His vanity and self-complacency vanished before this crushing realization of the hopelessness of his existence. Dazed and bewildered, he mingled blindly and blunderingly with the departing crowd, tossed here and there as if he were an invisible presence, stumbling over the impeding skirts of women with a vague apology they heeded not, and which seemed in his frightened ears as hollow as a voice from the grave.

When he at last reached the street he did not look back, but wandered abstractedly through by-streets in the falling rain, scarcely realizing where he was, until he found himself drenched through, with his closed umbrella in his tremulous hand, standing at the half-submerged levee beside the overflowed river. Here again he realized how completely he had been absorbed and concentrated in his search for his wife during the last three weeks; he had never been on the levee since his arrival. He had taken no note of the excitement of the citizens over the alarming reports of terrible floods in the mountains, and the daily and hourly fear that they experienced of disastrous inundation from the surcharged river. He had never thought of it, yet he had read

of it, and even talked, and yet now for the first time in his
selfish, blind absorption was certain of it.   He stood still for
some time, watching doggedly the enormous yellow stream
laboring with its burden and drift from many a mountain
town and camp, moving steadily and fatefully towards the
distant bay, and still more distant and inevitable ocean.
For a few moments it vaguely fascinated and diverted him;
then it as vaguely lent itself to his one dominant, haunting
thought.   Yes, it was pointing him the only way out, — the
path to the distant ocean and utter forgetfulness again!

The chill of his saturated clothing brought him to himself once more; he turned and hurried home.   He went
tiredly to his bedroom, and while changing his garments
there came a knock at the door.   It was the porter to say
that a lady had called, and was waiting for him in the sitting-room.   She had not given her name.

The closed door prevented the servant from seeing the
extraordinary effect produced by this simple announcement
upon the tenant.   For one instant James Smith remained
spellbound in his chair.   It was characteristic of his weak
nature and singular prepossession that he passed in an instant from the extreme of doubt to the extreme of certainty
and conviction.   It was his wife!   She had recognized him
in that moment of encounter at the entertainment; had
found his address, and had followed him here!   He dressed
himself with feverish haste, not, however, without a certain
care of his appearance and some selection of apparel, and
quickly forecast the forthcoming interview in his mind.
For the pendulum had swung back; Mr. James Smith was
once more the self-satisfied, self-complacent, and discreetly
cautious husband that he had been at the beginning of his
quest, perhaps with a certain sense of grievance superadded.
He should require the fullest explanations and guarantees
before committing himself, — indeed, her present call might
be an advance that it would be necessary for him to check.

He even pictured her pleading at his feet; a very little stronger effort of his Alnaschar imagination would have made him reject her like the fatuous Persian glass peddler.

He opened the door of the sitting-room deliberately, and walked in with a certain formal precision. But the figure of a woman arose from the sofa, and with a slight outcry, half playful, half hysterical, threw herself upon his breast with the single exclamation, "Jim!" He started back from the double shock. For the woman was *not* his wife! A woman extravagantly dressed, still young, but bearing, even through her artificially heightened color, a face worn with excitement, excess, and premature age. Yet a face that as he disengaged himself from her arms grew upon him with a terrible recognition, a face that he had once thought pretty, inexperienced, and innocent, — the face of the widow of his former partner, Cutler, the woman he was to have married on the day he fled. The bitter revulsion of feeling and astonishment was evidently visible in his face, for she, too, drew back for a moment as they separated. But she had evidently been prepared, if not pathetically inured to such experiences. She dropped into a chair again with a dry laugh, and a hard metallic voice, as she said, —

"Well, it's *you*, anyway — and you can't get out of it."

As he still stared at her, in her inconsistent finery, draggled and wet by the storm, at her limp ribbons and ostentatious jewelry, she continued, in the same hard voice, —

"I thought I spotted you once or twice before; but you took no notice of me, and I reckoned I was mistaken. But this afternoon at the Temple of Music" —

"Where?" said James Smith harshly.

"At the Temple — the San Francisco Troupe performance — where you brushed by me, and I heard your voice saying, 'Beg pardon!' I says, 'That's Jim Farendell.'"

"Farendell!" burst out James Smith, half in simulated astonishment, half in real alarm.

"Well! Smith, then, if you like better," said the woman impatiently; "though it 's about the sickest and most played-out dodge of a name you could have pitched upon. James Smith, Don Diego Smith!" she repeated, with a hysteric laugh. "Why, it beats the nigger minstrels all hollow! Well, when I saw you there, I said, 'That 's Jim Farendell, or his twin brother;' I did n't say 'his ghost,' mind you; for from the beginning, even before I knew it all, I never took any stock in that fool yarn about your burnt bones being found in your office."

"Knew all, knew what?" demanded the man, with a bravado which he nevertheless felt was hopeless.

She rose, crossed the room, and, standing before him, placed one hand upon her hip as she looked at him with half-pitying effrontery.

"Look here, Jim," she began slowly, "do you know what you 're doing? Well, you 're making me tired!" In spite of himself, a half-superstitious thrill went through him as her words and attitude recalled the dead Scranton. "Do you suppose that I don't know that you ran away the night of the fire? Do you suppose that I don't know that you were next to ruined that night, and that you took that opportunity of skedaddling out of the country with all the money you had left, and leaving folks to imagine you were burnt up with the books you had falsified and the accounts you had doctored! It was a mean thing for you to do to me, Jim, for I loved you then, and would have been fool enough to run off with you if you 'd told me all, and not left me to find out that you had lost *my* money — every cent Cutler had left me in the business — with the rest."

With the fatuousness of a weak man cornered, he clung to unimportant details. "But the body was believed to be mine by every one," he stammered angrily. "My papers and books were burnt, — there was no evidence."

"And why was there not?" she said witheringly, staring

doggedly in his face. "Because *I* stopped it! Because when I knew those bones and rags shut up in that office were n't yours, and was beginning to make a row about it, a strange man came to me and said they were the remains of a friend of his who knew your bankruptcy and had come that night to warn you, — a man whom you had half ruined once, a man who had probably lost his life in helping you away. He said if I went on making a fuss he 'd come out with the whole truth — how you were a thief and a forger, and " — she stopped.

"And what else?" he asked desperately, dreading to hear his wife's name next fall from her lips.

"And that — as it could be proved that his friend knew your secrets," she went on in a frightened, embarrassed voice, "you might be accused of making away with him."

For a moment James Smith was appalled; he had never thought of this. As in all his past villainy he was too cowardly to contemplate murder, he was frightened at the mere accusation of it. "But," he stammered, forgetful of all save this new terror, "he *knew* I would n't be such a fool, for the man himself told me Duffy had the papers, and killing him would n't have helped me."

Mrs. Cutler stared at him a moment searchingly, and then turned wearily away. "Well," she said, sinking into her chair again, "he said if I 'd shut my mouth he 'd shut his — and — I did. And this," she added, throwing her hands from her lap, a gesture half of reproach and half of contempt, — "this is what I get for it."

More frightened than touched by the woman's desperation, James Smith stammered a vague apologetic disclaimer, even while he was loathing with a revulsion new to him her draggled finery, her still more faded beauty, and the half-distinct consciousness of guilt that linked her to him. But she waved it away, a weary gesture that again re minded him of the dead Scranton.

"Of course I ain't what I was, but who's to blame for it? When you left me alone without a cent, face to face with a lie, I had to do something. I was n't brought up to work; I like good clothes, and you know it better than anybody. I ain't one of your stage heroines that go out as dependents and governesses and die of consumption, but I thought," she went on with a shrill, hysterical laugh, more painful than the weariness which inevitably followed it, "I thought I might train myself to do it, *on the stage!* and I joined Barker's Company. They said I had a face and figure for the stage; that face and figure wore out before I had anything more to show, and I was n't big enough to make better terms with the manager. They kept me nearly a year doing chambermaids and fairy queens the other side of the footlights, where I saw you to-day. Then I kicked! I suppose I might have married some fool for his money, but I was soft enough to think you might be sending for me when you were safe. You seem to be mighty comfortable here," she continued, with a bitter glance around his handsomely furnished room, "as 'Don Diego Smith.' I reckon skedaddling pays better than staying behind."

"I have only been here a few weeks," he said hurriedly. "I never knew what had become of you, or that you were still here" —

"Or you would n't have come," she interrupted, with a bitter laugh. "Speak out, Jim."

"If there — is anything — I can do — for you," he stammered, "I 'm sure" —

"Anything you can do?" she repeated slowly and scornfully. "Anything you can do *now?* Yes!" she screamed, suddenly rising, crossing the room, and grasping his arms convulsively. "Yes! Take me away from here — anywhere — at once! Look, Jim," she went on feverishly, "let bygones be bygones — I won't peach! I won't tell on you — though I had it in my heart when you gave me the go-by just now! I 'll do anything you say — go to your farthest hiding-place — work for you — only take me out of this cursed place."

Her passionate pleading stung even through his selfishness and loathing. He thought of his wife's indifference. Yes, he might be driven to this, and at least he must secure the only witness against his previous misconduct. "We will see," he said soothingly, gently loosening her hands. "We must talk it over." He stopped as his old suspiciousness returned. "But you must have some friends," he said searchingly, "some one who has helped you."

"None! Only one — he helped me at first," she hesitated — "Duffy."

"Duffy!" said James Smith, recoiling.

"Yes, when he had to tell me all," she said in half-frightened tones, "he was sorry for me. Listen, Jim! He was a square man, for all he was devoted to his partner — and you can't blame him for that. I think he helped me because I was alone; for nothing else, Jim. I swear it! He helped me from time to time. Maybe he might have wanted to marry me if he had not been waiting for another woman that he loved, a married woman that had been deserted years ago by her husband, just as you might have deserted me if we 'd been married that day. He helped her and paid for her journey here to seek her husband, and set her up in business."

"What are you talking about — what woman?" stammered James Smith, with a strange presentiment creeping over him.

"A Mrs. Smith. Yes," she said quickly, as he started, "not a sham name like yours, but really and truly *Smith* — that was her husband's name! I 'm not lying, Jim," she went on, evidently mistaking the cause of the sudden contraction of the man's face. "I did n't invent her nor her name; there *is* such a woman, and Duffy loves her — and *her* only, and he never, *never* was anything more than a friend to me.   I swear it!"

The room seemed to swim around him.   She was staring at him, but he could see in her vacant eyes that she had no conception of his secret, nor knew the extent of her revelation.   Duffy had not dared to tell all!   He burst into a coarse laugh.   "What matters Duffy or the silly woman he'd try to steal away from other men."

"But he didn't try to steal her, and she's only silly because she wants to be true to her husband while he lives. She told Duffy she'd never marry him until she saw her husband's dead face.   More fool she," she added bitterly.

"Until she saw her husband's dead face," was all that James Smith heard of this speech.   His wife's faithfulness through years of desertion, her long waiting and truthfulness, even the bitter commentary of the equally injured woman before him, were to him as nothing to what that single sentence conjured up.   He laughed again, but this time strangely and vacantly.   "Enough of this Duffy and his intrusion in my affairs until I'm able to settle my account with him.   Come," he added brusquely, "if we are going to cut out of this at once I've got much to do. Come here again to-morrow, early.   This Duffy — does he live here?"

"No.   In Marysville."

"Good!   Come early to-morrow."

As she seemed to hesitate, he opened a drawer of his table and took out a handful of gold and handed it to her. She glanced at it for a moment with a strange expression, put it mechanically in her pocket, and then looking up at him said, with a forced laugh, "I suppose that means I am to clear out?"

"Until to-morrow," he said shortly.

"If the Sacramento don't sweep us away before then,"

she interrupted, with a reckless laugh; "the river's broken through the levee — a clear sweep in two places. Where I live the water's up to the doorstep. They say it's going to be the biggest flood yet. You're all right here; you're on higher ground."

She seemed to utter these sentences abstractedly, disconnectedly, as if to gain time. He made an impatient gesture.

"All right, I'm going," she said, compressing her lips slowly to keep them from trembling. "You haven't forgotten anything?" As he turned half angrily towards her she added, hurriedly and bitterly, "Anything — for to-morrow?"

"No!"

She opened the door and passed out. He listened until the trail of her wet skirt had descended the stairs, and the street door had closed behind her. Then he went back to his table and began collecting his papers and putting them away in his trunks, which he packed feverishly, yet with a set and determined face. He wrote one or two letters, which he sealed and left upon his table. He then went to his bedroom and deliberately shaved off his disguising beard. Had he not been so preoccupied in one thought, he might have been conscious of loud voices in the street and a hurrying of feet on the wet sidewalk. But he was possessed by only one idea. He must see his wife that evening! How, he knew not yet, but the way would appear when he had reached his office in the building opposite hers. Three hours had elapsed before he had finished his preparations. On going downstairs he stopped to give some directions to the porter, but his room was empty; passing into the street he was surprised to find it quite deserted, and the shops closed; even a drinking saloon at the corner was quite empty. He turned the corner of the street, and began the slight descent towards his office. To his amaze-

ment the lower end of the street, which was crossed by the
thoroughfare which was his destination, was blocked by a
crowd of people. As he hurried forward to join them he
suddenly saw, moving down that thoroughfare, what appeared to his startled eyes to be the smokestacks of some
small, flat-bottomed steamer. He rubbed his eyes; it was
no illusion, for the next moment he had reached the crowd,
who were standing half a block away from the thoroughfare,
and on the edge of a lagoon of yellow water, whose main
current was the thoroughfare he was seeking, and between
whose houses submerged to their first stories, a steamboat
was really paddling. Other boats and rafts were adrift on
its sluggish waters, and a boatman had just landed a passenger in the backwater of the lower half of the street on
which he stood with the crowd.

Possessed of his one idea, he fought his way desperately
to the water edge and the boat, and demanded a passage
to his office. The boatman hesitated, but James Smith
promptly offered him double the value of his craft. The
act was not deemed singular in that extravagant epoch, and
the sympathizing crowd cheered his solitary departure, as
he declined even the services of the boatman. The next
moment he was off in mid-stream of the thoroughfare, paddling his boat with a desperate but inexperienced hand until he reached his office, which he entered by the window.
The building, which was new and of brick, showed very
little damage from the flood, but in far different case was
the one opposite, on which his eyes were eagerly bent, and
whose cheap and insecure foundations he could see the flood
was already undermining. There were boats around the
house, and men hurriedly removing trunks and valuables,
but the one figure he expected to see was not there. He
tied his own boat to the window; there was evidently no
chance of an interview now, but if she were leaving there
would be still the chance of following her and knowing her

destination. As he gazed she suddenly appeared at a window, and was helped by a boatman into a flat-bottomed barge containing trunks and furniture. She was evidently the last to leave. The other boats put off at once, and none too soon; for there was a warning cry, a quick swerving of the barge, and the end of the dwelling slowly dropped into the flood, seeming to sink on its knees like a stricken ox. A great undulation of yellow water swept across the street, inundating his office through the open window and half swamping his boat beside it. At the same time he could see that the current had changed and increased in volume and velocity, and, from the cries and warning of the boatmen, he knew that the river had burst its banks at its upper bend. He had barely time to leap into his boat and cast it off before there was a foot of water on his floor.

But the new current was carrying the boats away from the higher level, which they had been eagerly seeking, and towards the channel of the swollen river. The barge was first to feel its influence, and was hurried towards the river against the strongest efforts of its boatmen. One by one the other and smaller boats contrived to get into the slack water of crossing streets, and one was swamped before his eyes. But James Smith kept only the barge in view. His difficulty in following it was increased by his inexperience in managing a boat, and the quantity of drift which now charged the current. Trees torn by their roots from some upland bank; sheds, logs, timber, and the bloated carcasses of cattle choked the stream. All the ruin worked by the flood seemed to be compressed in this disastrous current. Once or twice he narrowly escaped collision with a heavy beam or the bed of some farmer's wagon. Once he was swamped by a tree, and righted his frail boat while clinging to its branches.

And then those who watched him from the barge and shore said afterwards that a great apathy seemed to fall upon him. He no longer attempted to guide the boat or struggle with the drift, but sat in the stern with intent forward gaze and motionless paddles. Once they strove to warn him, called to him to make an effort to reach the barge, and did what they could, in spite of their own peril, to alter their course and help him. But he neither answered nor heeded them. And then suddenly a great log that they had just escaped seemed to rise up under the keel of his boat, and it was gone. After a moment his face and head appeared above the current, and so close to the stern of the barge that there was a slight cry from the woman in it, but the next moment, and before the boatman could reach him, he was drawn under it and disappeared. They lay on their oars eagerly watching, but the body of James Smith was sucked under the barge, and in the mid-channel of the great river was carried out towards the distant sea.

. . . .

There was a strange meeting that night on the deck of a relief boat, which had been sent out in search of the missing barge, between Mrs. Smith and a grave and anxious passenger who had chartered it. When he had comforted her, and pointed out, as indeed he had many times before, the loneliness and insecurity of her unprotected life, she yielded to his arguments. But it was not until many months after their marriage that she confessed to him on that eventful night she thought she had seen in a moment of great peril the vision of the dead face of her husband uplifted to her through the water.

LANTY FOSTER'S MISTAKE

LANTY FOSTER was crouching on a low stool before the dying kitchen fire, the better to get its fading radiance on the book she was reading. Beyond, through the open window and door, the fire was also slowly fading from the sky and the mountain ridge whence the sun had dropped half an hour before. The view was uphill, and the sky-line of the hill was marked by two or three gibbet-like poles from which, on a now invisible line between them, depended certain objects — mere black silhouettes against the sky — which bore weird likeness to human figures. Absorbed as she was in her book, she nevertheless occasionally cast an impatient glance in that direction, as the sunlight faded more quickly than her fire. For the fluttering objects were the "week's wash" which had to be brought in before night fell and the mountain wind arose. It was strong at that altitude, and before this had ravished the clothes from the line, and scattered them along the highroad leading over the ridge, once even lashing the shy schoolmaster with a pair of Lanty's own stockings, and blinding the parson with a really tempestuous petticoat.

A whiff of wind down the big-throated chimney stirred the log embers on the hearth, and the girl jumped to her feet, closing the book with an impatient snap. She knew her mother's voice would follow. It was hard to leave her heroine at the crucial moment of receiving an explanation from a presumed faithless lover, just to climb a hill and take in a lot of soulless washing, but such are the infelicities of stolen romance reading. She threw the clothes-basket over

her head like a hood, the handle resting across her bosom
and shoulders, and with both her hands free started out of
the cabin. But the darkness had come up from the valley
in one stride after its mountain fashion, had outstripped
her, and she was instantly plunged in it. Still the outline
of the ridge above her was visible, with the white, steadfast
stars that were not there a moment ago, and by that sign
she knew she was late. She had to battle against the rushing wind now, which sung through the inverted basket over
her head and held her back, but with bent shoulders she at
last reached the top of the ridge and the level. Yet here,
owing to the shifting of the lighter background above her,
she now found herself again encompassed with the darkness.
The outlines of the poles had disappeared, the white fluttering garments were distinct apparitions waving in the wind,
like dancing ghosts. But there certainly was a queer mis-
shapen bulk moving beyond, which she did not recognize,
and as she at last reached one of the poles, a shock was
communicated to it, through the clothes-line and the bulk
beyond. Then she heard a voice say impatiently, —

"What in h——ll am I running into now?"

It was a man's voice, and, from its elevation, the voice
of a man on horseback. She answered without fear and
with slow deliberation, —

"Inter our clothes-line, I reckon."

"Oh!" said the man in a half-apologetic tone. Then
in brisker accents, "The very thing I want! I say, can
you give me a bit of it? The ring of my saddle girth has
fetched loose. I can fasten it with that."

"I reckon," replied Lanty, with the same unconcern,
moving nearer the bulk, which now separated into two
parts as the man dismounted. "How much do you want?"

"A foot or two will do."

They were now in front of each other, although their
faces were not distinguishable to either. Lanty, who had

been following the lines with her hand, here came upon the
end knotted around the last pole. This she began to untie.

"What a place to hang clothes," he said curiously.

"Mighty dryin', though," returned Lanty laconically.

"And your house? Is it near by?" he continued.

"Just down the ridge — ye kin see from the edge. Got
a knife?" She had untied the knot.

"No — yes — wait." He had hesitated a moment and
then produced something from his breast pocket, which he
however kept in his hand. As he did not offer it to her
she simply held out a section of the rope between her hands,
which he divided with a single cut. She saw only that the
instrument was long and keen. Then she lifted the flap of
the saddle for him as he attempted to fasten the loose ring
with the rope, but the darkness made it impossible. With
an ejaculation, he fumbled in his pockets. "My last match!"
he said, striking it, as he crouched over it to protect it from
the wind. Lanty leaned over also, with her apron raised
between it and the blast. The flame for an instant lit up
the ring, the man's dark face, mustache, and white teeth
set together as he tugged at the girth, and Lanty's brown,
velvet eyes and soft, round cheek framed in the basket.
Then it went out, but the ring was secured.

"Thank you," said the man, with a short laugh, "but I
thought you were a hump-backed witch in the dark there."

"And I couldn't make out whether you was a cow or a
b'ar," returned the young girl simply.

Here, however, he quickly mounted his horse, but in the
action something slipped from his clothes, struck a stone,
and bounded away into the darkness.

"My knife," he said hurriedly. "Please hand it to me."
But although the girl dropped on her knees and searched
the ground diligently, it could not be found. The man with
a restrained ejaculation again dismounted, and joined in the
search.

"Have n't you got another match?" suggested Lanty.

"No — it was my last!" he said impatiently.

"Just you hol' on here," she said suddenly, "and I 'll run down to the kitchen and fetch you a light. I won't be long."

"No! no!" said the man quickly; "don't! I could n't wait. I 've been here too long now. Look here. You come in daylight and find it, and — just keep it for me, will you?" He laughed. "I 'll come for it. And now, if you 'll only help to set me on that road again, for it 's so infernal black I can't see the mare's ears ahead of me, I won't bother you any more. Thank you."

Lanty had quietly moved to his horse's head and taken the bridle in her hand, and at once seemed to be lost in the gloom. But in a few moments he felt the muffled thud of his horse's hoof on the thick dust of the highway, and its still hot, impalpable powder rising to his nostrils.

"Thank you," he said again, "I 'm all right now," and in the pause that followed it seemed to Lanty that he had extended a parting hand to her in the darkness. She put up her own to meet it, but missed his, which had blundered onto her shoulder. Before she could grasp it, she felt him stooping over her, the light brush of his soft mustache on her cheek, and then the starting forward of his horse. But the retaliating box on the ear she had promptly aimed at him spent itself in the black space which seemed suddenly to have swallowed up the man, and even his light laugh.

For an instant she stood still, and then, swinging the basket indignantly from her shoulder, took up her suspended task. It was no light one in the increasing wind, and the unfastened clothes-line had precipitated a part of its burden to the ground through the loosening of the rope. But on picking up the trailing garments her hand struck an unfamiliar object. The stranger's lost knife! She thrust it hastily into the bottom of the basket and completed her work. As she began to descend with her burden she saw that the light of the kitchen fire, seen through the windows, was augmented by a candle. Her mother was evidently awaiting her.

"Pretty time to be fetchin' in the wash," said Mrs. Foster querulously. "But what can you expect when folks stand gossipin' and philanderin' on the ridge instead o' tendin' to their work?"

Now Lanty knew that she had *not* been "gossipin'" nor "philanderin'," yet as the parting salute might have been open to that imputation, and as she surmised that her mother might have overheard their voices, she briefly said, to prevent further questioning, that she had shown a stranger the road. But for her mother's unjust accusation she would have been more communicative. As Mrs. Foster went back grumblingly into the sitting-room Lanty resolved to keep the knife at present a secret from her mother, and to that purpose removed it from the basket. But in the light of the candle she saw it for the first time plainly — and started.

For it was really a dagger! jeweled-handled and richly wrought — such as Lanty had never looked upon before. The hilt was studded with gems, and the blade, which had a cutting edge, was damascened in blue and gold. Her soft eyes reflected the brilliant setting, her lips parted breathlessly; then, as her mother's voice arose in the other room, she thrust it back into its velvet sheath and clapped it into her pocket. Its rare beauty had confirmed her resolution of absolute secrecy. To have shown it now would have made "no end of talk." And she was not sure but that her parents would have demanded its custody! And it was given to *her* by *him* to keep. This settled the question of moral ethics. She took the first opportunity to run up to her bedroom and hide it under the mattress.

Yet the thought of it filled the rest of her evening.

When her household duties were done she took up her novel again, partly from force of habit and partly as an attitude in which she could think of *It* undisturbed. For what was fiction to her now? True, it possessed a certain reminiscent value. A "dagger" had appeared in several romances she had devoured, but she never had a clear idea of one before. "The Count sprang back, and, drawing from his belt a richly jeweled dagger, hissed between his teeth," or, more to the purpose: "'Take this,' said Orlando, handing her the ruby-hilted poniard which had gleamed upon his thigh, 'and should the caitiff attempt thy unguarded innocence'"—

"Did ye hear what your father was sayin'?" Lanty started. It was her mother's voice in the doorway, and she had been vaguely conscious of another voice pitched in the same querulous key, which, indeed, was the dominant expression of the small ranchers of that fertile neighborhood. Possibly a too complaisant and unaggressive Nature had spoiled them.

"Yes!—no!" said Lanty abstractedly, "what did he say?"

"If you was n't taken up with that fool book," said Mrs. Foster, glancing at her daughter's slightly conscious color, "ye'd know! He allowed ye'd better not leave yer filly in the far pasture nights. That gang o' Mexican horse-thieves is out again, and raided McKinnon's stock last night."

This touched Lanty closely. The filly was her own property, and she was breaking it for her own riding. But her distrust of her parents' interference was greater than any fear of horse-stealers. "She's mighty uneasy in the barn; and," she added, with a proud consciousness of that beautiful yet carnal weapon upstairs, "I reckon I ken protect her and myself agin any Mexican horse-thieves."

"My! but we're gettin' high and mighty," responded

Mrs. Foster, with deep irony. "Did you git all that outer your fool book?"

"Mebbe," said Lanty curtly.

Nevertheless, her thoughts that night were not entirely based on written romance. She wondered if the stranger knew that she had really tried to box his ears in the darkness, also if he had been able to see her face. *His* she remembered, at least the flash of his white teeth against his dark face and darker mustache, which was quite as soft as her own hair. But if he thought "for a minnit" that she was "goin'" to allow an entire stranger to kiss her — he was mighty mistaken." She should let him know it "pretty quick"! She should hand him back the dagger "quite careless like," and never let on that she'd thought anything of it. Perhaps that was the reason why, before she went to bed, she took a good look at it, and after taking off her straight, beltless, calico gown she even tried the effect of it, thrust in the stiff waistband of her petticoat, with the jeweled hilt displayed, and thought it looked charming — as indeed it did. And then, having said her prayers like a good girl, and supplicated that she should be less "tetchy" with her parents, she went to sleep and dreamed that she had gone out to take in the wash again, but that the clothes had all changed to the queerest lot of folks, who were all fighting and struggling with each other until she, Lanty, drawing her dagger, rushed up single-handed among them, crying, "Disperse, ye craven curs, — disperse, I say!" And they dispersed.

Yet even Lanty was obliged to admit the next morning that all this was somewhat incongruous with the baking of "corn dodgers," the frying of fish, the making of beds, and her other household duties, and dismissed the stranger from her mind until he should "happen along." In her freer and more acceptable outdoor duties she even tolerated the advances of neighboring swains who made a point of pass-

ing by "Foster's Ranch," and who were quite aware that
Atalanta Foster, *alias* "Lanty," was one of the prettiest
girls in the country.   But Lanty's toleration consisted in
that singular performance known to herself as "giving them
as good as they sent," being a lazy traversing, qualified with
scorn, of all that they advanced.   How long they would
have put up with this from a plain girl I do not know, but
Lanty's short upper lip seemed framed for indolent and fascinating scorn, and her dreamy eyes usually looked beyond
the questioner, or blunted his bolder glances in their vel-
vety surfaces.   The libretto of these scenes was not exhaus-
tive, *e. g.* : —

The Swain (with bold, bad gayety).   "Saw that shy
schoolmaster hangin' round your ridge yesterday!   Orter
know by this time that shyness with a gal don't pay."

Lanty (decisively).   "Mebbe he allows it don't get left
as often as impudence."

The Swain (ignoring the reply and his previous attitude
and becoming more direct).   "I was calkilatin' to say that
with these yer hoss-thieves about, yer filly ain't safe in the
pasture.   I took a turn round there two or three times last
evening to see if she was all right."

Lanty (with a flattering show of interest).   "No! *did*
ye, now?   I was jest wonderin' " —

The Swain (eagerly).   "I did — quite late, too!   Why,
that's nothin', Miss Atalanty, to what I'd do for you."

Lanty (musing, with far-off eyes).   "Then that's why
she was so awful skeerd and frightened!   Just jumpin'
outer her skin with horror.   I reckoned it was a b'ar or
panther or a spook!   You ought to have waited till she got
accustomed to your looks."

Nevertheless, despite this elegant raillery, Lanty was
enough concerned in the safety of her horse to visit it the
next day with a view of bringing it nearer home.   She had
just stepped into the alder fringe of a dry "run" when she

came suddenly upon the figure of a horseman in the "run," who had been hidden by the alders from the plain beyond and who seemed to be engaged in examining the hoof marks in the dust of the old ford. Something about his figure struck her recollection, and as he looked up quickly she saw it was the owner of the dagger. But he appeared to be lighter of hair and complexion, and was dressed differently, and more like a *vaquero*. Yet there was the same flash of his teeth as he recognized her, and she knew it was the same man.

Alas for her preparation! Without the knife she could not make that haughty return of it which she had contemplated. And more than that, she was conscious she was blushing! Nevertheless she managed to level her pretty brown eyebrows at him, and said sharply that if he followed her to her home she would return his property at once.

"But I'm in no hurry for it," he said with a laugh, — the same light laugh and pleasant voice she remembered, — "and I'd rather not come to the house just now. The knife is in good hands, I know, and I'll call for it when I want it! And until then — if it's all the same to you — keep it to yourself, — keep it dark, as dark as the night I lost it!"

"I don't go about blabbing my affairs," said Lanty indignantly, "and if it hadn't *been* dark that night you'd have had your ears boxed — you know why!"

The stranger laughed again, waved his hand to Lanty, and galloped away.

Lanty was a little disappointed. The daylight had taken away some of her illusions. He was certainly very good-looking, but not quite as picturesque, mysterious, and thrilling as in the dark! And it was very queer — he certainly did look darker that night! Who was he? And why was he lingering near her? He was different from her neighbors — her admirers. He might be one of those locaters, from the big towns, who prospect the lands, with a view of settling government warrants on them, — they were always so secret until they had found what they wanted. She did not dare to seek information of her friends, for the same reason that she had concealed his existence from her mother, — it would provoke awkward questions; and it was evident that he was trusting to her secrecy, too. The thought thrilled her with a new pride, and was some compensation for the loss of her more intangible romance. It would be mighty fine, when he did call openly for his beautiful knife and declared himself, to have them all know that *she* knew about it all along.

When she reached home, to guard against another such surprise she determined to keep the weapon with her, and, distrusting her pocket, confided it to the cheap little country-made corset which only for the last year had confined her budding figure, and which now, perhaps, heaved with an additional pride. She was quite abstracted during the rest of the day, and paid but little attention to the gossip of the farm lads, who were full of a daring raid, two nights before, by the Mexican gang on the large stock farm of a neighbor. The Vigilance Committee had been baffled; it was even alleged that some of the smaller ranchmen and herders were in league with the gang. It was also believed to be a widespread conspiracy; to have a political complexion in its combination of an alien race with Southwestern filibusters. The legal authorities had been reinforced by special detectives from San Francisco. Lanty seldom troubled herself with these matters; she knew the exaggeration, she suspected the ignorance of her rural neighbors. She roughly referred it, in her own vocabulary, to "jaw," a peculiarly masculine quality. But later in the evening, when the domestic circle in the sitting-room had been augmented by a neighbor, and Lanty had taken refuge behind her novel as an excuse for silence, Zob Hopper, the enamored swain of the previous evening, burst in with more astounding news. A posse of the sheriff had just passed along the ridge; they had "corraled" part of the gang, and rescued some of the stock. The leader of the gang had escaped, but his capture was inevitable, as the roads were stopped. "All the same, I'm glad to see ye took my advice, Miss Atalanty, and brought in your filly," he concluded, with an insinuating glance at the young girl.

But "Miss Atalanty," curling a quarter of an inch of scarlet lip above the edge of her novel, here "allowed" that if his advice or the filly had to be "took," she did n't know which was worse.

"I wonder ye kin talk to sech peartness, Mr. Hopper," said Mrs. Foster severely; "she ain't got eyes nor senses for anythin' but that book."

"Talkin' o' what's to be 'took,'" put in the diplomatic neighbor, "you bet it ain't that Mexican leader! No, sir! he's been 'stopped' before this — and then got clean away all the same! One o' them detectives got him once and disarmed him — but he managed to give them the slip, after all. Why, he's that full o' shifts and disguises thar ain't no spottin' him. He walked right under the constable's nose oncet, and took a drink with the sheriff that was arter him — and the blamed fool never knew it. He kin change even the color of his hair quick as winkin'."

"Is he a real Mexican, — a regular Greaser?" asked the paternal Foster. "Cos I never heard that they wuz smart."

"No! They say he comes o' old Spanish stock, a bad egg they threw outer the nest, I reckon," put in Hopper eagerly, seeing a strange animated interest dilating Lanty's eyes, and hoping to share in it; "but he's reg'lar high-toned, you bet! Why, I knew a man who seed him in his own camp — prinked out in a velvet jacket and silk sash. with gold chains and buttons down his wide pants and a

dagger stuck in his sash, with a handle just blazin' with
jew'ls. Yes! Miss Atalanty, they say that one stone at
the top — a green stone, what they call an ' em'ral' — was
worth the price o' a 'Frisco house-lot. True ez you live!
Eh — what's up now?"

Lanty's book had fallen on the floor as she was rising to
her feet with a white face, still more strange and distorted
in an affected yawn behind her little hand. "Yer makin'
me that sick and nervous with yer fool yarns," she said
hysterically, "that I'm goin' to get a little fresh air. It's
just stifling here with lies and terbacker!" With another
high laugh, she brushed past him into the kitchen, opened
the door, and then paused, and, turning, ran rapidly up to
her bedroom. Here she locked herself in, tore open the
bosom of her dress, plucked out the dagger, threw it on the
bed, where the green stone gleamed for an instant in the
candle-light, and then dropped on her knees beside the bed
with her whirling head buried in her cold red hands.

It had all come to her in a flash, like a blaze of lightning, — the black, haunting figure on the ridge, the broken
saddle girth, the abandonment of the dagger in the exigen-
cies of flight and concealment; the second meeting, the
skulking in the dry, alder-hidden "run," the changed dress,
the lighter-colored hair, but always the same voice and
laugh, — the leader, the fugitive, the Mexican horse-thief!
And she, the God-forsaken fool, the chuckle-headed nigger
baby, with not half the sense of her own filly or that sop-
headed Hopper — had never seen it! She — *she* who
would be the laughing-stock of them all — she had thought
him a "locater," a "towny" from 'Frisco! And she had
consented to keep his knife until he would call for it, —
yes, call for it, with fire and flame perhaps, the trampling
of hoofs, pistol shots — and — yet —

Yet! — he had *trusted* her. Yes! trusted her when he
knew a word from her lips would have brought the whole

district down on him! when the mere exposure of that
dagger would have identified and damned him! Trusted
her a second time, when she was within cry of her house!
When he might have taken her filly without her knowing
it! And now she remembered vaguely that the neighbors
had said how strange it was that her father's stock had not
suffered as theirs had. *He* had protected them — he who
was now a fugitive — and their men pursuing him! She
rose suddenly with a single stamp of her narrow foot, and
as suddenly became cool and sane. And then, quite her
old self again, she lazily picked up the dagger and restored
it to its place in her bosom. That done, with her color
back and her eyes a little brighter, she deliberately went
downstairs again, stuck her little brown head into the sitting-room, said cheerfully, "Still yawpin', you folks," and
quietly passed out into the darkness.

She ran swiftly up to the ridge, impelled by the blind
memory of having met him there at night and the one
vague thought to give him warning. But it was dark and
empty, with no sound but the rushing wind. And then an
idea seized her. If he were haunting the vicinity still, he
might see the fluttering of the clothes upon the line and
believe she was there. She stooped quickly, and in the
merciful and exonerating darkness stripped off her only
white petticoat and pinned it on the line. It flapped, fluttered, and streamed in the mountain wind. She lingered
and listened. But there came a sound she had not counted
on, — the clattering hoofs of not *one*, but many, horses on
the lower road. She ran back to the house to find its inmates already hastening towards the road for news. She
took that chance to slip in quietly, go to her room, whose
window commanded a view of the ridge, and crouching low
behind it, she listened. She could hear the sound of voices,
and the dull trampling of heavy boots on the dusty path
towards the barnyard on the other side of the house — a

pause, and then the return of the trampling boots, and the
final clattering of hoofs on the road again. Then there was
a tap on her door and her mother's querulous voice.

"Oh! yer there, are ye? Well — it 's the best place fer
a girl — with all these man's doin's goin' on! They 've
got that Mexican horse-thief and have tied him up in your
filly's stall in the barn — till the 'Frisco deputy gets back
from rounding up the others. So ye jest stay where ye are
till they 've come and gone, and we 're shut o' all that cattle. Are ye mindin'? "

"All right, maw; 't ain't no call o' mine, anyhow," returned Lanty through the half-open door.

At another time her mother might have been startled at
her passive obedience. Still more would she have been
startled had she seen her daughter's face now, behind the
closed door — with her little mouth set over her clinched
teeth. And yet it was her own child, and Lanty was her
mother's real daughter; the same pioneer blood filled their
veins, the blood that had never nourished cravens or degen-
erates, but had given itself to sprinkle and fertilize desert'
solitudes where man might follow. Small wonder, then,
that this frontier-born Lanty, whose first infant cry had
been answered by the yelp of wolf and scream of panther;
whose father's rifle had been leveled across her cradle to
cover the stealthy Indian who prowled outside — small
wonder that she should feel herself equal to these "man's
doin's," and prompt to take a part. For even in the first
shock of the news of the capture she recalled the fact that
the barn was old and rotten, that only that day the filly had
kicked a board loose from behind her stall, which she, Lanty,
had lightly returned to avoid "making a fuss." If his captors had not noticed it, or trusted only to their guards, she
might make the opening wide enough to free him!

Two hours later the guard nearest the now sleeping
house, a farm hand of the Fosters', saw his employer's

daughter slip out and cautiously approach him. A devoted slave of Lanty's, and familiar with her impulses, he guessed her curiosity, and was not averse to satisfy it and the sense of his own importance. To her whispers of affected, half-terrified interest, he responded in whispers that the captive was really in the filly's stall, securely bound by his wrists behind his back, and his feet "hobbled" to a post. That Lanty could n't see him, for it was dark inside, and he was sitting with his back to the wall, as he could n't sleep comf'ble lyin' down. Lanty's eyes glowed, but her face was turned aside.

"And ye ain't reckonin' his friends will come and rescue him?" said Lanty, gazing with affected fearfulness in the darkness.

"Not much! There's two other guards down in the corral, and I'd fire my gun and bring 'em up."

But Lanty was gazing open-mouthed towards the ridge. "What's that wavin' on the ridge?" she said in awe-stricken tones.

She was pointing to the petticoat, — a vague, distant, moving object against the horizon.

"Why, that's some o' the wash on the line, ain't it?"

"Wash — *two days in the week!*" said Lanty sharply. "Wot's gone of you?"

"Thet's so," muttered the man, "and it wa'n't there at sundown, I'll swear! P'r'aps I'd better call the guard," and he raised his rifle.

"Don't," said Lanty, catching his arm. "Suppose it's nothin', they'll laugh at ye. Creep up softly and see; ye ain't afraid, are ye? If ye are, give me yer gun, and *I*'ll go."

This settled the question, as Lanty expected. The man cocked his piece, and bending low began cautiously to mount the acclivity. Lanty waited until his figure began to fade, and then ran like fire to the barn.

She had arranged every detail of her plan beforehand.
Crouching beside the wall of the stall she hissed through a
crack in thrilling whispers, "Don't move! Don't speak for
your life's sake! Wait till I hand you back your knife,
then do the best you can." Then slipping aside the loosened board she saw dimly the black outline of curling hair,
back, shoulders, and tied wrists of the captive. Drawing
the knife from her pocket, with two strokes of its keen cutting edge she severed the cords, threw the knife into the
opening, and darted away. Yet in that moment she knew
that the man was instinctively turning towards her. But
it was one thing to free a horse-thief, and another to stop
and "philander" with him.

She ran halfway up the ridge, and met the farm hand
returning. It was only a bit of washing after all, and he
was glad he had n't fired his gun. On the other hand,
Lanty confessed she had got "so skeert" being alone, that
she came to seek him. She had the shivers; was n't her
hand cold? It was, but thrilling even in its coldness to
the bashfully admiring man. And she was that weak and
dizzy, he must let her lean on his arm going down; and
they must go *slow*. She was sure he was cold too, and if
he would wait at the back door she would give him a drink
of whiskey. Thus Lanty, with her brain afire, her eyes
and ears straining into the darkness, and the vague outline
of the barn beyond. Another moment was protracted over
the drink of whiskey, and then Lanty, with a faint arch-
ness, made him promise not to tell her mother of her esca-
pade, and she promised on her part not to say anything
about his "stalking a petticoat on the clothes-line," and
then shyly closed the door and regained her room. *He*
must have got away by this time, or have been discovered;
she believed they would not open the barn door until the
return of the posse.

She was right. It was near daybreak when they returned, and, again crouching low beside her window, she heard, with a fierce joy, the sudden outcry, the oaths, the wrangling voices, the summoning of her father to the front door, and then the tumultuous sweeping away again of the whole posse, and a blessed silence falling over the rancho. And then Lanty went quietly to bed, and slept like a three-year child!

Perhaps that was the reason why she was able at breakfast to listen with lazy and even rosy indifference to the startling events of the night; to the sneers of the farm hands at the posse who had overlooked the knife when they searched their prisoner, as well as the stupidity of the corral guard who had never heard him make a hole "the size of a house" in the barn side! Once she glanced demurely at Silas Briggs — the farm hand — and the poor fellow felt consoled in his shame at the remembrance of their confidences.

But Lanty's tranquillity was not destined to last long. There was again the irruption of exciting news from the highroad; the Mexican leader had been recaptured, and was now safely lodged in Brownsville jail! Those who were previously loud in their praises of the successful horse-thief who had baffled the vigilance of his pursuers were now equally keen in their admiration of the new San Francisco deputy who, in turn, had outwitted the whole gang. It was *he* who was fertile in expedients; *he* who had studied the whole country, and even risked his life among the gang, and *he* who had again closed the meshes of the net around the escaped outlaw. He was already returning by way of the rancho, and might stop there a moment, — so that they could all see the hero. Such was the power of success on the country-side! Outwardly indifferent, inwardly bitter, Lanty turned away. She should not grace his triumph, if she kept in her room all day! And when there was a clatter of hoofs on the road again, Lanty slipped upstairs.

" I thought you were that horse-thief "

But in a few moments she was summoned. Captain Lance Wetherby, Assistant Chief of Police of San Francisco, Deputy Sheriff and ex-United States scout, had requested to see Miss Foster a few moments alone. Lanty knew what it meant, — her secret had been discovered; but she was not the girl to shirk the responsibility! She lifted her little brown head proudly, and with the same resolute step with which she had left the house the night before, descended the stairs and entered the sitting-room. At first she saw nothing. Then a remembered voice struck her ear; she started, looked up, and gasping, fell back against the door. It was the stranger who had given her the dagger, the stranger she had met in the run! — the horse-thief himself! No! no! she saw it all now — she had cut loose the wrong man!

He looked at her with a smile of sadness — as he drew from his breast-pocket that dreadful dagger, the very sight of which Lanty now loathed! "This is the *second* time, Miss Foster," he said gently, "that I have taken this knife from Murietta, the Mexican bandit: once when I disarmed him three weeks ago, and he escaped, and last night, when he had again escaped and I recaptured him. After I lost it that night I understood from you that you had found it and were keeping it for me." He paused a moment and went on: "I don't ask you what happened last night. I don't condemn you for it; I can believe what a girl of your courage and sympathy might rightly do if her pity were excited; I only ask — why did you give *him* back that knife *I* trusted you with?"

"Why? Why did I?" burst out Lanty in a daring gush of truth, scorn, and temper. "*Because I thought you were that horse-thief.* There!"

He drew back astonished, and then suddenly came that laugh that Lanty remembered and now hailed with joy. "I believe you, by Jove!" he gasped. "That first night

I wore the disguise in which I have tracked him and mingled with his gang. Yes! I see it all now — and more. I see that to *you* I owe his recapture!"

"To me!" echoed the bewildered girl; "how?"

"Why, instead of making for his cave he lingered here in the confines of the ranch! He thought you were in love with him, because you freed him and gave him his knife, and stayed to see you!"

But Lanty had her apron to her eyes, whose first tears were filling their velvet depths. And her voice was broken as she said, —

"Then he — cared — a — good deal more for me — than some people!"

But there is every reason to believe that Lanty was wrong! At least later events that are part of the history of Foster's Rancho and the Foster family pointed distinctly to the contrary.

AN ALI BABA OF THE SIERRAS

JOHNNY STARLEIGH found himself again late for school.
It was always happening. It seemed to be inevitable with
the process of going to school at all. And it was no fault
"o' his." Something was always occurring, — some eccen-
tricity of Nature or circumstance was invariably starting up
in his daily path to the schoolroom. He may not have
been "thinkin' of squirrels," and yet the rarest and most
evasive of that species were always crossing his trail; he
may not have been "huntin' honey," and yet a wild bees'
nest in the hollow of an oak absolutely obtruded itself before him; he was n't "bird-catchin'," and yet there was a
yellow-hammer always within stone's throw. He had heard
how grown men hunters always saw the most wonderful
animals when they "had n't got a gun with 'em," and it
seemed to be his lot to meet them in his restricted possibilities on the way to school. If Nature was thus capricious
with his elders, why should folk think it strange if she was
as mischievous with a small boy?

On this particular morning Johnny had been beguiled by
the unmistakable footprints — so like his own! — of a bear's
cub. What chances he had of ever coming up with them,
or what he would have done if he had, he did not know.
He only knew that at the end of an hour and a half he
found himself two miles from the schoolhouse, and, from
the position of the sun, at least an hour too late for school.
He knew that nobody would believe him. The punishment for complete truancy was little worse than for being
late. He resolved to accept it, and by way of irrevocabil-

ity at once burnt his ships behind him — in devouring part
of his dinner.

Thus fortified in his outlawry, he began to look about
him.   He was on a thickly wooded terrace with a blank
wall of "outcrop" on one side nearly as high as the pines
which pressed close against it.   He had never seen it before; it was two or three miles from the highroad and
seemed to be a virgin wilderness.   But on close examination he could see, with the eye of a boy bred in a mining
district, that the wall of outcrop had not escaped the attention of the mining prospector.   There were marks of his
pick in some attractive quartz seams of the wall, and farther
on, a more ambitious attempt, evidently by a party of
miners, to begin a tunnel, shown in an abandoned excavation and the heap of débris before it.   It had evidently
been abandoned for some time, as ferns already forced their
green fronds through the stones and gravel, and the yerba
buena vine was beginning to mat the surface of the heap.
But the boy's fancy was quickly taken by the traces of a
singular accident, and one which had perhaps arrested the
progress of the excavators.   The roots of a large pine tree
growing close to the wall had been evidently loosened by
the excavators, and the tree had fallen, with one of its
largest roots still in the opening the miners had made, and
apparently blocking the entrance.   The large tree lay, as it
fell — midway across another but much smaller outcrop of
rock which stood sharply about fifteen feet above the level
of the terrace — with its gaunt, dead limbs in the air at a
low angle.   To Johnny's boyish fancy it seemed so easily
balanced on the rock that but for its imprisoned root it
would have made a capital see-saw.   This he felt must be
looked to hereafter.   But here his attention was arrested
by something more alarming.   His quick ear, attuned like
an animal's to all woodland sounds, detected the crackling
of underwood in the distance.   His equally sharp eye saw

the figures of two men approaching.   But as he recognized
the features of one of them he drew back with a beating
heart, a hushed breath, and hurriedly hid himself in the
shadow.   For he had seen that figure once before — flying
before the sheriff and an armed posse — and had never forgotten it!   It was the figure of Spanish Pete, a notorious
desperado and sluice robber!

Finding he had been unobserved, the boy took courage,
and his small faculties became actively alive.   The two
men came on together cautiously, and at a little distance
the second man, whom Johnny did not know, parted from
his companion and began to loiter up and down, looking
around as if acting as a sentinel for the desperado, who
advanced directly to the fallen tree.   Suddenly the sentinel uttered an exclamation, and Spanish Pete paused.
The sentinel was examining the ground near the heap of
débris.

"What's up?" growled the desperado.

"Foot tracks!   Were n't here before.   And fresh ones,
too."

Johnny's heart sank.   It was where he had just passed.

Spanish Pete hurriedly joined his companion.

"Foot tracks be ——!" he said scornfully.   "What fool
would be crawlin' round here barefooted?   It's a young
b'ar!"

Johnny knew the footprints were his own.   Yet he recognized the truth of the resemblance; it was uncompli-
mentary, but he felt relieved.   The desperado came forward, and to the boy's surprise began to climb the small
ridge of outcrop until he reached the fallen tree.   Johnny
saw that he was carrying a heavy stone.   "What's the
blamed fool goin' to do?" he said to himself; the man's
evident ignorance regarding footprints had lessened the
boy's awe of him.   But the stranger's next essay took
Johnny's breath away.   Standing on the fallen tree trunk at

its axis on the outcrop, he began to rock it gently. To Johnny's surprise it began to move. The upper end descended
slowly, lifting the root in the excavation at the lower end,
and with it a mass of rock, and revealing a cavern behind
large enough to admit a man. Johnny gasped. The desperado coolly deposited the heavy stone on the tree beyond
its axis on the rock, so that it would keep the tree in position, leaped from the tree to the rock, and quickly descended, at which he was joined by the other man, who
was carrying two heavy chamois-leather bags. They both
proceeded to the opening thus miraculously disclosed, and
disappeared in it.

Johnny sat breathless, wondering, expectant, but not
daring to move. The men might come out at any moment;
he had seen enough to know that their enterprise as well as
their cave was a secret, and that the desperado would subject any witness to it, however innocent or unwilling, to
horrible penalties. The time crept slowly by, — he heard
every rap of a woodpecker in a distant tree; a blue jay
dipped and lighted on a branch within his reach, but he
dared not extend his hand; his legs were infested by ants;
he even fancied he heard the dry, hollow rattle of a rattlesnake not a yard from him. And then the entrance of the
cave was darkened, and the two men reappeared. Johnny
stared. He would have rubbed his eyes if he had dared.
They were not the same men! Did the cave contain others
who had been all the while shut up in its dark recesses?
Was there a band? Would they all swarm out upon him?
Should he run for his life?

But the illusion was only momentary. A longer look at
them convinced him that they were the same men in new
clothes and disguised, and as one remounted the outcrop
Johnny's keen eyes recognized him as Spanish Pete. He
merely kicked away the stone; the root again descended
gently over the opening, and the tree recovered its former

angle. The two hurried away, but Johnny noticed that
they were empty-handed. The bags had been left behind.

The boy waited patiently, listening with his ear to the
ground, like an Indian, for the last rustle of fern and
crackle of underbrush, and then emerged, stiff and cramped
from his concealment. But he no longer thought of flight;
curiosity and ambition burned in his small veins. He
quickly climbed up the outcrop, picked up the fallen stone,
and in spite of its weight lifted it to the prostrate tree.
Here he paused, and from his coign of vantage looked and
listened. The solitude was profound. Then mounting the
tree and standing over its axis he tried to rock it as the
others had. Alas! Johnny's heart was stout, his courage
unlimited, his perception all-embracing, his ambition
boundless; but his actual avoirdupois was only that of a
boy of ten. The tree did not move. But Johnny had
played see-saw before, and quietly moved towards its highest part. It slowly descended under the changed centre of
gravity, and the root arose, disclosing the opening as before. Yet here the little hero paused. He waited with
his eyes fixed on the opening, ready to fly on the sallying
out of any one who had remained concealed. He then
placed the stone where he had stood, leaped down, and ran
to the opening.

The change from the dazzling sunlight to the darkness
confused him at first, and he could see nothing. On entering he stumbled over something which proved to be a bottle in which a candle was fitted, and a box of matches evidently used by the two men. Lighting the candle he could
now discern that the cavern was only a few yards long, the
beginning of a tunnel which the accident to the tree had
stopped. In one corner lay the clothes that the men had
left, and which for a moment seemed all that the cavern
contained; but on removing them Johnny saw that they
were thrown over a rifle, a revolver, and the two chamois-

leather bags that the men had brought there. They were so heavy that the boy could scarcely lift them. His face flushed; his hands trembled with excitement. To a boy whose truant wanderings had given him a fair knowledge of mining, he knew that weight could have but one meaning. Gold! He hurriedly untied the nearest bag. But it was not the gold of the locality, of the tunnel, of the "bed rock." It was "flake gold," the gold of the river. It had been taken from the miners' sluices in the distant streams. The bags before him were the spoils of the sluice robber, — spoils that could not be sold or even shown in the district without danger, spoils kept until they could be taken to Marysville or Sacramento for disposal. All this might have occurred to the mind of any boy of the locality who had heard the common gossip of his elders, but to Johnny's fancy an idea was kindled peculiarly his own. Here was a cavern like that of the "Forty Thieves" in the story book, and he was the "Ali Baba" who knew its secret! He was not obliged to say "Open Sesame," but he could say it if he liked, if he was showing it off to anybody!

Yet alas! he also knew it was a secret he must keep to himself. He had nobody to trust it to. His father was a charcoal-burner of small means; a widower with two children, Johnny and his elder brother Sam. The latter, a flagrant incorrigible of twenty-two, with a tendency to dissipation and low company, had lately abandoned his father's roof, only to reappear at intervals of hilarious or maudlin intoxication. He had always been held up to Johnny as a warning, or with the gloomy prognosis that he, Johnny, was already following in his tortuous footsteps. Even if he were here he was not to be thought of as a confidant. Still less could he trust his father, who would be sure to bungle the secret with sheriffs and constables, and end by bringing down the vengeance of the gang upon the family. As for himself, he could not dispose of the gold if he were to take

it. The exhibition of a single flake of it to the adult public would arouse suspicion, and as it was Johnny s hard fate
to be always doubted, he might be connected with the gang.
As a truant he knew he had no moral standing, but he also
had the superstition — quite characteristic of childhood —
that being in possession of a secret he was a participant in
its criminality — and bound, as it were, by terrible oaths!
And then a new idea seized him. He carefully put back
everything as he had found it, extinguished the candle, left
the cave, remounted the tree, and closed the opening again
as he had seen the others do it, with the addition of murmuring "Shut Sesame" to himself, and then ran away as
fast as his short legs could carry him.

Well clear of the dangerous vicinity, he proceeded more
leisurely for about a mile, until he came to a low white-
washed fence, inclosing a small cultivated patch and a neat
farmhouse beyond. Here he paused, and, cowering behind
the fence, with extraordinary facial contortions produced a
cry not unlike the scream of a blue jay. Repeating it at
intervals, he was presently relieved by observing the approach of a nankeen sunbonnet within the inclosure above
the line of fence. Stopping before him, the sunbonnet revealed a rosy little face, more than usually plump on one
side, and a neck enormously wrapped in a scarf. It was
"Meely" (Amelia) Stryker, a schoolmate, detained at
home by "mumps," as Johnny was previously aware. For
with the famous indiscretion of some other great heroes, he
was about to intrust his secret and his destiny to one of the
weaker sex. And what were the minor possibilities of con-
tagion to this?

"Playin' hookey ag'in?" said the young lady, with a
cordial and even expansive smile, exclusively confined to
one side of her face.

"Um! So 'd you be ef you 'd been whar I hev," he said
with harrowing mystery.

"No! — say!" said Meely eagerly.

At which Johnny, clutching at the top of the fence, with hurried breath told his story. But not all. With the instinct of a true artist he withheld the manner in which the opening of the cave was revealed, said nothing about the tree, and, I grieve to say, added the words "Open Sesame" as the important factor to the operation. Neither did he mention the name of Spanish Pete. For all of which he was afterwards duly grateful.

"Meet me at the burnt pine down the cross-roads at four o'clock," he said in conclusion, "and I'll show ye."

"Why not now?" said Meely impatiently.

"Couldn't. Much as my life is worth! Must keep watching out! You come at four."

And with an assuring nod he released the fence and trotted off. He returned cautiously in the direction of the cave; he was by no means sure that the robbers might not return that day, and his mysterious rendezvous with Meely veiled a certain prudence. And it was well! For as he stealthily crept around the face of the outcrop, hidden in the ferns, he saw from the altered angle of the tree that the cavern was opened. He remained motionless, with bated breath. Then he heard the sound of subdued voices from the cavern, and a figure emerged from the opening. Johnny grasped the ferns rigidly to check the dreadful cry that rose to his lips at its sight. For that figure was his own brother!

There was no mistaking that weak, wicked face, even then flushed with liquor! Johnny had seen it too often thus. But never before as a thief's face! He gave a little gasp, and fell back upon that strange reserve of apathy and reticence in which children are apt to hide their emotions from us at such a moment. He watched impassively the two other men who followed his brother out to give him a small bag and some instructions, and then returned within their cave, while his brother walked quickly away. He watched him disappear; he did not move, for even if he had followed him he could not bear to face him in his shame. And then out of his sullen despair came a boyish idea of revenge. It was those two men who had made his brother a thief!

He was very near the tree. He crept stealthily on his hands and knees through the bracken, and as stealthily climbed the wedge of outcrop, and then leaped like a wildcat on the tree. With incredible activity he lifted the balancing stone, and as the tree began to move, in a flash of perception transferred it to the other side of its axis, and felt the roots and débris, under that additional weight, descend quickly with something like a crash over the opening. Then he took to his heels. He ran so swiftly that all unknowingly he overtook a figure, who, turning, glanced at him, and then disappeared in the wood. It was his second and last view of his brother, as he never saw him again!

But now, strange to say, the crucial and most despairing moment of his day's experience had come. He had to face Meely Stryker under the burnt pine, and the promise he could not keep, and to tell her that he had lied to her. It was the only way to save his brother now! His small wits, and alas! his smaller methods, were equal to the despairing task. As soon as he saw her waiting under the tree he fell to capering and dancing with an extravagance in which hysteria had no small part. "Sold! sold! sold again, and got the money!" he laughed shrilly.

The girl looked at him with astonishment, which changed gradually to scorn, and then to anger. Johnny's heart sank, but he redoubled his antics.

"Who's sold?" she said disdainfully.

"You be. You swallered all that stuff about Ali Baba! You wanted to be Morgy Anna! Ho! ho! And I've made you play hookey — from home!"

"You hateful, horrid, little liar!"

Johnny accepted his punishment meekly — in his heart gratefully. "I reckoned you'd laugh and not get mad," he said submissively. The girl turned, with tears of rage and vexation in her eyes, and walked away. Johnny followed at a humble distance. Perhaps there was something instinctively touching in the boy's remorse, for they made it up before they reached her fence.

Nevertheless Johnny went home miserable. Luckily for him, his father was absent at a Vigilance Committee called to take cognizance of the late sluice robberies, and although this temporarily concealed his offense of truancy, the news of the vigilance meeting determined him to keep his lips sealed. He lay all night wondering how long it would take the robbers to dig themselves out of the cave, and whether they suspected their imprisonment was the work of an enemy or only an accident. For several days he avoided the locality, and even feared the vengeful appearance of Spanish Pete some night at his father's house. It was not until the end of a fortnight that he had the courage to revisit the spot. The tree was in its normal position, but immovable, and a great quantity of fresh débris at the mouth of the cave convinced him that the robbers, after escaping, had abandoned it as unsafe. His brother did not return, and either the activity of the Vigilance Committee or the lack of a new place of rendezvous seemed to have dispersed the robbers from the locality, for they were not heard of again.

The next ten years brought an improvement to Mr. Starleigh's fortunes. Johnny Starleigh, then a student at San José, one morning found a newspaper clipping in a letter from Miss Amelia Stryker. It read as follows: "The excavators in the new tunnel in Heavystone Ridge lately discovered the skeletons of two unknown men, who had evidently been crushed and entombed some years previously by the falling of a large tree over the mouth of their temporary refuge. From some river gold found with them, they were supposed to be a part of the gang of sluice robbers who infested the locality some years ago, and were hiding from the Vigilants."

For a few days thereafter Johnny Starleigh was thoughtful and reserved, but he did not refer to the paragraph in answering the letter. He decided to keep it for later confidences, when Miss Stryker should become Mrs. Starleigh.

THE FOUR GUARDIANS OF LAGRANGE

PART I

THE TRUST

IT certainly was a matter of serious import that so gravely interested the four most experienced and self-contained citizens of Lagrange. For nearly half an hour they had been sitting in the private room of Riker's grocery without exchanging a word. Even the silent communion of libation was wanting; their liquor stood untasted before them, a fact that aroused the serious concern of the barkeeper and the free comment of the outside bar. "Mebbe it's some new 'skin' game imported from 'Frisco, and they want to keep their heads level, " was suggested by a cautious gossiper.

The barkeeper shook his head. "Nary deck o' keerds thar — onless they plays 'm under the table, and that ain't their style."

"Ye did n't notice no lumps o' sugar, sorter lyin' round, keerless like, before each man," insinuated another, "and them chaps lyin' low and quiet, waitin' for some d——d fly to light and rake down the pile. I 've heerd," the speaker continued cautiously, "that heaps o' good money hez been lost in thet onchristian-like way."

"Yes," interpolated a third, "and *trained* flies, ez knew jest when to light, hez been rung in on greenhorns. Thar was a man down at French Camp, et they say picked up about seven thousand dollars outer ther camp with an innocent lookin' hoss fly, and et wuzent ontil one o' the boys accidently sot his glass down on thet harmless inseck thet the boys smelt a mice."

"'T ain't no game, I tell ye," reiterated the barkeeper stoutly. "Thar's suthin' more 'n flies and sugar on their minds. My belief is they 're reck'nin' to revive the old vigilants of '52. Thar's a lot o' dead beats in this yer camp," he continued darkly, with an aggressive recollection of certain unsettled scores, "ez mebbe will find out soon enough wot 's up."

Unfortunately, none of these surmises, however ingenious or reasonable, were correct. The simple fact was that a lately deceased miner had on his death-bed called to his side the above-mentioned four citizens of Lagrange, and solemnly confided to them the care of his only child in the "States," with the little property he possessed in trust for her maintenance. This trust was further burdened with the fact that the dying man had withheld from the child the news of the death of her mother, a year previous, and it now devolved upon the guardians to inform the orphan of her double bereavement. This was the first meeting of the guardians since they had last looked upon the face of their dead comrade. Hence their grave silence and perplexity.

At last the spell was broken. One of the party, a tall, thin, rickety man, who had been softly pacing the room with a certain deprecatory manner and a smile of imbecile acquiescence in everything and anything that shone out at the slightest expression, even of vexation or anxiety on the part of his companions, gradually neared the door, and laid a large, bony, good-humored hand on the lock. The act was instantly detected by one of the party, who coolly locked the door and put the key on the table. "Ye can't slip outer this, Rats," he said; "ye must sit down here with the rest of us, and see what 's to be done."

Captain Rats weakly succumbed, and began to apologize. "I warn't goin' back on ye, Horton," he began. "I only

reckoned as ye all seemed to be gitting along famous a-think-
ing, I 'd jest slip out and 'tend to some business, and allow
ye to make up yer mind without me — countin' me out,
and yourselves as my proxies. Fer wot 's agreeable to you
is agreeable to me. I 'm no sharp at this game."

"You 're a guardian," responded Horton decisively.

"In course. Thet 's so. But I allow it ain't no valid
app'intment. The very fact thet the old man app'inted
a d——d fool like me shows he warn't in his right
mind."

"That 's so, boys," ejaculated the eldest of the four,
with a sudden gleam of hopefulness. "The old man was
sorter flighty just afore he went off, and we can slip our
heads outer this lasso he flung over us by allowin' insanity,
you know."

"We can't slouch out of *this* kind of a trust though,
Colonel," said Joe Fleet, the youngest of the party, yet
with a leader's peremptoriness. "It ain't white to do it!"

The gleam faded from the Colonel's face.

"Thet 's so, it wouldn't be the squar' thing," he said
dejectedly; "kick me, boys."

"Couldn't we sorter club together and app'int a kind
of sub-guardian to take care o' the whole thing on a high
salary. I 'll come down heavy," suggested Horton.

"If you could get a chap to do your feelin' for you at
the same figure I don't know but it might suit," said Fleet
with decided sarcasm. "As for me I ain't rich enough to
buy up any chap's conscience."

"Ye may as well quit this foolin'," broke in the Colonel,
with a groan. "The game 's made, and we 're goin' to wade
in like men. Mebbe suthin' may turn up. Afore long
some one of us may get shot or buried in a tunnel, and so
get excused on the squar'. But just now we must wade
in."

"Oh, yes, ' wade in '!" said Horton derisively. "Do

you know the first thing we 've got to do? Why, write to
that gal, and tell her thet her father was a d——d old liar,
and thet her mother 's been dead a year, and thet now he 's
dead too, and thet the d——d old fool's property won't
bring five hundred dollars, and that we 're goin' to give her
five thousand dollars for charity, and adopt her, and if she 's
a loving sort of gal, and a high-spirited gal, she 'll like it,
and like us all the better. Oh, yes!" he continued with
sardonic shrillness, "it 's easy enough to do that, of course.
Wade in! Yes! Wade in — drop right out o' the ford into
deep water over yer head the first thing."

The men looked aghast at each other, and there was another ominous silence. "Could n't ye let it on easy?" suggested the Colonel despairingly, "sorter begin to-day with
the mother, and next month, when she 's feelin' better and
more able to bear it, kinder light gently down on her with
the decease of her father, and so on ontil, in the course of
a year or so, she 'll take the charity business quite peaceful?"

But Joe Fleet dismissed the idea fiercely. "Ef she 's
got any pluck she 'll take it in a lump. You go to work
driftin' into her feelin's like that instead of sinking your
shaft straight down, and you 'll hev her crazy here on your
hands in a week!"

The latter idea was so awful as to compel another gloomy
silence for its stern contemplation. "Could n't ye drop
it on her all in a lump, — money, deceased parients, et
cettery," suggested Captain Rats, with vague and imbecile
good humor, "kinder brisk and business like."

"It 's a gal," said the Colonel, shaking his head, "over
fourteen."

"Hold on, and give Cap'n Rats a show," interrupted
Fleet. "Ef there 's a man ez can do it, it 's him. Did n't
he edit the 'Record' up at Murphy's? Wade in and give
us a specimen."

The suggestion met with unanimous favor. Captain Rats was shamelessly pleased with this compliment to his literary abilities, and at once began: "'Honored Miss, — Not knowin' what a day may bring forth, we beg to inform you' — No," reflected the Captain slowly, feeling some unfavorable criticism in the air, "no, that won't do. Let's see! Ah! 'The death of your mother, followed by the illness of your father, resulting in his decease, and the entire loss' " —

"Ain't them bricks follerin' each other rather close?" suggested the Colonel faintly. The Captain stopped, rubbed his long chin thoughtfully, and looked at the others. It was evident that this was the prevailing impression.

"Well, yes; I was rather thinkin' so myself," he assented vaguely.

"And its bein' a gal, don't you want to heave in here and thar a little sentiment," said Horton, "and sorter touch her up gently? They say when you make 'em cry easy, they kinder like it, and get over it quicker."

"Jess so," returned Captain Rats cheerfully. "I was thinkin' that very thing, only jist now I was sorter samplin' it; showin' ye what *could* be done. A good way," he added, now completely lost in the fascinations of condoling composition, — "a very good, takin' sort of way is to tell it, and yet seem not to tell it; to kinder ring in a cold deck of information, and never let her see ye shuffle the keerds. Suthin' like this, ye know: 'Honored Miss, — Enclosed please find draft for five thousand dollars; same would have been sent before but for Wells-Fargo's office being closed the day of your father's funeral. The weather here is fine, but we suppose is fur different with you in the East, as your deceased mother often remarked to the writer. Business is dull, and ores are running light, most o' the claims on the North Fork sharing the fate of your late father's property.' Ye see," continued Captain Rats, with the glow of successful authorship mantling his cheek, "that kind of letter mout be written so that by the time she got through with it, it would seem as if she 'd knew it all before, and she could n't get nary soul to sympathize with her, and help her take on." The feeling of the majority was so strongly in favor of the last composition that they all turned impatiently to the only dissenter, Joe Fleet. But at this moment a knock on the door checked further discussion.

It was Jack Foster, expressman, — alert, vigilant, familiar, and fateful, — holding a letter.

"For John Meritoe," said the Sierran Mercury crisply. "As we don't have no office nor agent at his present address, we deliver at his last residence." He tossed the letter on the table, winked, and was gone.

It was for the dead man, the great first cause of their perplexity. For a few moments it lay there undisturbed, while the men looked at each other in silence. Then Captain Rats, with a decision and independence new to him, took it up. "Ther 's no one, boys, hez a better right to it than we has," he said. "I propose that we open it here afore each other and read it."

"As to opening it, I second the motion," said Joe Fleet's voice, "but we 'll see who it 's from before we read it," added that honorable man.

The letter was opened. It was signed "Fanny Meritoe."

"The girl herself," said Fleet promptly. "Read it."

With a hesitating voice, that at last seemed to almost simulate what might have been the hesitating youthful accents of the writer, Captain Rats began.

How shall I describe it? It was simple, it was girlish, it was affectionate, it was real. Against its candid frankness and simplicity poor Rats's previous rhetoric assumed the appearance of the most monstrous duplicity and deceitful sophistry. It was evident that the writer had seen but little of her real father, and that the rather commonplace, homely, often somewhat despicable figure known to the men who now listened to her yearnings was not the ideal parent of her dreams. At last Captain Rats finished. There was a slight huskiness in the Captain's voice, a slight dimness in his eyesight as he ended, and a blur upon the fair page that was not there when he began.

The Colonel had dropped his head between his hands. Horton had never taken his eyes from the paper. Fleet, who had walked to the window and had been apparently absorbed in staring at the staring sunlight without, suddenly turned, advanced to the table, and held out both his hands. In another moment they were locked in his companions', and the four men, holding hands, closed round the table and the letter that lay in its centre.

"We don't want no letter of condolence, Captain Rats," said Joe Fleet sturdily, "for there ain't anythin' to condole for. I don't see just how it is, or how we can fix it, but I *know* that girl's parents *ain't* dead, ez long, please God, as we are living!"

The men pressed each others' hands in silence, until Captain Rats, with a burst of revelation, disengaged his, and suddenly brought it against his right leg with resounding emphasis.

"That's it — and it makes the whole thing clar. We don't write no letters of condolence — for why? We goes straight on and writes ez if we was the old man. He's let on enough to me about hisself and his affairs to make it as easy as fallin' off a log. We'll just chip in whar he let off. We'll take his hand as it is, play out his little game, win or lose; and if four sharps like us can't make it easy for that child and rake in the pot every time, we'll leave the board. Yes, gentlemen," continued Rats, taking up the letter, "I'll answer this to-night myself, I, Captain Rats, late Meritoe, deceased."

PART II

HOW THE TRUST WAS FULFILLED

When the combined guardians of Lagrange first practiced to deceive, they did not forecast the tangled web whose pleasant intricacies and sinuosities they were presently to weave. And when Captain Rats calmly announced to his gentle confederates his intention of writing his first letter — *in loco parentis* — to the orphaned girl with his left hand, explaining to her the thereby changed chirography through the ingenious fiction of an accident that had happened to his right, it was accepted with acclamation. "You see," said the Captain sententiously, "every man slings ink with his left hand at about the same gait. The style ain't pretty nor plain, but she 'll never find out it ain't the old man's."

The possibility of detection thus obviated, — and, indeed, it afterwards appeared that the simple-minded girl dwelt more anxiously upon the discomforts of the accident to her father than on his changed and almost illegible hand, — various other gentle frauds and deceits were introduced in the correspondence. A certain emulation of the Captain's skill and importance as a correspondent grew up among the other guardians. They began to make suggestions of their own, until at last steamer day brought them generally together, in conclave, in the back room of the saloon, where the fortnightly epistle was dictated finally by all. Captain Rats's pride, which at first resented this interference, was finally placated by the compromise that the composition or "wording" of the letter should be his own, although the subject matter might be a various contribution.

The result of this unhallowed collaboration was a series of the most extraordinary letters ever inflicted on a single

correspondent.   It was not long before their fame reached
beyond the horizon of their fair recipient.   "Do you know,
papa dear," wrote the simple girl from the seclusion of
Madame Brimborion's academy, "do you know, your letters are so very, *very* interesting, I could not help showing
them to some of the girls here!   Your account [the Colonel's] of the fight with the bear was so *real* that I almost
saw it.   I laughed till I cried over the funny story of the
Chinaman mending your clothes [a characteristic contribution from Horton], but then I did cry, really, too, papa,
over what you [Fleet] said about your feeling that Sunday
you saw the sunset from the poor little forlorn cemetery on
the hill.   Oh, papa! it was just lovely — and so sad —
so very sad!   Mary Ricketts said it was just like Shake-
speare, and she knows, oh, so much, and is considered very,
very smart!   They all think I ought to be so fond of my
dear papa, as if I wanted anything to make me love him!
She, Mary, asked me if you were very old, and I said you
could n't be very — are you ?   Then that was very good
about the mines that you [the Colonel] wrote.   Mme.
Brimborion asked permission to copy that part where you
[the Colonel] describe the manner of reducing ores; she said
it was so instructive and valuable.   Dear papa, how much
you do know!   But I think I like you better when you 're
a little, just a little — sad, and say such sweet things about
the landscape and your longings.   I 'm sure you 're a real
poet, papa, ain't you ? "

It is scarcely necessary to say that when this letter was
read Fleet coughed slightly, colored perceptibly, muttered
something vaguely about "really having forgotten it all,"
but remembered only that he had dictated to Captain Rats
some suggestions that he "thought might please the young
thing," etc. ; nor that a slight feeling of jealousy crept into
the breasts of all but the complacent Captain.   Indeed, the
Colonel is said to have afterward remarked aside to Horton

that he was of the opinion that Fleet's "flapdoodle" and "purp stuff" was n't exactly the thing "to ladle out" to a young girl that was already "overdosed with chewing gum and licorice;" and Fleet is reported to have cautioned Captain Rats against the freedom of some of the Colonel's stories. "Ez fur as the wordin' goes," explained Captain Rats, "I plays my own cards; so don't you get skeert. On'y the other day, tellin' that story about the coon hunt, the Kernel allowed the dogs was 'hell bent' on gettin' the coon. Lord love ye! do ye think I set that down for that little gal's eye? Not much! I jist sat down sorter keerless and quiet like, and sling her this: 'Meanwhile, the noble hounds, justly emulating the feverish impatience and ambitious spirit of their master!' Lord, it's easy enough to turn the Kernel into decent English — ef you 've got the *sabe*! Why, it 's jist wonderful how keerless men is in their composition. Why, even *you*, Fleet, I hed to take *you* down last letter. Don't ye mind ye was lettin' on about Night walkin' in her scant robes on the hill? Did ye think I was goin' to hand that over to that child? No, sir. I stopped it! How? Why, I jest said, 'suitably appareled.' That's all. It's easy when you know how."

Another unlooked-for result naturally followed the baleful excellence of this correspondence. Miss Fanny grew more and more anxious to behold again the author of her being and of these extraordinary letters. One or two vague hints to that effect, thrown out in her correspondence, were received with alarm by her guardians, and it was finally resolved that the next letter should be composed in such a manner as to effectually check this wanton desire. For this purpose all the guardians assembled. Considerable excitement was manifested. I grieve to record the fact that much liquor was drunk, and that Captain Rats was somewhat exalted and discursive. But your true gentleman is never more fastidious and refined than in his cups; and the gentle Captain Rats, during the whole letter (save an occasional slip), held his rhetorical hat deferentially in his hand.   A copy of this epistle has been preserved, and runs as follows: —

MY OWN DARLING CHILD, — Your esteemed and precious favor came promptly to hand, and contents noted. We — that is, your sainted mother and myself — are glad to hear that the draft for two hundred and fifty dollars came promptly to hand, and trust that the balance of one hundred and fifty dollars, which you retained after paying Mme. Brimborion's bill, will be sufficient for you to purchase laces, furbelows, bonnets, shoe-ties, and hosiery suitable to the season and the fashions.   We (that is, your mother — who is still unable to write by reason of a sore finger — and myself) hope you will not spare any expense to clothe yourself equal to your schoolmates.   We note what you say about Mary Rickett's new silk dress, that cost seventy-five dollars.   You are to see that seventy-five, and go her fifty or one hundred better, drawing on us for the balance, if short.   Raise the Rickett girl or bust.   We trust you are careful of your health, and do not partake too frequently of confectionery, and that your French and music lessons are the same.   We trust that you wrap up warmly when you go out, and are careful about your flannels in that dreadful Eastern climate, and always wear your rubbers.   The wheat crop this year will average nearly forty bushels to the acre, or supply each inhabitant of the State with forty-four barrels of flour, and still leave one hundred thousand bushels for exportation.   With the Pacific Railroad finished, and the effete nations of Europe and Asia knocking at the Golden Gate for breadstuffs, the time is not far distant when the State will be entirely self-producing.   We often picture you, dear child, sitting at your tasks, your bright eyes occasionally dropping in reverie

as you think of your parents so far away. Do you ever
wander with us through these dim woods — God's first
temples — and breathe with us the infinite peace of solitude,
or reflect that long before we had our being or existence
these grand old monarchs looked down on others as they
do on us? Do you? We hope — that is, your mother and
myself trust you do, although we earnestly beg and implore
you not to dream of visiting us here. For the society is
quite unfitted for a person of your age and sex. Murder
not unfrequently stalks abroad, and sluice robbing is as
common as the red hand of the assassin. Scarcely a day
passes that we do not consign some victim to the silent
tomb. Consumption is epidemic, and smallpox, too, often
has marked the loveliest of your sex for his prey. The
face of beauty fades quickly through a pestilential fever now
quite common, and the exquisite daughter of one of the first
families has been taken for an Indian squaw by reason of
the same. Freckles are paramount. The hair withers and
falls out, — the teeth likewise the same. Much as we hope
to once more behold that darling face, we could not expose
you to such certain ruin. Your mother fainted on reading
your request to visit her. I fear, in her present state of
health, a visit from you would be fatal! If you value your
parents' love, banish this idea from your mind. In a few
years, probably, we will be able to once more clasp you in
our arms by the Atlantic shores.

YOUR AFFECTIONATE PARENTS.

Six weeks had elapsed, and the dutiful answer to the
above, confidently looked for by the guardians, was due.
Nevertheless, as the time approached, some nervousness on
the part of Fleet was manifested by that gentleman's unrest, and his frequent visits to Captain Rats, to whom all
letters addressed to their deceased friend were delivered.
"Nothing from the young lady yet, I suppose?" Fleet

would say indifferently. "No," the Captain would respond quietly. "I reckon it 'll take her about two weeks to get over her disappointment. Then she 'll write sassy — like as not — or mebbe not at all." Fleet turned pale, then red, and then bit his mustache. "You don't think, Captain," he asked with an affected laugh, "that we were a little — just a little too hard ? " "Not too much for peace and quietness," replied the Captain gravely. "Women don't take a halfway 'no;' they can't believe a man means it," he added, "any more than *they* do." Nevertheless, the Captain himself grew a little anxious, and having to visit Sacramento, left strict orders with his comrades that he was to be recalled promptly on the arrival of Miss Fanny's reply.

But his visit was not interrupted, and it was nearly three weeks later that he mounted the box seat of the Pioneer stage coach to return to Lagrange. As he settled himself beside the driver, after the interchange of a few complimentary epithets, his eye glanced down toward the wheels, and was attracted by an open letter and part of a female head obtruded from the coach. The fair reader had evidently thus sought to evade the gloom of the coach's interior and possibly the prying eyes of her fellow passengers, while she perused it. But why did the Captain's withered cheeks instantly change color, and why did he convulsively clasp the railing by his side ? The letter was in his own handwriting, and had been mailed to Miss Fanny nine weeks before!

It was impossible, even by the utmost craning, and at the risk of his life, to see anything more than a bit of lace, some artificial flowers, a front of blonde hair, and the fatal letter. Yet his guilty conscience instantly recognized in these scant facts the formidable presentment of the deceived orphan. Had she discovered their trick, and was she now on their trail, with this terrible indictment in her hand ?

Or was she still in ignorance — an ignorance which a single chance question and answer now might dispel, amid faintings, shrieks, tears, and wailing? Captain Rats grew apoplectic with bewilderment; he dared not even ask a question of the driver, who was already beginning to survey him with a sardonic leer, and had audibly sought information if he, the Captain, called this kind of conduct proper at "his time o' life." "Let the gal alone, Rats! Don't you see it ain't a love letter from you she 's porin' over?" he added, a statement that again covered the Captain with guilty blushes. But a sudden jolt of the vehicle, a little shriek, and the fluttering of the letter to the road, jarred from the reader's fingers, gave the Captain a providential opportunity. To jump from the box to the road and seize the truant epistle was the work of a moment. When he approached the coach to restore it to its fair owner, another passenger had appropriated his own seat on the box, and thus gave color and reason for his exchange to the "inside." The young lady thanked him, the coach again started forward, and Captain Rats fell into the seat beside her. Here was the supreme moment! With a profuse apology, the Captain drew his knees together, slipped into a respectfully diagonal position, so as to oppose the narrowest point of contact with her, and carefully dusted his knees and her dress softly with his handkerchief. The shyest nymph would scarcely have been startled, the coldest and most antiquated of duennas would not have been discomposed by the submissive respect of the Captain. The young lady, who evidently was neither, turned a pair of calm large gray eyes on her neighbor, and sat expectant. But how the Captain improved his chances I must refer the reader to his own account of the interview, delivered gravely the same evening to his brother guardians.

"When I saw we was in for it, boys," he said, rubbing his knees upward softly, "I kinder measured the gal afore

I commenced, to see what sort of a hand she might hold.
But you could n't hev told anything by her looks.   And
short of axing her a downright saucy question, you could n't
get a word out of her about her own business, nor what
she war up to.   And then — well," continued the Captain,
with a languid smile of conscious success, "I calkilated that
this was one o' them peculiar cases that wanted skill and
science, and I jist applied 'em, and in course I won.
Thet's all.   Yes," said the Captain, with a yawn of sti-
fled indifference, "it's all right now, boys.   Everything's
explained."

"But how?" queried the others eagerly.

"Well," said the Captain lazily, "I sorter slipped into
a gineral conversation about the opery, the fashions, and
po'try, and sich.   Speakin' o' literatoor, I told her of a
yarn I'd read t' other day in a magazine, and then, kinder
keerless and easy, I jist up and told her the whole story
about her father and us and herself, giving her the name o'
Seraphina, calling you and Horton ' Oscar ' and ' Roderigo,'
and Fleet ' Gustavus,' and myself ' Rodentio,' which is
Latin for ' Rats.'   Well, if I do say it myself, it was n't no
slouch of a story, fur I was kinder clipper and fresh, and
the other passengers was jist about as much interested as
she was.   Then I sorter looked in her eye, you know, this
way," and Captain Rats here achieved a peculiar leer, "and
said that I allowed it was n't true, and asked her what she
thought about it as a story.   And she said it might be true
and it might not, but it was quite interesting.   Them's
her very words, gentlemen."

"Well, go on," said the Colonel eagerly.

"That's all!"

"All!   All!" shrieked the guardians together.   "Did n't
she say anything else?   Did n't you" —

"Nary," said the Captain coolly.   "But it's all right,
boys!   You 'll see."

Horton seized Captain Rats by one shoulder, and the Colonel grappled the other. For a few seconds they shook him furiously.

"Where is she now, you blank, blank mule? Answer us!"

"Why, I reckon she's over at the Union Hotel with Fleet. I forgot to say that he happened accidental to be there when the stage kem in. She seemed to be kinder easy and nat'ral with him, and I" —

But before Captain Rats had finished his speech the two men rose furiously and dashed out of the room bareheaded. And even as the Captain sat there, mute and astonished, yet with his usual vague smile of acquiescence lingering around his mouth, Horton returned, shook his fist fiercely at the Captain, seized his hat, and vanished. In another moment the Colonel also reëntered hastily, grasped his hat, kicked Captain Rats, and dashed out again.

As the door slammed on the last of his fellow guardians, Captain Rats slowly emptied his glass, thoughtfully placed one knee on a chair, and rubbed it in silence. Presently a more decided smile came into his eye, and crept to his mouth as his lips slowly fashioned this astounding reflection: —

"That's so — that's *it!* Fleet was allers kinder soft on the gal! Like as not — like as not — he's up and writ to her on the sly."